*f*P

Life After Life

A Story of Rage and Redemption

EVANS D. HOPKINS

FREE PRESS
NEW YORK LONDON
TORONTO SYDNEY

FREE PRESS
A Division of Simon & Schuster, Inc.
1230 Avenue of the Americas
New York, NY 10020

FREE PRESS and colophon are
trademarks of Simon & Schuster, Inc.

For information about special discounts for bulk purchases,
please contact Simon & Schuster Special Sales:
1-800-456-6798 or business@simonandschuster.com

Designed by Paul Dippolito

Manufactured in the United States of America

1   3   5   7   9   10   8   6   4   2

Library of Congress Cataloging-in-Publication Data
Hopkins, Evans D.
Life after life: a story of rage and redemption / Evans D. Hopkins.
p.   cm.
1. Hopkins, Evans D., 1954–.   2. Black Panther Party—Biography.
3. Prisoners—Virginia—Biography.   4. African Americans—Virginia—Biography.
5. Ex-convicts—Biography.   I. Title.
HV9468.H75 A3   2005
305.896'0730755'092—dc22   2004065018
[B]
ISBN: 978-1-4516-4612-2

In memory of my mother, Marguerite Hopkins,
and my son, Roderick Anthony Hopkins;
for my father, Daniel Hopkins; and for my loving Shelia,
who has been my inspiration . . .

NOTE TO THE READER

This book is a memoir of my experiences. The names of some persons have been changed, as have certain physical characteristics and other descriptive details.

Life After Life

Life after life
I have led,
Through sadness and loss
It seems I've bled

Words upon page, woven
Sorrow and rage into song
Of transcendence and woe,
With hope that reader may know

Love can endure
Through suffering and pain—
And emerge as redemptive story,
To be read once, and again. . . .

CONTENTS

PART ONE · EARLY LIVES

CHAPTER ONE

The Roots of Rage

The A&P in Danville, Virginia, has a special significance in my memory. It was the only place my mother would shop. The other food stores in Danville during the early 1960s had found ways to let it be known that "Negro business" was unwanted—and, as genteel colored folk, we tried never to go where we weren't wanted. At the age of six, I wasn't aware of this discrimination. I simply loved going to the store with Mama, to this public gathering place where there were white people shopping along with us—and, of course, wearing all the white aprons.

There, every week, I was able to help Mama pull household necessities from the shelves, her meager-budget list dictating the various missions between the aisles she would send her smart little boy on—smart enough to snatch the correct sizes of Sugar Pops and pancake mix and Log Cabin syrup in a single foray away from her basket. My reward would be her smile, and the supreme gift of a quarter, to purchase a comic book on my own, at the checkout lanes manned with some of the white people segregated southern culture had taught me at once to revere, envy, and fear. Rushing out to my father's '55 Chevy, I would wait alone in the car and read the treasure I had garnered from the store: mainly copies of Classics Illustrated—my earliest introduction to literature.

The A&P parking lot was beside the old city jail, and I would spend minutes that seemed like hours with my face close to the windshield, looking up at the hundred-year-old building's faded grayish white façade. I would see the men inside with their arms sticking out through rusted iron bars, watch them waving or screaming or flinging notes to girlfriends or family members standing at the fence along the edge of the lot.

The jail took on a more frightening aura when I turned nine. It was then that police locked away hundreds of demonstrators during the Civil Rights marches of 1963, where firemen opened up on the crowds with water hoses, when deputized garbage men attacked them with clubs, and dogs were set upon those who came to the courts building to protest the mass jailings.

My family was embroiled in this struggle, and the image of the jail became embedded in my young mind, a fearsome symbol of the consequences of social change. But, as imaginative a child as I was, I could never have foreseen that one day I would be looking out at that A&P parking lot from the inside of the old jail, awaiting trial for bank robbery.

Life came to me early in the morning of June 23, 1954, in the delivery room of the small one-story hospital the city of Danville reserved for its colored citizenry. At thirty-six years of age, my mother had been told by her doctor that she shouldn't deliver another child after my sister, who had been born the year before. But my father's seed had somehow defeated the diaphragm she'd been given, and I was conceived.

My mother, Marguerite, was the daughter of Danville's foremost Negro businessman, while my father, Daniel Grover Hopkins, was a war veteran who worked in the local cotton mill, as well as on the farm that his sharecropper father had purchased with his labor. Always something of a go-getter, Daniel had met Marguerite Swanson in a typing class sponsored by Dan River Mills, the town's primary employer, in that bygone era when corporations felt responsible for nurturing the entire community.

My father had dark brown skin, and my mother was very light, as was my sister, Susanne. My complexion was closer to my father's, and a self-consciousness of color became a part of my world, from earliest memory. In a world where white was thought better than black, could yellow be better than brown? Could one's mother be better than one's father, or one's sister better than oneself, simply because of skin hue?

For the first five years of my life the Hopkins family lived in the city with my mother's family, in "the big house" on the block. The two-and-a-half-story brick structure was built—or perhaps I should say *rebuilt*—by my mother's enterprising father, Benjamin Swanson, back in the 1920s. When he bought the house, it was situated a block away, on a "whites-only" street. Never one to be deterred, he and his construction crew of sons tore down the structure, then reconstructed it brick by brick in the "colored colony" called Brucetown.

During my early years there was a wonderfully nourishing attitude of learning in the home. All of Grandfather Benjamin's children had attended college, and the books left over from their studies filled our library. Classical music and jazz permeated the house. My uncle Julian's wife, Vivian, was a teacher, and she and my mother would read to my sister and me every night, from *The Cat in the Hat* and other children's books. Aunt Vivian took a special interest in me and would spend afternoons, after teaching, reading to me. One day, when I was four, she presented me to my mother, saying, "Listen to Derrell read for you!" (I was called by my middle name then, and throughout my school years.) The joy of having a loving, attentive aunt reading with me during the evening, and then the ritual of my mother reading stories to us at bedtime, helped form my young imagination.

Everything became drama, and stories I was told became grand tapestries of black life. My grandfather was the seminal patriarchal character, a man of color who had managed to own most of the land on the two streets of Brucetown, along with other properties on the city's south side. While he had passed before my birth, from the tales about him I learned that he was the tacitly acknowledged illegitimate son of the scion of a wealthy white family that owned a huge tobacco plantation and a cigarette factory, a family that boasted of having a member who had been the governor of Virginia, as well as secretary of the navy, in the early part of the twentieth century. (In fact, this family was so rich that they had a chunk of the county named after them, called Swansonville.)

My grandfather's mother, Letitia, was a mulatto of legendary beauty. Her escape from post–Civil War serfdom came when she was cast off the plantation, after bearing a son who "looked too much like the young master." Upon discovering his father's identity, sixteen-year-old Benjamin marched out to Swansonville and demanded to meet his father. He subsequently changed his name to Swanson, and—a most religious man who would loudly praise the Lord each morning from his porch—he was known to travel regularly to the northern part of the county in order to worship with white family members.

Most of the Swanson progeny fled to professional careers in the less-segregated North after finishing college. However, my mother returned home to nurse her ailing mother after my grandfather passed away. My uncle Julian became the family realtor, taking care of the real estate my grandfather had bequeathed. Every week, in his blue Ford station wagon, he could be seen making his rounds, collecting rent. Perhaps our status in the community did not endear my sister and me to our playmates, for I don't recall mixing a great deal with the children who lived around us. Most of them were from fairly poor families, and lived in the small houses that had been built and rented out by my grandfather, who had also owned and run the neighborhood general store. My family's status in the neighborhood may have been the foundation of the notion that being in the forefront of things was quite natural for me.

My earliest dream was of hiding out behind our house, holding court with my outlaw band of five-year-olds after we'd robbed a bank or stagecoach or something. I'm not sure whether this dream stemmed from those early days of television or from some infantile concept of the joys (and fears) of sinning.

On the heels of this dream came a real adventure with my earliest friend, Berkley Crews, who was a year older than I and lived across the street. Berkley and I discovered an old tin barn-garage while exploring a forbidden zone of overgrowth separating Brucetown from the bordering white community. We liberated an ancient toolbox filled with old rusted tools, for it seems that at ages five and six we had a rather undeveloped idea of private property, and may have even thought we were raiding "the enemy" on the other side. We had no idea that the stuff belonged to my reclusive uncle Benny, who lived up the street from the big house.

Without fear or shame, we proudly dragged our treasure of old saws and drills and pipes and such down the street to our homes, only to receive what we'd always remember to be unjust whippings from our parents.

As a black child of the South in the 1960s, I found the realities of race to be a bewildering blend of stereotypes and situations that tore at my psyche at every turn. I could sense from the talk in the homes of "respectable colored folk," before the civil rights era, an attitude of acquiescence to our oppression, of just trying to get along until things got better. This served only to reinforce, in my young mind, the idea that those in power might well be of a superior race.

Certain memories stand out, like one Saturday's excursion downtown with my mother to get a new suit and shoes. The trip began with the wait for one of those fearful buses my parents normally avoided, in order to be spared the indignity of having to go to the seats in the back. When we reached downtown, we went first to a shoe store, but Mama could only give the clerk my size and then pick out a style of shoe, for black customers weren't allowed to try them on. Then we walked to Belk's department store, one of the few places where blacks were allowed to try on the clothes. We entered from a side door—the entrance to the store for blacks, though there were no "COLORED ONLY" signs posted to tell us it was the entrance we were supposed to use. All the salespeople were white, and the nicest white lady fitted me with a splendid navy blue blazer, gray slacks, a pale yellow shirt, and a paisley clip-on tie. While my mother paid for the items, I wandered into another part of the store, where a red-faced man with a crew cut snarled, in a deep drawl, "You'd better get back there with your mama, boy."

Leaving the store, I asked Mama why the man was so mean. Stopping on the sidewalk, she bent down and put her hands on my shoulders and looked into my eyes. "Some people are just brought up that way," she said, trying to disguise the hurt she felt in having to explain white hatred to me. "It's not that the man didn't like you. Some people just don't know how to act, and it will take some time for them to change. But things will change, son, I promise you."

Later we stopped by Woolworth's and Mama treated me to a hot dog, and I dared to try onions and a bit of chili on it. (Woolworth's was thought to be progressive because it had a separate lunch counter for blacks at the back of the store, whereas the Kresge's across the street still served only take-out to blacks.) She also asked for a root beer for me, so that I wouldn't have to go to the rear of the store to the colored-only drinking fountain, and sat quietly as I ate. She didn't order anything for herself, since she'd depleted the money allowed for this outing. Whirling around on the bar stool between bites, I felt strangely privileged to have this treat, yet bewildered by the differing rules of Jim Crow.

When I was six my father moved our family to the country, into a nice little brick home that he'd had built with the help of a GI loan, on land left to him by his father. About seventy-five yards away, in an old farmhouse, my father's mother lived, in her eighties and confined to a wheelchair. Soon after we moved, Pop was inspired to take the tractor from the family farm into town, where he started his landscaping business. As he still worked second shift at the mill (becoming the factory's first black supervisor—a strong point of pride for him), for several years I seemed never to have much time with him.

When my sister and I were old enough to attend school, my mother began teaching at Stony Mill Elementary, the little two-room school for black students that was two miles from our new home. This barnlike clapboard building was the one my father had gone to in the 1920s. In fact, it was the *only* school my father had been able to attend, since there was no high school for blacks in Pittsylvania County until the 1950s. Pop's father hadn't allowed him even to finish the grade school, taking him out early to work on the farm, for he could see no future in education for his bright son in the segregated world of southside Virginia.

My sister and I did not go to that school, however. Faced with the inferior facilities in the county, we attended a modern (though segregated) elementary school in the city, where we tended to excel over most of our classmates, due in large part to the head start we'd received at home. Every day we would ride into town with my father in his truck, passing the busloads of white children on their way to the large whites-only elementary school a few miles away. They would gawk at us from the bus windows, many giving us the finger and mouthing curses.

On Sundays, riding home from church in the summer, we'd get similar treatment from kids in cars outside Pine Lake, a small whites-only resort less than a mile from our home. Sweltering in the heat of the South, we seethed at this lack of privilege, only to take a bit of solace later in the day when we would hike with our cousins, who lived farther down the gravel road, a mile through dense woods to the muddy Sandy River for a dip in the cooling waters.

Growing up in the country helped to shape my idea of freedom. The property owned by my grandfather, and bequeathed to his children, stretched from the other side of the gravel road in front of our home all the way to the small river behind the house; I could hike all afternoon and still not cover it all. The wooded hills gave me refuge on lonely days (there were only six black families on the road, and few playmates my age), and I would go rock hunting or collect insects and leaves for school projects, nurturing my sense of wonder. Summers were really wonderful, for cousins from northern cities would come to share in my adventures. We would run among the old orchards at my grandmother's, pick blackberries from vines at the side of the road, and hide between rows of tobacco on parcels of land the family rented out to farmers, making fires to roast apples picked earlier from the ancient apple trees.

It was there, in the country, that I developed a love of firearms. At age eight I received a BB rifle, then a semiautomatic pellet pistol at ten, and a high-powered pellet rifle at eleven. At thirteen, for Christmas, I finally got my prize: a 12-gauge pump shotgun. That day Pop took me out into the December snow, and I shot my first rabbit, nailing him as he sprinted at a dead run, just before he could escape into the woods. The blast of that big gun filled me with a sense of power, a feeling of what it meant to be a man. And while skinning it for supper wasn't so much fun ("If you're man enough to kill it, you got to be man enough to deal with the blood and guts of it, too," Pop said to me), the joy of spending that afternoon with my father was what really mattered, for I felt I was growing up just like he had.

I built a gun rack for my room, and my pump hung up there along with my father's old single-barrel. My hunting bow and arrows also hung in the rack; by that time I had become a serious country boy, and would bow hunt for deer before the winter hunting season commenced.

Often our two German shepherds would bark in the middle of the night, and the family would think that a prowler was about. Perhaps, living in the country with whites all around, we were afraid because the Ku Klux Klan was still active in the area, with reports of their cross burnings surfacing every so often.

"We have to be on guard in case a convict escapes from a road gang, 'cause they'll kill everybody in the house to get away," Pop would say to me, not wanting to frighten me by saying we were on the lookout for the Klan. "So we'll just keep birdshot loaded in one of the shotguns, so in case you have to shoot somebody, you won't hurt them too bad." But there must have been a fearful—or dangerously lethal—streak in me even then, as I remember filching a round of deadly 00 buckshot from Pop's drawer and sneaking it into the gun's chamber, in case there was real trouble.

This was around the time that I watched shows like *Peter Gunn* and *The Man From U.N.C.L.E.,* with all of the scary black-and-white imagery of early television. I began reading James Bond books, or anything else in the espionage genre, perhaps a little too early for such a young psyche. I also got into books relating to crime, like Truman Capote's *In Cold Blood,* and from there developed a particular interest in the death penalty. In the sixties the electric chair was still used, and I recall pondering the fate of men on death row, rotting away while awaiting execution. I remember, even at that preadolescent stage, asking myself: *What would be worse: life in prison, or death in the electric chair?*

Growing up as a black child of the South in the sixties, one's sensibilities were warped by history textbooks that gave the view that slavery wasn't that bad in Virginia, and a view of Africa that would have us believe we should feel lucky to have been rescued from the primitive jungles of our homeland. Only later would I learn of the horrors of slavery and Reconstruction, of all the brutality and the lynchings. When I'd later come to realize how badly I'd been lied to, encountering the truth of what my race had endured would be even more infuriating.

I was able to expand my worldview, to a degree, on weekends when our parents would take my sister and me to the little two-room colored-only library, which mainly had books discarded from the segregated main library, housed two blocks away in the old Sutherlin mansion the city touted as "The Last Capitol of the Confederacy." (The city had the nerve to take pride in the fact that it was here, in the antebellum home of a rebel colonel, that Confederate president Jefferson Davis had hidden out for the seven days before Robert E. Lee's surrender, after having been run out of Richmond by the Union Army.)

In the hours I spent at that library I discovered literature, learned the beauty of words, and found worlds I'd never imagined in the works of Hans Christian Andersen, Daniel Defoe, and Robert Louis Stevenson. And then there were books on the English hero I most revered, Robin Hood. The story of a nobleman who would reject his status in order to rob from the rich to give to the poor struck a chord of righteousness in my heart, for it was easy for me to look upon the world in black-and-white—the rich white world, and the world of poor blacks—even though my middle-class status was actually in between the two poles.

In 1963, when I was nine, there were mass demonstrations in Danville, protests against the segregation of the bus lines, of the department stores—and, perhaps most pointedly, of the city library. It was then that my social consciousness began to develop, with the firsthand accounts I heard of boycotts and marches, of the swinging police clubs and attacking dogs, of folk being knocked down by the force of fire hoses in the streets of my town—all melded with the terrible photos and television accounts of similar turmoil throughout the South.

The Civil Rights Movement in Danville was headquartered at High Street Baptist, a large church with grand architecture that my mother's family had belonged to since before the turn of the century. The unity and fervor of everyone made a great impact on me, for I could not believe how people could seem so unafraid of being brutalized, or thrown into the old jail; how they could be so defiant of white authority. This feeling of oneness with the people was heightened when I attended a mass meeting at the city armory with my parents, when Martin Luther King, Jr. came to speak. A thousand black people filled the auditorium, and I was awed by so many people coming together in common cause.

I felt proud that my family, and our church, was at the heart of the struggle for equal rights. I was inspired by the fact that my uncle Gregory had been a civil rights pioneer, having been the first black to integrate the University of Virginia. My father and most of my uncles had served in the military, so I loved the idea of one day becoming something of a soldier, and felt that the struggle for civil rights was but an aspect of patriotism, and that it would be my duty to one day be involved in the struggle for justice.

But I was still a child, and while marchers were out in the streets, I played with other children on the steps of the church basement. We would sing a little ditty about the city's hated chief of police, Earl McCain, to the tune of "Joshua Fought the Battle of Jericho," which still rings in my ears: "Chief McCain is the chief dog . . . chief dog . . . chief dog. Chief McCain is the chief dog, and he comes from a couple of dogs." As we had been taught not to swear or to hate our enemies, we felt a great daring in our defiant play. (We had no way of knowing the threat we were under, but it would hit home a few months later, when four black girls would be bombed to death in a Birmingham church.)

Our minister at High Street was the Reverend L. W. Chase, one of the primary leaders of the Movement in Danville, as was my uncle, the Reverend Doyle Thomas, and a young minister, Bishop Lawrence Campbell.

During the height of the demonstrations police actually raided High Street Church, breaking down the doors in an attempt to arrest the Movement leaders. Unable to find anyone in the church

(Bishop Campbell and other leaders, having heard the commotion downstairs, had fled out the back door), police went to the parsonage next door, and arrested Reverend Chase while he was taking a shower. They wouldn't allow him to dress, but he managed to don his wife's bathrobe before being ignominiously hauled off to the old jail, in handcuffs, and charged with defying a hastily passed city ordinance against public demonstrations. Upon his release on bond, Reverend Chase refused to accept a ride home. To protest the indignity to which he had been subjected, he walked from the old jail back to the parsonage, through the streets of downtown, still dressed in his wife's robe—an image indelibly captured in a newspaper photo that made him a hero to all of us.

After several days of demonstrations came Bloody Monday. Police had locked up a score of protesters earlier in the day, and when demonstrators arrived at the jail for a prayer vigil for those arrested, they were attacked by police and garbagemen who had been deputized and given billy clubs, and by firemen with high-pressure hoses.

I remember seeing bloody men and women come staggering into High Street Church for first aid. The black hospital was filled with wounded protesters that night, and when those arrested went to court, they were tried before Judge A. M. Aiken, who would take a pistol from beneath his robe before each session and place it on the bench, in an effort to intimidate any who would defy the racist laws. But all of this only solidified the resolve of those involved in the Movement, and city leaders would eventually have to give in to our demands, but only after dictates from the courts.

While the buses and stores had been forced into integration, the library remained the last bastion of white supremacy in Danville. When the courts finally mandated that the library integrate, I was overjoyed. I remember arranging to ride into town with a teacher after school, and rushing to the main library to delve into the books that had been denied to me. But once inside the library, I discovered that all of the tables and chairs had been removed. In a final attempt to maintain segregation, city officials had decided that while blacks would have to be allowed into the library, they would not be permitted to sit and study alongside whites. When I recall the shock of seeing the spitefulness of whites evidenced by the bare floors of that library, I begin to understand how anger turns into rage.

By the time I reached the fifth grade, a new county elementary school had been built beside the old two-room one, and Susanne and I transferred from the city school. For the next few years we would have the unenviable pleasure of going to a school where our mother taught, providing an additional pressure to achieve.

When I reached high school age in the late 1960s, court-ordered integration had arrived, and my sister and I were among the first eleven black students to attend Tunstall, the area's all-white high school. Riding on the school bus was a harrowing ordeal. On the first day of school, after mounting the bus steps and seeing no vacant seats, I decided to stand at the front, only to be accosted by a large white senior in a football jacket. My sister came to my rescue, threatening him with the vilest of curses. Throughout the school day, and in the ensuing weeks, I felt ashamed about not having attacked the older boy; having my sister defend me wasn't exactly what I needed for my developing sense of manhood, either. I endured a number of threats, epithets, and assaults during that first year of high school, which didn't help my view of whites.

But I had to admit that the school was obviously better funded and staffed than the black high school, and I received a better education there. I was always on the honor roll, just as I had been throughout my earlier school years, and I learned firsthand that white kids weren't really innately intellectually superior, as we'd been led to believe. This was no small discovery, for until we *proved* such lies to be false, black students in the forefront of integration lived with the subconscious fear that the lies of racial inferiority might indeed, in some small and unknown way, be damnably true.

During these high school years I had two teachers, both of them white, who praised the papers I wrote, thereby giving me the first idea that I might become a writer of some kind. Yet, the staffs of the yearbook and the school paper, as well as the audiovisual and journalism clubs, were all-white enclaves, so I never got on that career track. However, along with a number of other black students, I was part of the marching and concert bands, in which we believed that our excellence helped to debunk the prevailing attitude of black inferiority.

I also joined the debating society and actually won all my debates that first year, in one instance, ironically, taking the *affirmative* position that the United States should be in Vietnam. One day, however, while sitting in the section of the cafeteria where the black students customarily sat, I tried to impress the upperclassmen by boasting of my victories, causing a senior named Harold Breedlove to take issue with me. Instead of being proud of what I felt was an accomplishment for us, he blasted me. "Why are you defending the white man's war? Why should a black man fight in Vietnam, when we aren't yet free over here?"

After some thought, I decided to quit the debate team, for the war and the Civil Rights Movement had begun to change my perspective. At the end of the football season, those of us in the band made a pact to refuse to stand up and play "Dixie," as had been part of our regular routine. That act of defiance almost got us kicked out of the band.

My attitude of quietly enduring the indignities of integration had changed by my third year of high school. Elbowing by whites in the crowded hallways had always been commonplace, but one day I decided to strike back. This led to a fight with an older white boy, for which I was suspended from school, having no way to prove that he had assaulted me first. The black eye I wore did not hurt nearly as much as the injustice of the suspension, or the psychological pain of having my father visit the school principal, only to be rejected after pleading my case.

Adolescence brought about a change in my relationship with my father. He had continued to work second shift in the mill while working during the day to build his landscaping business. During summers I would work with him, but I had come to view his cordial manner with his mostly white clientele as subservient. I failed to see the value in his labor, as it seemed our family never quite had the things families of black professionals had. I knew that if it weren't for my mother's schoolteacher salary, we would not have been able to make ends meet.

One morning, after just turning fourteen, I rode in to work with Dad, and we stopped for breakfast at a diner that had only recently been forced to integrate. I ordered scrambled eggs and sausage, and Pop ordered fried eggs and bacon. When our plates were nearly dropped onto the counter before us by a surly waitress, I showed Pop how my sausage was close to being raw, and he noted that his eggs were still runny, though he'd asked that they be cooked well.

When he complained to the waitress, she claimed that there was nothing wrong with my sausage, and that Pop hadn't told her he wanted his eggs hard. "You people always comin' in here complainin'," she said. "You lucky we even servin' you nigras at all."

Angrily, Pop demanded to see the manager. We sat there for ten minutes waiting for him to emerge from the kitchen. When Pop tried to explain the situation calmly, the manager cut him off, saying, "Look, you boys got the food you ordered. Now either pay for it, or I'm calling the po-lice."

Pop knew that if the Danville police got involved, we would end up being the ones at fault. He went ahead and paid for the food, telling me, "Come on, Derrell, we'll get something to eat somewhere else."

I felt bad for my father, caught up in the old system of the South, this just another in a long line of humiliations I knew he'd had to endure. But I was angrier than I'd ever been and had wanted to see him fight this small battle through to the end. Growing up during segregation, we'd been taught that being colored simply meant you just had to deal with such things. We had been told by our parents that if we just waited until integration came, eventually it would be all right. But integration was already supposed to be here, I thought, and my father was still viewed as a boy, just like me. With that incident I began to think that going along to get along was not the way to go about changing the order of things.

In 1968, my view of the black middle class I once wanted to belong to began to change, as a more militant attitude developed among black youth. My mother had had my sister and me join an elite national social club called Jack and Jill, which was organized by black professionals to give their children social and cultural opportunities denied to them by segregation. But we seemed never to mix well with others in the club, who seemed to have their noses up in the air because their parents were educators, and other members of the upper crust (which wasn't *all that* upper) in Danville. Our growing disdain for the snobbery of the black bourgeoisie was, in part, due to our status as the country kin of our cousins up North, who were the sons and daughters of lawyers, doctors, dentists, and school administrators. It always seemed as if we were trying to prove ourselves to be just as good as they were.

Attitudes regarding social struggle really changed after the assassination of Martin Luther King, for many African-Americans began to lose hope that the country would ever achieve racial justice through the nonviolent means Dr. King had advocated. This growing anger among the youth coincided with the Black Pride movement, which taught that we should be proud of our blackness and our African heritage—in direct opposition to past teachings, wherein we had been taught to believe ourselves inferior: having "bad hair," no historical culture, and "primitive" ancestry. My sister and I were swept up in this cultivation of pride, and we began wearing large Afros and African dashikis, the black pride music of the period providing a drumbeat for our transformation.

During 1969 and 1970 I experienced a transition in political consciousness with my introduction to literature by and for black men, which began to give me the feeling that *I* might be able to *do that*—either write or organize for the Movement. Many were works that dealt, in part or fully, with prison: Malcolm X's autobiography, Eldridge Cleaver's *Soul On Ice,* and George Jackson's *Soledad Brother,* the book of letters from a California prison that had made Jackson a cause célèbre. Because of the mass jailings of civil rights demonstrators in Danville, the possibility of imprisonment was already part and parcel of my idea of social struggle. Soon, overcoming this fear would become part of my rite of passage into manhood.

I was still active in the church during this time and had organized a Youth Sunday, and even a Junior Deacon Board. I quickly came into conflict with the complacent attitudes of those in my church, which mirrored the views of most of the older blacks in Danville and everywhere else in the South. One Youth Sunday, I decided that, instead of inviting someone from outside the church, as had been the custom, I would be the guest speaker. I proceeded to deliver a message I had picked up from the recorded speeches of Malcolm X and H. Rap Brown.

The next week, at a meeting of the church membership, it was decided that only ordained ministers would be allowed to speak from the pulpit. At that meeting I denounced the church, renounced my faith, and angrily walked out. At fifteen years of age I'd found the courage to reject the complacency of my elders; I would now find a way to forge a new path into the world.

CHAPTER TWO

Coming of Age

When Arthur Ashe captured the U.S. Open title in 1968, he burst into the realm of a sport all but closed to blacks and captured my imagination. Sports had long been used by African-Americans to break down doors of prejudice, and he became my champion, proving that we could excel in all sports—even this one, which was said to be too intellectual for us.

I was brought to the game by Ronald Charity, who had achieved some renown as the man who had taught Ashe to play on the segregated courts of Richmond, Virginia. Charity had moved to Danville after marrying Ruth Harvey, a pioneering civil rights attorney and a friend of my family. Charity was a handsome, charismatic man, and I came under his sway after receiving several lessons from him. Being slight of frame, I'd never done well in football, or even basketball. But this "genteel" sport seemed to fit my athletic abilities well. After Charity's pronouncement that I was showing real promise, I became a serious junior player.

Tennis gave me a sense of physical freedom I'd never experienced before. I felt as if I'd discovered a world one might control, without artificial barrier. I fell in love with the game, and I relished having a partner in Isiah Cardwell, one of my earliest friends from elementary school. He became, within the domain of this game, the brother I'd always wanted. We felt as if we were battling the white man in his sport, one of the last bastions of his social domain. Tall, lean, and angular, I developed a ballet-like style of play, and when I was on the court I felt as if I were on stage.

Charity gave me expensive professional rackets just like the ones Ashe used, and my rapid development made me feel that I might achieve the sort of success Ashe was having. I bore a resemblance to the tennis star with my horn-rimmed glasses and slight build. Hitting off of the backboard at the exclusive, all-girls Averett College one day, an attractive student (who had probably heard that Ashe was going to be in town) asked me if I were he. I pretended that I was indeed the tennis great, impressing her with my powerful serve and fluid backhand, and flirtatiously hinting that I might have time to give her a lesson "the next time I'm in town."

Isiah and I practiced and played with zeal, intent upon following in Arthur Ashe's footsteps—except that *we* would use our fame to speak out for black people, as Ashe was failing to do at that time. We began to play junior tournaments with modest success. But we encountered a subdued racism on the courts, and trips to tournaments in Washington, D.C., and Maryland made us realize that the walls against blacks would be hard to break down no matter how good we were. We had started late and were playing against white boys who had had lessons before they had attended school, private coaches, and expensive equipment. At posh country clubs where some of the events were held, we saw the class inequities that existed in a world of which we'd had no concept. (One young player, for instance, was flown to and from the various tournaments on the junior circuit in a private helicopter.)

Meanwhile, Isiah and I were delving deeper into the black militancy of the age, reading radical books like *The Wretched of the Earth,* by the famed psychiatrist Frantz Fanon. In writing about the peoples of Africa, he had said that the basis for antipathy for the colonialist by those who were colonized stemmed not only from a feeling of injustice at inequality, but also from basic envy. Witnessing the opulence of the upper crust, Isiah and I began to see where Fanon was coming from.

Ashe was our supreme hero, and in 1969 we finally got a chance to meet him when he came to Danville to do a promotion at Safari Unlimited, an African clothing store that he co-owned with Charity. Dressed in a resplendent dashiki, but with a beaded choker around his neck in the All-American red, white, and blue, Ashe told us that we had a hard row to hoe if we wanted to play professional tennis. "This is my *livelihood*," he said. "Don't think that professional sport is something you do for fun. This is how I make my living."

That statement dented our dreamy bubble, for we had wanted to believe that professional sport was only an extension of fun. Then, as we left him, Ashe flashed the peace sign to us. This really dashed our illusions, as we thought of ourselves as militants by then, and the peace Ashe so wanly represented to us was the direct opposite of our beliefs. We suddenly saw our hero as a sell-out. But rather than question ourselves, after the meeting we were all the more certain that tennis needed the likes of us to carry on the Cause.

During the summer of 1970, my family visited relatives in Washington, D.C., and it was then that my cousin Carroll Jr. told Susanne and me about the Black Panther Party. Organized in 1966 in Oakland, California, by Huey P. Newton and Bobby Seale, the Party had spread to major cities across the nation and had more than a thousand members at the time. Carroll explained how we had seen only "the White Man's Propaganda" about the Party: photos of men and women in black berets and leather jackets with rifles and shotguns who had been labeled by the media as "extremists" and a "hate group," with FBI director J. Edgar Hoover calling the Panthers "the greatest threat to the security of the United States."

Carroll took us into the basement of his home and gave Susanne and me our first copy of the Panther newspaper. The cover featured the famous photograph of seventeen-year-old Jonathan Jackson, brother of *Soledad Brother* author George Jackson, with an assault rifle in his hand during an abortive attempt to rescue three San Quentin prisoners at the San Rafael County Courthouse in California. I had read about the resulting shoot-out, which had left Jonathan Jackson, the judge, and the prosecutor dead—and how University of California professor Angela Davis had become the country's most famous fugitive, accused of supplying the arms to the young Jackson.

Reading that paper on the ride back to Virginia filled me with pride in the Panthers' spirit of resistance, and Jonathan's daring action made me think that at sixteen, I was not too young to engage in militant struggle. I was impressed by the Panthers' platform and program, which showed them not to be a hate group, as the media called them, but an organization calling for self-defense against the rampant police brutality of the period, and advocating the political and economic rights of black people. In that newspaper, I felt I had encountered real *truth,* and I was eager to learn more, and really get involved in what had become known as the Black Liberation movement.

Carroll began sending Panther papers to Susanne and me in Virginia which we used to organize a small group of high school students, including Isiah, our childhood friends Mike Fisher and Ricky Holman, and Carl Williams and "Pete" Watkins. I named the group the Black Awareness Alliance, reasoning that after we *educated* our people we would change the name to the Black *Action* Alliance. (Perhaps I was a little too serious, as I got pissed when one of our group mentioned that our acronym was the sheepish BAA.) I was a reluctant leader, however, feeling that though I possessed intelligence and dedication, I didn't really have the charisma needed for real leadership.

One afternoon during the spring of 1971, Isiah and I were on the tennis courts at George Washington High School in Danville— the city school to which I had transferred because Tunstall High did not have a tennis team—practicing for tryouts for the team.

Susanne drove by in her little green Fiat, along with Carl, Pete, and Ricky. "Derrell," she yelled out, "we just heard on the news that the pigs vamped on the Panthers in Winston-Salem." (Winston-Salem, North Carolina, is a medium-size city ninety miles southwest of Danville, and *vamp* was the term used by the Party for the frequent police attacks upon their dwellings, which often led to gunplay.) "We're going down there to check on them," she said. "Come on, get in the car and come with us."

"No," I told her, "we can't do without this practice; tryouts start in a few weeks." Angry—and Susanne was the angriest of us all back then—she sped away.

They returned from Winston-Salem with several bundles of Panther papers, which we hid in Mike's basement, where we hoped his parents wouldn't discover them. We then sold them door-to-door and on the street downtown, in order to help the Party in Winston, and "to educate the community as to the true nature of oppression," as the Panther platform put it.

Isiah and I continued concentrating on our tennis, while Susanne and the others kept going back and forth to North Carolina to meet with the Panthers. Then one day she skidded to the curb next to the court with Ricky in tow, in a state of panic. "We were just talking to the Panthers on the phone," she said in a rush, "when all of a sudden there was a bunch of clicks. Then, one of the pigs actually *came on the line,* started *laughing,* and said, 'We're gonna get you little niggers.' "

I tried to get her to calm down, but she was hearing none of it. "Don't you see, Derrell? They might be getting ready to vamp on *us* now. We've got your shotgun in the backseat, and we're going to Winston to find out what we should do. Are you coming with us or not?"

My sister never seemed more magnificent than she did then, the spring wind blowing her soft Afro—to my mind and heart, a true warrior woman, ready to do battle. I looked at Isiah, who nodded his consent. This time we went with them.

We took a backroads route to Winston-Salem, fearful that we were being followed, and arrived just after dark at a four-room house on the outskirts of the city, where Party members were living communally. We parked a hundred yards from the house just in case the police were watching. As we got out of the car, with me carrying my shotgun, a car started up and began to drive toward us. "It's the pigs!" Ricky shouted, and we all ducked behind the little Fiat, and I threw my weapon under the car.

It turned out that it was not a police car, after all, just an old station wagon that rolled right by us. As spooked as we were, we left the shotgun under the car and went ahead into the Panther house.

I'm not sure what I'd expected to see, but the Panthers were hardly as I had pictured them. They did not wear leather and berets; in fact, their clothing and surroundings revealed them to be as impoverished as the people they were trying to help. There were no sandbags at the windows, as had been claimed in news reports, though one young Panther stood watch with a carbine in hand, nervously looking out a curtained window in case the police had been following us.

A senior member of the chapter, a two-hundred-pound, jet-black thirty-two-year-old whose nickname was Coon, came out to calm us down. "You will have to learn to resist the scare tactics the pigs use to fill you with fear," he said. "In our struggle fear is the greatest enemy."

When I told him that we'd left the shotgun under the car, he said, "Maybe you need a little example of courage. You two come with me," pointing to Isiah and me; and then he walked out into the cool spring night, and we followed. After he had me crawl under the car to retrieve the weapon, he took it, jacked the round from its chamber into his palm, and then said, "This shotgun shell and this gun are only tools—tools that have been used against us, tools that we now, as the vanguard of the people, *choose* to have the courage to use for our defense, and for our liberation."

He suddenly threw the shotgun to me, which I fumbled to catch with both hands. "See, it don't bite, and it won't kill you to hold it," he said. "What you got to worry about is the fact that the pigs are holding them, too, so you got to make sure *they* don't kill you." He added that it wasn't illegal to possess a shotgun, as long as it wasn't concealed. "You have to rid your minds of your slave mentality, if you're going to be Panthers," he said.

Then he took out a cigarette and lit it, calmly exhaling smoke into the air, as I struggled not to tremble while holding a gun in the middle of the city, beneath a streetlamp. I stood in awe of this fearsome-looking brother who seemed to have no fear. And I suppose Isiah felt about the same, for in the minutes of silence while Coon enjoyed his smoke, and the discomfort he had to know we felt from his lesson, Isiah decided to broach the question we had agonized over, about whether our tennis was as important as the call of the Struggle. I was reluctant even to *tell* the Panthers that we engaged in a bourgeois sport like tennis, but I guess Isiah was too mesmerized to care.

"Comrade brother," he began. We have a question to ask." I knew what was coming, and tried to bump Isiah with my elbow, hoping he would change the subject. But he kept going.

"Derrell and I play tennis, and have become pretty good at it," he said. "We think we have the chance to do more for the Revolution by becoming tennis stars, and then use fame and money to help the Struggle. Do you think that's the way we should go?"

Coon fixed us with a cold stare, then asked us both, in a soft whisper, "Little brothers, do you think you can play your way to freedom?"

Isiah and I gave up tennis after that night. We began traveling to Winston-Salem with Susanne and others in the group, attending P.E. (political education) classes, in which the Panthers presented us with their socialist, internationalist view of the world. They put forward their theories on the assassinations of JFK and Martin Luther

King, giving us an analysis of why the United States was in Vietnam, telling of the misdeeds of the FBI and CIA.

They said that the police forces acted like armies of occupation in the black community, showing as evidence of police brutality an array of graphic morgue photos, which showed the body of a North Carolina man with bullet wounds he'd received, while unarmed, from the .357 magnums that had just begun to be issued to police forces. They told us how they'd been harassed and assaulted by police, how their office in nearby High Point had been vamped on, resulting in a shoot-out during which a sixteen-year-old member was wounded, and how their last office had been firebombed in the night.

Instead of being frightened by these accounts, I was fired up even more. Back then, people did not want to believe how racist the nation's police forces were. I felt as if the truth had been hidden from me, and I was infuriated to learn that the police, who were supposed to protect us, were committing such brutality. The concept of self-defense mixed with the allure that guns held for me, and I had begun to romanticize the use of violence in pursuit of a noble cause—with Malcolm X's credo, "By any means necessary," prominent in my thoughts.

But I'd become involved with the Black Panther Party during the change from its earlier days of violent rhetoric, when Huey Newton and the leadership had decided that the Party would "put away the gun" and begin to "work within the system." Along with the desire to "serve the people, body and soul," as the Panther motto put it, I felt that the subservient attitude of my race had to be abolished, and I relished the idea of a proud, militant defiance of the System. I believed that I was needed in the universal fight for justice, and I began to feel a sense of belonging to a movement that was akin to something spiritual, a feeling that I had lost after leaving the church.

Along with Susanne and the rest of our young cadre, Isiah and I began working in the Danville community after school, selling papers, holding meetings wherever we could find space, and organizing rallies. One rally was held at a teen nightspot called The Top of the Stairs. We disseminated leaflets that said the featured speaker would be the head of the Winston-Salem chapter, a well-known former collegiate basketball star named Larry Little. With this the police began to focus their energies against us, spreading the word that if the meeting was held, "the blood of the Panthers would flow from the top of the stairs to the bottom." Though fearful, we did not let the threat stop us, and the police action against us was limited to their constantly driving by the nightclub in an effort to intimidate.

In mid-May we held another rally, on the frayed grass of the ball field of the community called the Old Projects, a public housing assembly from the 1940s where, while selling papers door-to-door, I'd been moved by seeing poverty as I'd never before witnessed it in my sheltered life. I spoke to a large group of residents, blasting a police raid that had taken place a few days before in the area, referring to them as "the goddamn pigs." I felt strangely conflicted: at once the firebrand energized by the power I seemed to wield with a megaphone in hand, but still the nice boy ashamed of using profanity in front of women and children.

We were able to recruit more students to sell the Panther papers on the main streets of downtown. But the police began harassing us. One day I was in front of Woolworth's with a bundle of papers under my arm when one of the city's three black policemen confronted me and asked gruffly, "What do you think you're doing?"

"I'm exercising my freedom-of-speech rights," I told him boldly, though I was scared to death, this being my first direct confrontation with the law. Proffering a paper, I dared ask, "Would you like a paper, so you can read the *truth* about oppression?"

"I'll do just that," he said, then snatched the paper from my hand.

"That's stealing!" I screamed at him as he walked away, enraged by this abuse of power. I soon learned that this was a concerted effort by the police. When all of the sellers converged at the end of the day, one of us was missing: Carl had been arrested on the charge of loitering and was being held at the old city jail.

I immediately went there, stormed into the office, and declared, "I demand that you release my comrade immediately!" The white jailers looked at me as if I were a madman, amazed at the audacity of this skinny teenager. Hearing me from his holding cell, Carl began screaming, "Right on! I demand that you call my father now!" His father was a prominent attorney and NAACP official in the city, and that may have been the only thing that saved me from joining Carl behind bars. An hour later the situation was diffused when Carl's mother came to post bond for him.

After that, word got around to our parents that we were involved with the Black Panther Party, but we refused to stem our activities. The Panthers had instructed us to organize the students at our school, since they felt that youth should be an integral part of forcing change. Larry Little told us, "Remember the sacrifice of the two black students who were killed by police at Jackson State in Mississippi, and the four students who were slain at Kent State," reminding us of how those incidents had sparked antiwar protests on other campuses all over the country the year before.

We decided to focus on a major grievance at our school that had been simmering since the beginning of the school year. The black high school, John M. Langston (named after a Reconstruction-era black congressman), had been integrated into the white one, the result being a complete loss of school identity for black students. We resented attending a school named after George Washington, a slave owner who, to our thinking, was a symbol of our continued oppression. We held a secret meeting in Mike's basement while his parents were away and decided to stage a walkout to demand that the name of the school be changed immediately, and that a black studies program be implemented. We drew upon the Panther platform and program for inspiration, which called for "a true education as to the nature of this oppressive society."

It was a Wednesday, and I convinced the group that the protest should be held on that Friday, which would give us Thursday to spread the word, with the hope that a majority of the black students would join in. This would also give me time to call Harold, a leader of the white students with whom I'd taken pains to cultivate a relationship. (Harold was a steadfast radical, having sold our group a hunting shotgun we felt we needed to protect ourselves in case of an assault by the police.) I believed I could convince him that the white students should also support our effort; I had embraced the Party's teaching that ours needed to be a nonracial revolution and should include all segments of society.

On Thursday, I walked the six blocks to school as usual, only to be greeted with the sight of little more than one hundred black students gathered on the knoll outside the school. But it was *only* one hundred, of a student population of well over a thousand. It seems that one of the sisters at the meeting the night before had gotten to school early and spread the word that the walkout was on for *today*. In response, school officials had locked the doors, trapping those who were already inside, the majority of whom had no knowledge of what the walkout was about.

I didn't know what to do. Squad cars began to form a cordon around the students, with policemen jumping out in riot gear, bandying clubs. I found Carl among the disorganized group, and we decided that we had to act as if all this were planned. We had to assume leadership of the small group and press for our demands.

When it seemed that the police were about to move in to disperse us, a group of white students, led by Harold, found a way out of the building and joined us on the hill.

This intervention changed the situation's dynamic, since the police were reluctant to attack with white students among us. The assistant principal, a black man named James Slade, came out to talk to us, and Carl and I were ushered to the principal's office. There, we insisted that an agreement be drawn up and a referendum be held on changing the identity of the school to reflect the nature of its integration.

We were told that our "requests" would be considered if we instructed the protesters to disperse. Otherwise, officials would dismiss school for the day in order to avoid a confrontation. Realizing that the police would, in all likelihood, have already attacked had it not been for the presence of the white students, we reluctantly agreed.

Carl and I were suspended for three days for our actions. The referendum was held, and school officials allowed a change of the school colors and mascot, and said that they would consider starting a class in "multicultural studies" the following year. However, they refused to drop the name George Washington.

Police harassment and pressure from parents soon took a toll on the ranks of my small cadre. Party members in Winston-Salem had warned me that, as a leader, I might expect this. By the end of the school year in 1971, my fellow travelers had dwindled away. Susanne let it be known that she was going off to college. Isiah went to Georgia, and Carl, Pete, and the others began to shy away. It became obvious that I would not be able to establish a Panther chapter in Danville. Ironically, it was I, the one most reluctant to get involved, who had become the most steadfast.

Though I felt abandoned and alone, I believed that I had a new family eighty miles south. The die was cast; I had made my decision. I had researched the law and knew that as soon as I turned seventeen, I would be legally free to leave home and join the Party in Winston-Salem.

In mid-June, just prior to my birthday, I gathered enough resolve to tell my parents that I was leaving home. I knew that my father would never understand. We had already clashed over my involvement with the Panthers, which he had learned about when I was suspended from school. I thought that I would fare better with my mother. It was her side of the family with background in civil rights; and, in a quiet way, she more or less ran things.

I went to talk to her at my father's office, a tiny two-room affair more like a small cabin than an office, built with used lumber that my ever-enterprising father had salvaged from a house he'd been hired to tear down. Mama had stopped teaching in order to become his secretary, a job I thought was a bit beneath her station, though her efforts would eventually help him to become a businessman of some prominence.

I explained to her that I was moving to Winston-Salem to join the Black Panther Party. "Don't worry, I'll finish high school in Winston," I said, in an attempt to allay her fears, adding, "The high school I'll be going to is one of the best in the state. And they have two good universities there, so please don't think that I'm not going to get an education." (Actually, I had considered dropping out of school altogether, to give my full time to being a revolutionary, since part of my indoctrination taught that most education was little more than brainwashing by the System; but Party leaders had explained to me that I needed to learn more bourgeois skills—typing, writing, etc.—in order to use them for the Struggle.)

Mama's response surprised me: "Derrell, I understand why you feel the need to go. I even understand why you feel you *have* to go. But I'm not just thinking of you, of all the dangers you may face. I'm thinking of *me*," said the woman who had sacrificed so much for her husband, her children. "What about me? Susanne is going off to college in the fall, and I want you here with me, with us. Have you thought about that, about what *I* might need?"

Her words tore into me. Yet, I had determined to harden my heart, as a warrior should, to what I'd been taught were the bourgeois constraints of family ties. I left the office before my father returned from the job he was on, so that she'd be able to talk to him before I'd have to face him.

That evening, I'd arranged to have Coon come up and talk to my parents with me. He was, as usual, persuasive. He told my parents that he would serve as guardian for me, that I would live with him and his wife while I finished high school. He also explained how the Party had changed, how it was primarily a community organization now, working within the system to effect change and eschewing the violent rhetoric of the past.

After he left, I talked with my father alone. He sat regally in the great armchair in the living room, a proud man trying to stay composed, to feel that he was still in control in the face of this rebellion by his only son. His tone was officious, like that of a deacon speaking to his congregation. "I don't agree with what you want to do, Derrell," he said. "But I've talked with your mama, and we've decided that we won't stand in your way."

On the day after my seventeenth birthday, Pop picked me up at my uncle Harry's, where I'd been staying part-time while going to school in the city, and drove me to the bus station for the trip to Winston-Salem. We rode in silence much of the way. When we got to the station, Pop parked and said, "You know, Derrell, you've always been hardheaded, always wanted to have your own way."

He paused, looked out the window, as if his next words would be a bit painful. "Maybe that's the one way you take after me," he said, revealing a bit of the disappointment he felt, because I was not ready to follow in his footsteps. Then, looking me in the eye, he said, "You're very intelligent, son, but you need to understand that real intelligent people tend to think things should be as they *want* them to be, rather than the way things really are."

I saw my father in a new way then, and was astonished at the depth of thought from this simple man. "Your problem, Derrell, is that you've always tended to be a dreamer. Just don't let it get to you when you find that the world won't change just because you want it to."

I thought about his words while riding the eighty miles to Winston-Salem, the scenery and blurred lines on the highway making me feel as if I were traveling a million miles from home, journeying into a new life. In the baggage hold of the bus were most of my clothes, in a suitcase lent to me by my mother. Beside me was a clothes bag, the two suits I owned providing padding for the 16-gauge shotgun I'd kept hidden from my uncle, beneath a rug under my bed—the weapon the young Danville comrades and I had bought after the Panthers had told us that Party rules mandated having a firearm available for self-defense.

This is interstate transport of a concealed firearm, I thought during that trip to my new home. But I was on my way to join the Revolution, and I was determined to overcome youthful trepidation. *It is time to become a man.*

CHAPTER THREE

Panther in Training

I stepped from the bus after the two-hour trip from Danville, the smell of diesel fumes and exhaust filling my nostrils, the garment bag with the shotgun slung over my shoulder. After retrieving my small suitcase, I emerged from the bus station overhang into the sun.

No one was there to meet me. The Panthers' phone line was still disconnected, so they did not know the time of my arrival. And, in any case, they had felt that the police might monitor any call, and hence might be there to intercept me, a teenager with a concealed weapon. As trepidation tried to peel away at my resolve, I embarked on the two-mile trek to the Panther apartment with a sense of mission borne of adolescent idealism.

My walk from the bus station took me through downtown Winston-Salem, where I looked up at the tall buildings like a tourist. Passing through part of the industrial section, with the gigantic smokestack of the R.J. Reynolds factory, my now-politicized mind began to think of the modern-day slaves who toiled there, processing the legal drug of tobacco. It was Sunday, and the streets were mostly deserted, which suited my idea of myself as a lone soldier: a spy or intelligence agent of some sort, resigned to an isolated life of secrecy for the cause. But I could not help but wonder—and fear—if the FBI had me under surveillance.

My arrival at the Panther pad interrupted their afternoon P.E. class, and I was greeted as if I were a young hero of the revolution, a guerrilla who had crossed a frontier. The entire membership of the North Carolina chapter was there, which included not only the Winston-Salem branch but those who staffed the Party's outpost in the nearby city of High Point, and three community workers all the way from Wilmington, as well.

The fifteen members crowded into the front room of the three-room apartment they called a "shotgun shack." (I was so green I'd never heard the term before my visits to Winston-Salem, hadn't known the description came from the joke, "You can fire a shotgun blast through the front door and it will go straight out the back.") As I took a place in the corner, sitting on the rough hardwood floor (since the few places on the old couch and all of the worn vinyl and metal kitchen chairs were taken), I decided that there was a dark humor involved here, in light of the shotguns in evidence at every window.

The coordinator of the chapter, Larry Little, was taking the group through the catechism of the Ten Point Platform and Program, which all new members were required to learn and be able to recite. "Point number one!" he demanded of Papa Doc, the stuttering, semiliterate brother, called upon first with the easiest question, in order to spare him the embarrassment of not knowing the more difficult points.

"We want f-f-freedom," Doc said. "We want the power to d–determine the destiny of our black community." Then he beamed with relief and pride.

"Point number two, Judge!" said Larry.

"We want housing, fit for the shelter of human beings," Judge said. He was a large man who wore thick, very dark shades because he was half blind, though he was a gifted artist in charge of putting out posters and leaflets as head of the Ministry of Information for the chapter.

Bernard Patterson, a high school dropout I had recruited in Danville, and who had moved down to Winston a few weeks before to help with refurbishing the new headquarters, was called upon next.

"We want an education which teaches us the true nature . . . of this . . ." Bernard paused to gather his thoughts, to try to glean some help from memory, as he had a serious reading disability. "That teaches us the true nature of this de-cadent American society," he plowed on, "and teaches us our true role in society . . ."

I looked around at the others in the room. A few of them had given up promising academic careers, but most had diverted their lives from a basic struggle to survive to embrace a new kind of vow of poverty, in order to "serve the people, body and soul," as the Panther motto put it.

I felt most inspired by the poorer comrades, having taken to heart the Panther dictum that the revolution could be fomented by the segment of society Karl Marx had termed the lumpen proletariat. At the same time, they seemed to prize the intellectual—those who, like Party founder Huey Newton, could interpret Marxist philosophy and turn it into a philosophical tool for the liberation of the oppressed. Having grown up a well-mannered son of the black middle class, wherein one never *dared* oppose the established order in a militant fashion, I looked forward to being able to transform my intellect into a source of power.

Nelson Malloy, the co-coordinator, was called on for the next point: "We want freedom for all black men and women held in federal, state, and local jails and prisons. We want trials for all black men and women by a jury of their peers." This was a point of the platform program I'd especially come to believe in, after reading about the injustices of the legal system George Jackson had outlined in his books. Black men in prison were seen as the most oppressed of all, and it was believed that they, being the most *lumpen* of the lumpen proletariat, could be organized to come back into the community and be essential to the Revolution.

"Comrade Derrell, point number ten," Larry bellowed, snapping me out of my reverie.

"We want land, bread, clothing, housing, and truth," I said, then went on to recite the preamble of the U.S. Constitution that ended the Panther Platform and Program. "When in the course of human events . . . a government evinces a design for despotism . . . it becomes necessary to dissolve the bonds which hold that nation in subjugation . . . it is their right, it is their *duty* to dissolve such a government . . ." Still patriotic from my Boy Scout days, I felt that I was following in the historical footsteps of the revolutionaries who had formed the nation, and that I was now working to bring the nation back to its founding ideals, in the company of these brothers and sisters.

The P.E. class then dealt with the most recent article by our revered leader, Huey P. Newton, whose title at the time was Chief Theoretician and Servant of the People. (For short, comrades affectionately called him the Servant.) His piece dealt with the movie *Sweet Sweetback's BaadAssss Song,* a groundbreaking film by Melvin Van Peebles, who would later be called the father of modern black cinema for his theretofore unheard-of depiction of a black man battling racist white policemen. The intersection of politics and popular film, in order to combat the demeaning images of blacks on screen at that time, was inspiring, as I was beginning to envision myself as a writer who might reach people with a popular message of revolution.

After the P.E. class there was the customary Sunday dinner of fried chicken. It was like the homecoming meal at my father's country church, and I loved the bonhomie of family and togetherness, loved the attention I received as the newest and youngest member—as well as the way some of the comrade sisters seemed to be sizing me up for the communal bedding situations. There were several bottles of Thunderbird available. Laced with grapefruit juice it was used to make a concoction called Bitter Dog, said to be the chosen drink of Lil' Bobby Hutton. (He was the Party's first martyr, a sixteen-year-old killed in a shoot-out with police in Oakland in 1969.) The drink added to my sense of the moment, though I could handle only a few swallows.

Rapping with the brothers was thrilling, for they talked in such jazzy, urban vernacular. I was still a country boy in many respects, and really wanted to be cool, to take on the devil-may-care attitude that I'd come to believe was the essence of "blackness." And it was not lost on me that the coolest brothers got the women.

Coon, who had done so much in recruiting me with his visit to my parents, seemed to take me under his wing. When we'd finished eating and drinking, he put his arm around my shoulders, steered me away from the group, and whispered, "Come with me. There's someone I want to introduce you to. Maybe you'll finally get your nuts out of the sand." At Coon's house, I met Charlotte, who was visiting there. After I had a little more wine with her, she and I enjoyed a night of marvelous sex like I'd never known.

Full Party membership had to be earned, so I was considered a Panther in training, or a community worker. Official membership in the party had been closed down when Huey Newton was released from prison. He'd been held for three years for the death of an Oakland police officer in 1967, in a shooting incident in which Newton had also been badly wounded. After a nationwide "Free Huey" campaign by black and white radicals nationwide had helped win a reversal of his conviction, he came out to discover that, in addition to the thousand real Party members, dozens of unofficial chapters had also sprung up, with hundreds of young men and women claiming to be Panthers—many of them creating all sorts of mischief.

My job as community worker began in earnest the day after I arrived. The most pressing task was to liberate the High Point

Four—four teens who had been arrested following a shoot-out at the Party's headquarters in High Point some months before. Police had tried to serve an eviction notice during, the predawn hours, a practice they'd often used in other cities to provoke a confrontation. A gunfight ensued, and a police officer was seriously wounded, as was Larry Medley, hit by a shotgun slug in the chest.

A rally was planned to take place in a recreational park in High Point, and leaflets had to be mimeographed and distributed, banners and posters prepared. I was assigned to work with Judge, and using my so-called bourgeois skills I helped Judge come up with some rather polished leaflets, posters, and banners.

The July rally was truly inspiring. We gathered some two or three hundred participants, who responded as a chorus with "right on!" to the dynamic rhetoric from speakers who ranged from chapter leader Larry Little to the state leader of the SCLC, along with Mrs. Lee Faye Mack, a Winston-Salem community activist in the mold of Fanie Lou Hamer, and the well-known civil rights lawyer Jerry Paul. I reveled in the moment, remembering how I had journeyed to this park and swimming pool with my church's Sunday school, because there were no such resorts in Virginia open to blacks. Larry Little delivered a powerful speech, declaring that "the power of the people will free the High Point Four from their repressive incarceration, by *any means necessary.*"

"Right on!" the crowd chanted in response to his incendiary voice, and waved banners and posters emblazoned with large black panthers and FREE THE HIGH POINT FOUR! Meanwhile, I was utilizing new skills to run the public address system. "The power of the people will overcome the man's technology," Larry screamed to the assembled. I felt proud to be among this community of black folk, in seeing my people making a stand, and proud of the Party's role in energizing them. I was at once falling in love with the Party, and more deeply in love with black people.

Following the speakers, there was music, with singing by the Mack family: Lee Faye Mack with her older daughters, Party members Hazel and Clara, and her younger daughters, Bunchy and Ruth. Wearing African headdresses, they represented black womanhood to me. The fifteen-year-old Ruth especially caught my eye, and I resolved to learn more about her at my earliest opportunity.

After the rally, the pressing task was to get the new headquarters renovated, with the goal of opening by the end of the summer so that the breakfast program could begin. I worked with the other comrades to clean up the old house that had been purchased by Mrs. Mack, who was, in a sense, with her standing in the community and position with various poverty programs in the city, the queen mother of the Party. For the first time I enjoyed physical labor, painting and hammering and lending to the communal effort to get the two-story building in shape.

Panther chapters were organized into various ministries, with smaller units called cadres. There was the Ministry of Education, which coordinated the P.E. classes and Liberation School (a sort of after-school program for the youth). There was the Ministry of Information to handle "the dissemination of propaganda to the masses." (The word *propaganda* was explained as not a bad thing, but simply getting one's view out into the world. "The Oppressor had his propaganda, and we have ours.") And then there was Distribution, which handled the sale of the Party newspaper. The newspaper was the primary source of income for most chapters, augmented by donations from sympathetic businesses to the Free Breakfast for Schoolchildren and other Survival Programs—the programs that were part of the Party's new focus on serving the community, so that "we might survive until revolution comes."

I was assigned to work with Russell, who was head of Distribution. Each week I'd ride with him to the airport to pick up the boxes of papers shipped from Oakland, and then we'd organize their sale across the state and region. I even went back to Danville on occasion, since our work when I was there had established a market for the paper. These visits also gave me a chance to see my family, let them know I was okay, and maintain my bond with them.

Because there were only the two shotgun-shack apartments for comrades to live in, I usually stayed at the new headquarters with Russell, who was also the chief of security, due to his ROTC training when he attended A&T State University, in Greensboro. We slept on mattresses on the floor of a back room, and someone was always required to be awake "pulling security." Russell was a splendid example of a man at twenty-three, muscular at six-foot-four with a face like a lion cub with a thick, untrimmed mustache. He explained to me the necessity of staying on guard: "The pigs firebombed our last headquarters, and attacked the one in High Point in the middle of the night. That won't happen again.

"Party mandate number one rules that no one can breach the security of our doors," he said, describing attacks on other headquarters around the country, particularly the infamous predawn attack in Chicago that killed famed Panther leaders Fred Hampton and Mark Clark in December 1969. "If we are attacked by police forces, we are to defend our dwellings with all the firepower at our command," he said, presenting me with an M-1 carbine. I took this role of militant defender to heart, taking the extra magazine he gave me "in case the shooting got hot," and taping it upside-down to the magazine in the carbine's breech, in the fashion I'd seen in war movies.

I felt that I was indeed now part of a war, and I would drill with my weapon as I walked from the back of the building to the front, peering out from the side of makeshift curtains to make sure no police or white vigilantes were lurking in the shadows. Sometimes I'd take the rounds out of the M-1 so that I could dry-fire at imagined targets.

Russell, being a real military buff, had numerous books about urban guerrilla warfare, and used them to instruct me about the dedication of the communist insurgent. "Check out these writings by Kim Il Sung, the leader of North Korea," he said. "He teaches about the art of *juche*—using what you have to fashion the weapons you need. The North Korean revolutionaries are so dedicated," he added, "that they have vowed to do without sex until they liberate the southern part of their country." He also had me read from "The Mini-manual of the Urban Guerrilla," a South American pamphlet that described, among other things, how to make a mortar out of a shotgun, a broom handle, and a Molotov cocktail.

Russell told me how Huey and other Party leaders had recently visited China and North Korea, and that the Black Panther Party was the vanguard of world revolution by virtue of its position in the belly of the beast—the monolith of U.S. imperialism. The Party also taught that whites and people of color were all brothers and sisters, that the divisions in the world were based upon class, not color, and that color and race were used by the oligarchies—the families who historically owned and controlled most of the wealth of the world—to divide the working classes who actually produced the goods and services.

With Russell's Marxist teachings I became engaged by the concept of worldwide revolution, loving all the history and idealistic philosophy, and loving the words with which the Panther Party defined the world. It gave me a way to understand things like the ongoing war in Vietnam, and how black people had come to be enslaved, how we were still subjugated by the mental bonds ensuing from their enforced cultural and educational ignorance. These ideas fed into my desire to be at the forefront of universal change: We would save the world by organizing the black community to rise up and destroy the racist power structure in America.

"Revolution in our lifetime" was Russell's favorite Party slogan, and the force of arms would one day provide the means for achieving full liberation, he said. "More than thirty Panthers have lost their lives," he said, "and we must all know that someday we, too, might have to make the supreme sacrifice for the people."

As I dutifully stood watch against nocturnal attack, Russell's words would ring in my mind, and I felt the possibility of death as a constant. But being part of an army of young men and women who were also standing guard against aggression gave me comfort, and I felt the spirit of comrades wounded or slain in such battles during my solitary vigils.

Being on the road with Russell was exciting. We were distributing the truth to the masses, in areas that had never seen black men and women daring to tell the truth regarding oppression. Because our chapter had only one basic vehicle—a run-down Volkswagen van donated by Quakers—Russell and I usually caught the bus to various cities and college campuses in North Carolina, with a box or two of Panther papers in tow. We then hitchhiked back to Winston-Salem, to save the hard-earned quarters we had collected from hawking our papers.

Greensboro was our closest target, while Durham, Raleigh, and Chapel Hill—with the North Carolina Triangle universities of Duke, N.C. State, and the University of North Carolina—were more favored cities. Often, on weekends when the trips required staying overnight, supporters in the community, or even in the college dormitories, would put us up for the night. It was a beautiful sign of acceptance and trust.

The growing metropolis of Charlotte, North Carolina, seemed to be the most productive place for selling the papers, and I honed my street-corner techniques there. I practiced my quick line as one might the Peter Piper tongue twister in a speech class: "Would you like to buy a Panther paper—learn the real news—only twenty-five cents—help out the Black Panther Party survival programs—get the real news here and now."

One trip to Charlotte coincided with a parade through town by Richard Nixon. Catching sight of the relatively unprotected President, I imagined his chest in the crosshairs of a telescopic sight. I was thinking of the writings of George Jackson in his second book,

Blood in My Eye, in which he envisioned his younger brother Jonathan taking aim on the President with an antitank weapon. "Why don't we just declare war on the power structure," I asked Russell, "and go ahead and show we can kill these people at will?"

I was surprised at Russell's answer, as he was the chapter's most militant member. "Look around you, little brother. He's the fuckin' President. He's got all sorts of protection you can't even see. Don't you know that the FBI is watching us, even now?"

I looked around and saw only the sidewalks lined with flag-waving supporters of the war, and people just enjoying the sight of a living president. "You've got to remember," Russell said over the din of cheers and the occasional heckle of war protesters, "that a lot of our rhetoric is to inspire folk to believe that resistance *is possible.*"

He paused for a moment then, looked around at the scene before us, and evidently decided to bring some semblance of reality to my adolescent mind. "In reality," he said, "they've got a hundred Nixons to take that bastard's place. We are just setting the stage for a stronger, future warrior class to emerge. And no matter what we say, we have to be ready for years, if not decades of struggle, before the people are ready to rise up against the power structure."

He then added, "We are like the Irish Republican Army, creating what they call 'a terrible beauty' of resistance, for future generations to remember."

However, Russell's militancy seemed at odds with the current thrust of the Party, and the emphasis of "serving the people, body and soul" through the survival programs. "Revolution is a process," Huey Newton wrote after his release from prison, "a process of moving from A to Z. The people have to be educated and prepared for the struggle ahead." This reflected the division in the party that had occurred in 1971, when the New York chapter broke away to follow the ultramilitant positions of Eldridge Cleaver. An offshoot of that Party faction, the underground Black Liberation Army, was said to be carrying out armed attacks against police in New York and other places during this time.

Though I considered myself a warrior preparing for such revolutionary conflict, my heart was with the idea of community service through the Party's survival programs: Free Breakfast for Schoolchildren, Free Food, Free Clothing, Free Health Clinics, and others. I believed that these programs were set in an ideal not unlike the Christian ethos of my youth, though I was now embracing a new religiosity: that of socialist ideology, which Panther doctrine taught was rooted in the communal spirit of early African civilization.

I related the militancy of bringing about radical change through force to my "sermon" in church, which spoke of how Christ used force to expel the moneylenders from the temple. The Party was attempting to do the same thing, on a broader scale: expel the capitalist oligarchy from control over the lives of the masses. And while I had come to believe that the idea of God was used to keep the people in subjugation, by having them dream of a pie in the sky by and by, I still felt that the ideals of Christian justice were enduring. They needed only to be related to the secular world to bring about a communal utopia on earth, to bring "All Power to the People"— the Party's chief slogan, repeated as a salutation whenever members met, as well as replacement for *goodbye* at every departure.

Our new headquarters was slated to open with a grand celebration. I helped Judge put out leaflets and posters welcoming folk to attend the opening. The day before, we put the last touches on a large sign in front of the new office, painted in the Panther colors of powder blue and black, as was the building. A large panther was emblazoned on the sign, along with the motto SERVING THE PEOPLE, BODY AND SOUL. The finishing touch was a new layer of cement for the sidewalk leading to the new office, and Judge gave me the honor of inscribing, in the fresh cement, three lines taken from the "Warrior's Oath" of Panther folklore:

If ever I break my stride
Or falter at my comrade's side . . .
THIS OATH WILL SURELY KILL ME!

The next day, the grand opening of the office was a tremendous success, attended by more than five hundred people—evidence of the popularity of work done by the Party at previous offices. As part of our food program, everyone received a free bag of groceries. The office was replete with posters: Huey Newton sitting in an African wicker chair with a spear in one hand and a shotgun in the other; Chairman Bobby Seale speaking to a throng of folk in Chicago as part of the Days of Rage against the Vietnam War; and the most popular poster of all, Angela Davis, a hero of the Movement in general, and the Party in particular, for the BPP had been instrumental in galvanizing the support that had recently won her freedom. In the middle of the hallway was a poster of Fred Hampton, the Panther leader and martyr who was slain in a midnight raid by Chicago police in 1969, emblazoned with the words HE CAME FROM THE MOUNTAINTOP, DOWN TO THE VALLEY. I really related to this idea, for it spoke to how Fred had come from a middle-class family like mine, yet he'd chosen to throw in his lot with the masses. And then there was the poster of George Jackson, my beloved hero.

After the crowd had gone, we gathered for a celebratory Sunday dinner. With our group being so large, a few sat in the kitchen where the former schoolteacher, Mary, stood at the stove, frying the rest of the chicken. Others of us were in the hallway, including the tall, fiery Larry; Nelson, the diminutive organizer with the supersmooth manner; and Hazel, the group's secretary, who was several months pregnant at the time. We were high on the events of the day, laughing and joking ("This chicken will never fly again," said Nelson, after reducing the bird on his paper plate to mere bones), and I reveled in the earthy humor. I was given compliments for my contributions to the information surrounding the event, which was credited with our having had such a large turnout. "Just give the job to Can-Do-Derrell," Hazel said, "and you can be sure it will get done."

Then the discussion turned to George Jackson and his international bestseller, *Soledad Brother.* Given an indeterminate sentence of one-year-to-life for the robbery of a California gas station when he was seventeen, he was at that time under indictment for the murder of a prison guard who had been killed in retaliation for the killing of three militants by guards at Soledad Prison. Jackson had just been named Field Marshal of the Party by Huey Newton. "Comrade George is truly the greatest writer of us all," said Nelson, a comrade I'd become especially close to, as he always found time to talk to me, like an older brother of sorts. He was echoing what Newton had written about Jackson in his endorsement of his book.

Somehow, perhaps due to the Bitter Dog we were drinking along with our dinner, I had the nerve to comment, "Well, you got to look at all that time he has to read and study while in prison. If I had all of that time to write, I probably would become a great writer, too."

They looked at me with some astonishment, that I would display such arrogance as to even *insinuate* that I could become a writer on the level of the great George Jackson. And while most comrades there would forget about that moment, seeing the remark as merely adolescent hubris, others would one day recall the day and tell me that I had been foreshadowing my future, as desire.

Weeks later, on August 21, the chapter received word: George Jackson had been shot and killed by guards at San Quentin Prison during a purported escape attempt. Three inmates and three guards were also slain.

We were all devastated by the news, and none more than I. In the immediate aftermath of his death, a grand memorial service, attended by a thousand people, was held in Oakland. Then a week later prisoners at Attica State Prison in upstate New York staged a rebellion, taking several guards hostage, largely in response to the killing of George Jackson. I identified with these men, so I was crushed to learn on September 13 that New York State police had quashed the rebellion, and that thirty-one inmates and guards had lost their lives.

The next day, when news that the guards and prisoners had been killed by gunfire from the state troopers, I said to my comrades, "Their deaths will not be in vain." A few days later we received a package of posters with our weekly shipment of papers. I looked at the visage of my smiling hero, and, fighting back tears of sadness and rage, I set off alone to tack up the posters all around Winston-Salem. They proclaimed GEORGE JACKSON LIVES!

I felt compelled to make sure that he would, indeed, continue to live. I would carry on Jackson's work as a writer, and soon after I began sending articles to the Black Panther Party newspaper in Oakland. I would now become the writer George could no longer be.

In the fall, just before the beginning of the school year, I received a new assignment. I was given charge over the chapter's Ministry of Information after Judge left the Party—or "defected," as it was termed. ("You're either part of the solution or part of the problem," was the mentality of the period.) I took my new position seriously, and when I enrolled in the prestigious R. J. Reynolds High School, in the heart of the white community, I took classes in typing ("So I can write as fast as I can think," I told comrades), art ("So I can better disseminate the Party's vision on leaflets and posters"), and advanced English ("So I can become a better writer").

Before walking the two miles to school, I'd awaken from the upstairs communal room at headquarters (it couldn't exactly be called a bedroom, since there were no real beds, only three mattresses atop box springs) and help serve breakfast to neighborhood children. Carrying thin paper plates laden with hot grits and eggs burning through to the palms of my hands, I was energized by the smiles and jabbering of the children in the front room, which was set up with metal chairs and tables covered with clean paper tablecloths.

At my new school, however, I had trouble connecting with other students. They really didn't know what to make of me. I was new to the city and the school, was quiet and unassuming, but was rumored to be one of the Panthers. One day, after I'd been attending classes for a few months, a sister in my history class came up to me and said, "Aren't you with the Black Panthers?" She had seen me selling papers around town, and seemed interested in the Party's work, so I opened up to her a bit. Our conversations led to her telling our teacher that I was a Panther, and the teacher invited me to speak to the class one day. At the time I was still quite shy, but I felt it my duty to proselytize to the people whenever the opportunity arose.

I spoke on the Ten Point Platform and Program, trying to give my fellow students an understanding of what the Party was all about. The teacher, however, did not take well to my message.

"It sounds to me as if your group is basically communist—or at least Marxist in philosophy," she said. "Is this not the case?"

"We are not communist," I responded. "Nor do we think of ourselves as Marxist—as even Karl Marx said that he didn't consider himself a Marxist, only a social scientist. We are just social scientists of our day," I said, starting to preach a bit with a fervor I hadn't had much chance to use before. "We are an evolution of the communal spirit that believes human life is sacred, that the downtrodden peoples of the world must rise up to take control of our lives. We simply believe power should belong in the hands of the people, as is mandated by the Constitution you teach us in this class."

Defiantly, I asked her, "Do you think it should be any other way?" A heated discussion followed, and afterward students approached me with questions about the Party and its teachings. But I guess word got around the school, for I received no more invitations to use classes as forums.

I took only enough courses to graduate, so that I would have my afternoons free to work in the community, mainly doing door-to-door work in the housing projects and poor communities. I was enthusiastic about helping residents to understand that they could help take part in changing the system. I took particular pleasure in visits to one white family who lived in an old trailer on the outskirts of the projects. The elderly matriarch was receptive to our message, since her family had been aided by our free clothing and food programs. It turned out that her father had been a Russian immigrant socialist in New York, and she was able to share with me tales of the plight of the working class in the early 1920s. I felt that by talking to her and her family, I was embodying the Party's view that we were engaged in a collectivist class struggle that knew no racial boundaries.

As a chapter Minister of Information (a title I cherished) I became passionate about photography, learning to develop film at a nearby community center called The Summit. I would capture scenes of everyday life in 35-mm black-and-white and be enchanted as I developed the images, seeing them appear in a chemical tray under the red light of the darkroom. Along with photography I learned the art of silk-screening posters, aided by the black owner of a sign company near the office. I soon felt the power of this burgeoning artistry reach out all over the city, in posters and leaflets. Combined with the knowledge that my photos and articles were appearing around the country in the Party newspaper, I was hooked on the ability to expand my ideas out into the world.

My mother and father continued to give me support during this time, sending a little money here and there for school supplies and lunch, knowing that times weren't easy for us. They came to visit soon after the school year began, with the gift of an Underwood manual typewriter. I wrote to them regularly, typing out letters late at night in the upstairs room referred to as the Ministry. Along with the daily reports that all Party members and community workers were required to file at the end of each day, and the articles for the paper, I began the habit of writing daily.

In October Bobby Seale came to speak at Winston-Salem State University to much fanfare, packing a full house into the school's gymnasium. I took pictures and helped set up the sound system, which seemed to link me to the greatness that the famous BPP chairman embodied. My mother and father traveled from Danville to attend, bringing as a special present a three-quarter-length leather coat, as protection against the coming winter. It was, to my mind, validation of their love and the role I was playing in the struggle.

On Wednesday evenings we had our Liberation School, where we would bring in children from the community and work with them on basic reading skills, while teaching them black history, so that they might understand and have pride in their relationship to the world. Ruth Mack began helping out with the children as one of our community volunteers, and I really dug the way she related to the children. She was sixteen, with a dark chocolate complexion. She had something of a reputation as a firebrand, having led a walk-out at her high school the preceding year.

After the class I saw her sitting on the low stone fence in front of the headquarters, with a white girlfriend. While I didn't think there was anything wrong with that, I just wanted to have something to say to her. Knowing that people might see white and black hanging out together and get the wrong idea, I approached her and said, "Sister, can I speak to you for a minute?" I told her that I thought it might be inappropriate for her to be seen in front of headquarters talking to a white girl, "'Cause you have to know, little sister, that people will think there might be some kind of drug thing going on."

Now why did I say that? She very nearly cursed me out. "You got the nerve to approach me with that chauvinistic bullshit. How dare you try to tell me who I can or cannot talk to, or be seen with." Chastened, I retreated into the headquarters, and thought, *There's more to this girl than meets the eye.*

At the time, I had had very little in the way of relationships with women. Most of the sisters in the collective were older, and in relationships with the older brothers in the Party. I did not have the time to date in the normal high-school sense; so, to break it right down, I wasn't getting any, contrary to what I thought the deal would be from my first sexual initiation to collective living. But everybody around me seemed to be "getting down."

Brothers in the organization were taught never to treat women as "masturbatory objects" just for male gratification. And the Party had this thing about sisters "having free will," and they reveled in the free spirit of the age, and relished repeating the slogan, "Sisterhood is powerful." Often they wore hot pants and halter tops when going out to sell papers; this flaunting of sexuality left me one horny teenager. Although my comrade sisters had no trouble showing their bodies, they still maintained a reserve when it actually came to giving it up to the somewhat nerdy me.

I tried to get something going with a sister in the community named Jeannie, who was all of nineteen with two children, and lived just up the street. She took a liking to me, and would hang around the office helping with odd chores, in order to catch my eye—which she did indeed. I began walking her home in the early evenings, and finally late one night, in the dead of winter, I succeeded in getting invited into her home.

"Shhh, we don't want to wake Mama," she told me, as our kisses led to my disrobing her while I threw off my fake fur coat (which I'd pulled from the free clothing program), turtleneck sweater, two-tone pants, and knee-high leather boots. We were doing all right on the couch for a while, but my six-foot-one frame extended beyond the end of it, and I made the mistake of using a noisy end table for a bit of leverage, paying no heed to the squeak-squeak-squeak of the table legs.

"Let me get on top," the more experienced Jeannie told me;

evidently I was not working hard enough. That's when we heard a voice from the doorway.

"Jeannie, is that you? What you doin', chile?" her mother said, and I could hear her hand scraping the wall in search of the light switch. Luckily, she thought better of turning on the lights, and said, "I told you about that stuff. You need to go to a motel or something. Don't let me catch you doin' this no more in this house."

And so it was that I could be seen running down the street that night, shirt, underwear, and socks in one hand, holding up my two-tone pants with the other, with a bare chest under my fake fur coat in the dead of winter, unzippered boots flapping as I ran.

I then decided to focus on my attraction to Ruth. But my attempts to win her affections didn't go well at first, as she always seemed pissed off at me whenever we'd happen to see each other.

Miz Mack, as we called Ruth's mother, owned a '69 Dodge Dart that she lent to the chapter for various purposes. One day I walked up the five blocks from headquarters to their home to get the car for use in picking up donations to the clothing program. Ruth was fuming because she had no way to get to the shopping center about five miles away.

"Come on, little sister," I told her, knowing that she wouldn't like the appellation, since her childhood nickname had once been "Tiny."

"Is that suppose to be a 'short' joke?" she replied. "Because as far as age I'm almost as old as you are."

"No," I assured her, trying to be smooth, "I'm just offering to give you a ride."

On the way I got her to open up about the walkout at her high school she'd helped lead at the end of the school year, and I told her about my experiences at GW in Danville the year before. I told her that I'd watched her working with the children in Liberation School and admired her way with them. "You're a natural teacher," I said, "you really show your love, and you're obviously very bright."

This garnered a smile as she got out of the car, and she offered to buy me a hamburger to thank me for the lift. Next thing I knew, we were sitting on the stone wall in front of the office every chance we got. I'd talk to her for hours on the office's pay phone, to the point where Larry and Nelson had to just about ban me from "monopolizing" our communication—"You know we got to get calls from Central, and what you gonna say on the phone anyway, knowing the FBI got it tapped?" By spring I was in love for the first time, dreaming of a future with this strong-willed black girl, if only I could find a way to pull her fully into the Party—or at least get her to give up some drawers for the cause, as I used to say, for she still refused to go all the way with me.

That spring of 1972 the chapter received word that our comrade Joseph Waddell had died at Central Prison in Raleigh. A boxer in superb condition, he supposedly had collapsed from a heart attack out in the prison yard. Larry, Nelson, and Coon immediately called a press conference and charged prison authorities with murdering Joe Dell, as he was known by family and friends.

We held a big funeral for Joe Dell, with everyone dressed in black khaki field jackets, black pants, powder-blue shirts, and berets. I was one of the pallbearers, and it was the first time I had been in full Panther regalia. After the funeral Larry announced a surprise meeting of the entire chapter. "This meeting is to recognize that our comrade, Derrell Hopkins, from this point on is promoted, by recognition of the Central Committee in Oakland, to full membership in the Black Panther Party."

I was stunned, but immensely pleased. It was one of my proudest moments, to be officially made a Black Panther at age seventeen, to have my work and dedication rewarded at the time we were recognizing the passing of a dedicated member who had died in prison—whose passing would have gone unregarded had it not been for the love of his Panther family. I felt a renewed dedication to our revolution, and to struggling for the freedom of all our brothers incarcerated in America's dungeons.

At the end of the school year my guidance counselor recommended that I apply for the National Achievement Scholarship because of my high SAT scores. I wrote an essay that earned me semifinalist status, which opened the door for all sorts of scholarship opportunities. The chapter leadership thought that I should attend Winston-Salem State, so that I could organize the students there. I submitted an application for their prestigious Reynolds scholarship and felt certain of winning. However, we soon learned from a supporter, who was on the board of the university, that the FBI had paid a visit to the school and told administrators that the Panthers in Winston-Salem had gone to Virginia to recruit the brightest student they could find, and that I had been delegated to "take over the school." Soon after, my scholarship application was denied.

I was incensed. But, not to be deterred, I approached my parents to pay for my tuition. In the meantime, when I turned eighteen in June, I had to register for the draft. The Vietnam War was still in full swing, and the organization's opposition to the war was unequivocal. When I went in for examination, I wrote on the forms, at some length, about my opposition to the unjust war. I also wrote, "But rather than allow you to imprison me as a conscientious objector, if inducted I will go into the army, and even to Vietnam, and as a member of the Black Panther Party, I will organize the rank and file of the army to understand the true nature of this oppressive imperialist war."

I never heard from the army again.

As fall approached, I prepared for college, while continuing to put out information for the chapter, and working with our programs. By now my romance with Ruth had become intense. But it was a stormy relationship, as she was definitely a free spirit, hard to control. The chapter leadership felt that our relationship was not in the best interest of my work, and her family opposed our being together, thinking it might take her away from her education.

In late summer there came a general call for all chapters to send comrades to California to assist in Chairman Bobby Seale's burgeoning campaign for mayor of Oakland. It was said that members sent out west would work there until the election in the spring of '73, thereby making Oakland a centralized base of operations for the thirty or so Party chapters nationwide.

I wanted to go and to write full-time for the Party newspaper, something I'd dreamed of. But I did not want to let down my parents, who had already paid the tuition for me to go to Winston-Salem State. I didn't want to leave Ruth, either. I recall considering the situation while traveling, alone by bus, from Durham, after selling a load of papers. The bus stopped in front of a music store, the outside loudspeaker blaring Marvin Gaye's "What's Going On?" I looked at the poster of Gaye in the store window, in a leather raincoat with water pouring down upon his bare head, symbolic of the state of the world.

His song embodied my indecision, as well; yet, somehow, he helped me make up my mind. I would travel to Oakland, to find out what was really going on. I was a partisan writer, going where the big story was, a revolutionary journalist like Hemingway during the Spanish Civil War. I would journey to California, home of my hero, George Jackson, and there I would begin to make my mark.

CHAPTER FOUR

Manchild in Pantherland

A rriving at San Francisco International that August evening in 1972, the air was much cooler than I had imagined, as I'd thought of California as all sunshine and tropical heat. After leaving ninety-degree weather in North Carolina, however, the change was refreshing.

I was greeted by Aaron Dixon, a tall young man with angular features and a mustache and goatee that made him look like a handsome Lucifer. "You must be Comrade Derrell, from Winston-Salem," he said, having had no trouble picking me out from the predominance of white faces at the airport. Aaron smiled all the time and obviously loved to talk, explaining to me as he packed my belongings into a blue Ford station wagon that he was the OD (officer of the day) at Central Headquarters, and his job was to retrieve the newest additions to the Bay Area.

As soon as we got on the road, he began to regale me with exciting stories of how the organization was gearing up for Chairman Bobby's mayoral campaign. "We're going to seize power, legitimately, and take over the city," he said, as he wove through the freeway system from the airport, then through San Francisco itself and across the

Bay Bridge into Oakland. We developed a rapport right away, as he related tales of how he had helped to found the Party's chapter in Seattle with his brother, and drew me out of my country-boy awe by asking me to tell him all about the chapter in Winston-Salem.

"You'll like it out here," he said. "This is a whole new world, comrade brother. You have no idea how much power and pull we have here, how much real support we have in the community."

It was surely a new world to me, a bigger metropolitan area than I'd ever encountered before. As I viewed the Pacific Ocean giving way to the vast bay and freeways surrounding Oakland, I knew that I was entering a new life.

It was nearly dark when we arrived at Central Headquarters in East Oakland, the city and the office glowing with light and life. I didn't know what Central would be like—maybe a house in the community, like our office in Winston—but it turned out to be ad-joining two-story storefront buildings, on the main thoroughfare of East Sixteenth Street.

Aaron introduced me to everybody working at Central: the printers who put out the leaflets and posters and memoranda; the distribution workers who packaged up the newspapers and mailed out subscriptions; and upstairs in the Ministry of Information, the brothers and sisters who staffed the newspaper, worked the typeset-ting machines, and ran the library and photography lab.

After taking me on a quick tour, Aaron said, "I've heard that you're a writer and will probably be working with the editorial cadre, and that'll start tomorrow. But I'm getting ready to go on the garbage run now, and we usually take new comrades on the run with us, so they can see all that we have going." He then winked and added, "And I know you want to meet some of these fine com-rade sisters out here."

Aaron made it seem like we were about to embark on an adven-ture, so I gladly jumped into a big cargo truck with him. As we rode down Eighty-fifth Avenue, he explained the situation to me: "The city cut off our garbage services after we had a beef with them about the bill, so we decided to collect all the trash from all the offices and houses ourselves."

"Just how many facilities does the Party have out here?" I asked.

"Counting Berkeley and Richmond, maybe ten or so. But that doesn't include San Francisco or Palo Alto, but we don't have to do pickups there." Suddenly this trip had begun to sound much less glamorous.

The first stop was at the East Oakland office, where, after being greeted by eight comrades who lived in the house, Aaron instructed me to join him in donning galoshes. We proceeded to dump the funkiest garbage I could imagine from cans into the back of the cargo truck. When I saw the squirmy creatures crawling all over the week-old garbage, and oozing from the plastic bags, I was ignorant enough to ask Aaron, "What are those little white worms?"

He had a fit laughing. "The comrades in Winston told me that you came from a bourgeois family," he said, "but I got to say that I never ran across anybody who's never seen a maggot before."

From there we traveled to the facility on Twenty-ninth Street, called the Intercommunal Youth Institute, a three-story building in the heart of a middle-class white community. The Institute housed the organization's school, along with the main campaign headquarters. There, I received the warmest greeting, for most of the teachers at the Institute were female. (Thirty or more children, most of them the progeny of Party members, also lived there in a dormitory setting, but they were in bed by then.) Many of the sisters were, at this time of evening, clad only in nightclothes, which really set my adolescent sexual fantasies to working. I seemed to catch the interest of a sister named Gina, who flirted with me a bit. Right away I felt that I had made a personal connection on my new ground.

Next we went to houses and facilities in West Oakland, then downtown to The Lamp Post, which, Aaron told me, was run by the Party. "It used to be owned by Huey's cousin, but now it's staffed with Party members and used as a source of income."

From there we went to houses in North Oakland, followed by

Berkeley, where the BPP ran the George Jackson Free Health Clinic, one of the Party's main survival programs, which offered free health care to the surrounding communities. Then we drove all the way to Richmond, a small city several miles north of Berkeley, where the organization had its Child Development Center for the infants and toddlers of Party members. By the time Aaron and I returned to Central, I'd met nearly a hundred of the Panthers in the Bay Area and was completely worn out from my stint as a garbageman.

Back at Central, I found the sleeping arrangements fairly primitive, just as they were in Winston, and was glad to find a mattress in the back of the building. Though weary, I was happy to be in the heart of the living, expansive family of my comrades, wholly engaged in a sophisticated struggle for liberation.

The next day I was officially assigned to write for the newspaper. My first assignment was to accompany Aaron and the paper's deputy editor, Michael, to cover the beginning of the trial of the San Quentin Six. The Six were accused of taking part in the killing of prison guards at San Quentin the preceding year, on the day that George Jackson had been slain.

We traveled along the lovely Northern California coast in the same blue station wagon in which Aaron had fetched me from the airport, until we arrived at the harbor city of San Rafael. Riding past the quaint yacht marina, I spotted a Highway Patrol helicopter above us. The scenic beauty and the idea of freedom and civilization began to transform as we drove around great gray cliffs streaked with red and arrived at the San Rafael County Civic Center, its parking lot filled with police cars and uniforms of all kinds.

Moving into the building past an array of metal detectors, checkpoints, and still more uniformed men and women mixing with the crowd, we entered a courtroom and took seats up front near a wall of thick bulletproof glass that separated the spectators from the chamber proper. With a notepad on my lap as we waited for the proceedings to begin, I stared at the six brown-skinned men in beige prison khakis sitting in the dock, handcuffed and shackled to their chairs by an elaborate set of chains.

I remembered then how the Panther comrades in North Carolina had called the courtroom "the den of fascism."

"Why do you call it that?" I'd asked Larry Little, sitting beside him in the courtroom where he was on trial for illegal possession of a weapon.

"Because this is the heart of fascism," he had whispered to me, "where the powers-that-be conduct their legal lynchings, twisting their so-called laws so they can incarcerate us while pretending that they are righteous. This is how they maintain their power, where they repose and plan and connive and plot like the den of thieves they are."

The words *den of fascism* had stuck in my mind, as had so much of the first, fiery rhetoric I'd heard during the time of my initial recruitment by those silver-tongued zealots, so filled with the fervor of new truth. The term had seemed to give the courtroom an almost supernatural power, an aura of menace and evil portent. And I felt it now, watching the selection of the twelve white men and women who would pass judgment upon these prisoners of color, remembering how this was the place I'd read about, in that first Panther paper my cousin had given me, how this was where Jonathan Jackson had died in a hail of police gunfire.

Now I'm actually here, I thought, *writing for the Panther paper, a revolutionary war correspondent on the front line of struggle. The son of Daniel, in the lion's den.*

After the hearing we had to stop by San Quentin, where Michael was supposed to meet with lawyers for Johnny Spain, a Party member who was one of the San Quentin Six. Aaron and I waited outside the gates to the fortress prison for two hours, talking about the trial and George Jackson. Astounded by the security around the place, with its several fences of barbed wire surrounding gigantic walls that encircled what looked like a smokestack factory, bounded on three sides by the northern part of the San Francisco Bay, I told Aaron, "It's hard to believe George tried to escape from this place."

"Yeah," he said, "it had to be a carefully planned conspiracy to assassinate him. Just look at the place. You have to wonder how the thousands locked up inside could ever survive, much less write the way Comrade George did."

Along with covering the trial of the San Quentin Six, I was given the task of transcribing tapes of the last interview George Jackson had given to the Berkeley PBS radio station, KPFA. I had also been given the job of librarian, which entailed filing all of the past issues of the newspaper and keeping the Party's library in order. It was in the library, located upstairs at Central, with a window facing Eighty-fifth Avenue, that I sat down to transcribe Comrade George's last public words.

He spoke of the need to understand the relationship of armed struggle to political endeavor. "My politics," he said, in a supercool street cadence, "are Panther politics. I subscribe to *foco motor* theory, like Castro—meaning that the political ends dictate the means of struggle." I studied George's words, trying to discern the delineation he saw between the necessity for armed struggle and the pursuit of political ends by peaceful means. It boiled down to the old debate between followers of Martin Luther King and Malcolm X, about how black people should achieve liberation.

While the Party had its base in the militant rhetoric of armed struggle, we were now following the nonviolent path, using political means to change the system from within. But there were still guns all around. One of my duties at Central was pulling security, for we were still commanded to remain vigilant against attack by police throughout the night, just as we had been in Winston-Salem. Despite having tempered our rhetoric, there remained a hard edge that said, in no uncertain terms, that we would defend ourselves.

I became tight with another young comrade in the editorial cadre named Danny, who was about the same age as me. We both liked to write late at night, and would sneak off for a few minutes to smoke marijuana, as smoking in the office was forbidden. Danny had this wild and humorous view of life, and saw revolution as something of a joke played by fate on the rich elites, *and* on us—believing that the hard work of our writing the truth was a way of exacting ironic revenge against the powers-that-be. Along with a brother named Taps from Chicago, and Sherry from Baltimore, we were the hotshot writers for the paper. We'd conduct intellectual raps about politics, as well as the foibles of the Party leadership, for we saw ourselves as part of the rank and file.

During our walks around the block to smoke, I would trip on the nightlife of brothers and sisters gathered in front of bars and chicken joints in the area, young brothers selling matchboxes of weed for five dollars apiece, or "white crosses"—amphetamines some of us would sometimes buy to stay awake as we wrote. This was the first limited view I had of night culture of the black community, and I loved what I saw, romanticizing the characters dressed in the flamboyant costumes of the early seventies: bell bottoms, platform shoes, wide-brimmed hats. These were authentic members of the lumpen proletariat, I thought, the people we were fighting for, the ones we would recruit to get down and dirty "when the revolution came."

I worked hard to prove myself as a writer, though I really didn't know much about how to professionally report. Neither did the other members of the editorial cadre. Most of the articles in the Party paper were rewritten from reports gleaned from other news agencies, either Establishment sources like *The New York Times* or AP wires, or alternative sources like Liberation News Agency or agencies that reported the liberation movements in Africa. Also, we had articles sent in by the chapters around the country. The art was to give all of them the slant of the "Party line." Hence, a story would come in and be clipped by the assistant editor, Michael, who determined the relevance of the report to our revolutionary struggle and then assigned it to the writer he thought best suited to write the piece. Our pieces appeared without bylines, for it was thought that all we wrote was part of a collective effort—plus, we didn't want the police and FBI to have the names of any Party members if we could help it.

At the top of the list of subjects were incidents of police brutality, which were common all across the country. Most of the policemen at that time were white, and came from suburbs surrounding the black communities in which they served. Then there were reports of rent strikes and community actions for welfare reform, accounts of political activities by our chapters or by the small number of black officials, and any general story thought to be of interest to black folk.

Our stories would almost always end in rhetoric. A story about police brutality that featured the so-called innovation of SWAT teams in L.A. might end with, "Though the forces of oppression believe they can repress the righteous anger of the people, the spirit of the people is greater than the Man's technology." Or we'd close with one of our mottos, like REVOLUTION IN OUR LIFETIME, or BLOOD TO THE HORSE'S BROW. (Danny and I never used the latter, but we amused ourselves while getting high by wondering just where such a phrase had come from. Danny, having had a couple of years of college, finally determined that it might reach back to Shakespearean legend, and how horsemen were determined to fight to the very end, until even their horses were brow-deep in blood.)

After I was at the paper a couple of months, a new editor was brought in who would change our slapdash way of reporting. He was David Graham DuBois, the son of famed NAACP founder and author-sociologist W. E. B. DuBois. He had been the editor of the English-speaking daily newspaper in Cairo, Egypt, and he brought a new professionalism to our paper. David became my mentor, educating me in how to report a story without the blatant biases we normally injected into our pieces. Taking a special interest in my work, he took the time to instruct me on the nuances of using detail and color, and how to engage the reader.

In my capacity as librarian I took over the tape room, a small alcove at Central that consisted of little more than a desk and several
little-used reel-to-reel tape recorders. I became the Party's historian,
with the job of cataloging all the tape recordings of past radio interviews and speeches by Huey Newton, Bobby Seale, and other leaders, and filing issues of the paper that dated back to the Party's
inception in 1966.

It was through this that I learned all about the early attacks upon
the Party during the years when the organization proclaimed the
most stringent revolutionary rhetoric ("Death to the fascist pigs!"
was the cry of the day). More than two dozen Panthers had died in
shoot-outs with police, or through internecine conflicts engendered
by the FBI's COINTELPRO program. COINTELPRO (short for
Counter-Intelligence Program) used Watergate-style dirty tricks to
foment dissension within the Party, and with rival organizations,
with the FBI using agent provocateurs to instigate trouble, and
doing things like sending false letters to Party leaders to bring about
the Newton/Cleaver split.

Though most of the twenty-six Panthers cited in the old papers
were killed in aggressive actions by the police, I was able to read between the lines and see how a few had actually been slain while attempting to ambush policemen, or during "actions to reappropriate
the wealth" (i.e., robbing from the rich to support the liberation of
the poor).

Assigned to help me in the tape room was a sixteen-year-old
named Dewey Johnson, the brother of Bobby's secretary, Leslie,
who had been shipped out to California to get him away from gang
activity in his hometown of Philadelphia. Now Dewey was sho'nuff
a wild child, a thin, brown-skinned teen with an enormous wavy
Afro that extended a full four inches, in a sort of natural pom-
padour, from his forehead. Always hyped up, he explained to me
how, when the Party first came to Philly, he and other gang members thought that the Panthers were just another gang, since gang-
banging was all they knew about. Before Dewey I'd been the

youngest Panther in the Bay Area, so I welcomed having someone younger to train, someone I could help develop. And since Dewey was a stone lumpen, bringing him around would be evidence that we could take the most hardcore "street nigguh" and turn him into a disciplined revolutionary.

The tape room became our personal domain, and we organized it into a high-performance sound studio, with three reel-to-reel recorders hooked up to a mixer, two cassette machines, and superbad speakers. The high-energy Taps would storm into the room with the latest jazz recordings, introducing me to vintage John Coltrane. On the system we played Earth, Wind and Fire (a group I believed to deliver divine messages, despite the Marxist atheism I supposedly embraced), Sly and the Family Stone, Tower of Power, the Ohio Players, and other funk groups of the day. I believed Stevie Wonder's albums had a spiritual message as well. It was a glorious time to live and write for the Cause, to feel the spirit of the Movement through the music of the times, to believe in the wonderment of life and the possibilities for grand change.

Life at Central was still rough, and I slept on thin-sheeted mattresses most of the time. While the officer of the day, or the comrade sisters who worked at Central, cooked decent meals in the evenings, we were usually on our own during the early part of the day. Most mornings we cooked eggs left over from donations to the breakfast program, and lunch was hard to come by. Mama faithfully sent money to me every month, and that sustained me with California fruit and granola, as I had begun to get into the West Coast health food thing.

Many nights, when I was not writing for the paper, I would travel to North Oakland to visit Gina, with whom I'd developed a relationship. It didn't bother me to know that the Party hierarchy lived in nice houses in North Oakland, and that Huey lived in a penthouse on Lake Merritt. At the time, I believed the story that they needed to be where they would have extra security, that the comforts they had were deserved for their positions of leadership.

My writing and my work in handling the organization's tape recordings caused David DuBois to give me the assignment of covering Bobby Seale's run for mayor, which heated up in the winter of 1973, as we headed for the election in mid-April. Bobby was the face of the Party, famous for his book *Seize the Time,* and for having been a defendant in the Chicago Eight trial in 1969 (in which the judge had ordered him bound and gagged, to keep him from speaking out against the injustice of the trial of those charged with inciting the riots that took place at the Democratic convention of 1968). He'd also achieved a degree of fame for having been charged with the murder of a police agent in New Haven, a completely bogus charge of which he was eventually acquitted.

Along with Bobby, the flamboyant Panther chairwoman, Elaine Brown, was running for city council. My job was to tape their campaign speeches and every public utterance, to transcribe them into articles for the paper, and to blend them into political radio ads. I became part of the Seale/Brown entourage, with Bobby riding with his driver and bodyguard in his long Buick "Deuce and a Quarter" while I traveled with Elaine and her driver and bodyguard, along with the paper's photographer, Melanie, a Creole beauty from Louisiana with a haughty manner. (I developed a thing for Melanie. But, like most of the Panther sisters who were older, I couldn't get her to think of me romantically, though we did develop a nice Platonic friendship.)

We would rise at 6 A.M. to begin campaigning with Bobby and Elaine at bus stops, where they shook hands with workers as they went off to their jobs. We would have cadres of Panthers there, dressed nicely in jackets and ties or dresses, passing out sophisticated brochures, and registering people to vote. Then the campaign entourage would begin a whirlwind schedule of events, from meetings with welfare reform advocates to confabs with Democratic Party politicos, to evening soirees at posh restaurants. I would lug along my Uher broadcast-quality reel-to-reel recorder, and with microphone in hand try to capture our candidates' every word, while taking notes on the local color for weekly articles I would write on weekend nights for the paper.

I was able to see some of how big-city politics worked, and was mesmerized by the brilliance of Bobby's speeches. At one stop he would tone down his approach to gatherings of power brokers, delivering a message about the sophisticated economics of Oakland's premier position as a container-port facility; then he'd turn around and become the firebrand when speaking to community groups about social programs that would expand under his administration. What he sometimes lacked in polish he made up for with his dynamic style.

Still very much an adolescent at nineteen, I dug coming into contact with the security cadre that surrounded Bobby and Elaine. The "Squad," as they were called, were the toughest brothers in the Party, the drivers and bodyguards of the leadership, always armed with heavy-caliber handguns. Unsmiling and cold, they personified militant dedication. They were sworn to protect our leaders, even if it meant taking a bullet for them. A part of me longed to belong to their select number, to carry a loaded automatic and be prepared at any moment to exchange gunfire with police or any attacker. I still felt pride in the fact that while we claimed to have "put the gun away," it was still there for self-defense.

It was an exciting time, with an aura of historic destiny: we were going to take over major American cities *from within,* starting with Oakland as a base of operations. Having the renowned Hollywood producer Bert Schneider, who had achieved fame with the film *Easy Rider,* personally filming the campaign heightened this sense of destiny. As soundman for the campaign, I became a little starstruck while working with Schneider and his crew, and was fascinated by the process of filming a documentary: the sophisticated equipment used, the planning of shots and scenes, the capturing of sound and image for posterity. I saw myself as taking a vital part in living history, and relished being featured in many scenes of Schneider's film. Writing about those moments for the Party paper, which was read by strangers in places I'd never been, gave me a tremendous charge.

My job as reporter gave me press credentials, and my assignments allowed me to interview various celebrities, including the Pointer Sisters, the football star-turned-actor Bernie Casey, and my hero from my tennis days, Arthur Ashe. I interviewed Ashe at a ritzy tournament held at a country club in Northern California. He remembered our earlier meeting in Danville, and took extra time with me, talking informally as he did stretching exercises before his match with the world's number-one player, Bjorn Borg. The interview became a bit charged when I asked him about his controversial trip to South Africa the year before, which defied world sanctions against taking part in sports events in that country, because of the nation's racist policy of apartheid.

He calmly explained to me, "You have to realize, I was a tennis prodigy, and knew nothing but tennis until I was well into adulthood. I had little knowledge of the world, and felt that if I didn't go to South Africa to see what was *really* happening there, I wouldn't know what I could do about it." Indeed, Ashe soon became one of the foremost opponents of apartheid, and would be credited with being a motivating force in bringing world opinion to bear in changing the country's racist regime.

It was a great pleasure to work with David DuBois. Not only was he the son of an African-American icon, but his mother, Shirley Graham DuBois, had also been a pioneering writer and activist. David shared with me many of his experiences in the struggle, telling of his encounters with people like his close friend Maya Angelou and even Malcolm X. One evening he took me to a concert by his old friend Abbey Lincoln, the famous jazz singer, and I was invited to join them for cocktails after the concert. Later, while driving me back to headquarters in his little Toyota, he talked to me about the novel he was writing, which featured a fictionalized meeting between the book's hero and Malcolm X in Cairo, drawn from David's experiences.

"But why write fiction," I asked him, "when the real world around us is so compelling?"

"With fiction you can sometimes write what is most real," he said. "You can relate worlds from your imagination that can move people much more than the reporting of reality." His words started me thinking about the possibility of becoming something more than a revolutionary reporter, of the possibility of one day becoming a literary writer, as well.

When Election Day arrived, April 17, the Party was successful in getting out the vote in the black communities, and forced a runoff between Bobby Seale and the sitting mayor. (Sadly, Elaine Brown was beaten in her bid for city council.) Without other candidates to divide the votes of the incumbent Republican, we knew it would be a difficult battle. But battle hard we did. The runoff in May saw Bobby defeated, but we had shown ourselves to be a political force to be reckoned with in Oakland. Still, the bubble of hope that all Bay Area Panthers had built up for a victory had been deflated, and we were momentarily left without a clear vision of our future.

After the election I returned home to Danville to see my family, attending a wedding of a cousin in Connecticut with them. Then I worked for two weeks in Winston-Salem, where my home chapter was organizing a grand free food giveaway in the housing project closest to our office. I was greeted as something of a returning hero by my old comrades, and was glad to see that my old tennis partner, Isiah, was working with them for the summer. He and I teamed up to handle all of the publicity and information tasks: writing and printing the leaflets and silk-screening the posters, banners, and the one thousand grocery bags that proclaimed A CHICKEN IN EVERY BAG.

I also hooked up again with Ruth. While I still had a relationship with Gina in Oakland, I found that I was still very much in love with Ruth. After two torrid weeks with Ruth, who had just finished high school and was on her way to college, I found it hard to return to California. She and I promised to stay in touch, and I looked forward to reuniting with her after my stint in Oakland.

When I got back to Oakland, I discovered a change in the general atmosphere. The leadership had mandated that all members engage in military-style morning assemblies, with exercise, marching drills, three-mile runs, and then inspections of living quarters by Bobby Seale, a former army man, or his designated drill sergeants. All available Panthers were required to go out into various Bay Area cities to collect donations, which were needed to keep the Party afloat after the loss of moneys that had come in during the campaign. The donations were said to support the George Jackson Free Health Clinic, with its sickle cell anemia education and testing program, the first of its kind in the country to address the deadly disease that primarily affects people of color. But the money was basically used to keep all of the Party's programs afloat, especially the new Youth Institute, an accredited facility that now educated more than one hundred children.

I enjoyed getting out in the community, collecting donations, and selling the paper I helped put together. Trips to the well-to-do enclaves of Northern California, and ritzy places like Carmel to the south, with its glorious beaches and blue ocean, expanded my view of the world and of how those with money lived.

I especially liked going to San Francisco, with its colorful hippies, and to Berkeley, where I coordinated a program called *Third*

World News at the alternative radio station, KPFA. In Berkeley I hooked up with various counterculture types, including a brother named Musa, who, as it turned out, was from Winston-Salem. He had great reefer, and lived in an apartment with a white girl who worked as a masseuse, keeping Musa up in rather grand style. I admired the way he seemed to have it all together, and we became good friends. I looked forward to assignments to go to Berkeley either to sell papers or to work at the radio station, for it meant the opportunity to go by Musa's crib and get turned on to some of his good herb.

During this period I learned how to make long-distance calls with stolen credit card numbers. One day I used one of the numbers to call Ruth at her college. When I reached her dorm, a friend of hers came on the line. "Ruth left school and went back home about two weeks ago," she said. "I think she was sick or something."

"What was wrong with her?" I asked, worry beginning to wash over me.

The girl was quiet for a moment, then said, "I really don't want to say. Maybe you need to call her at home."

I reached Ruth at her mother's home in Winston-Salem, and when I asked her what was wrong, she told me, "I'm pregnant, Derrell, with our child."

Stunned, I didn't really know what to say. I was a world away from her, and more than a world away from being able to deal with the responsibilities of being a father, of taking care of a woman and child.

"What do you want to do?" I asked Ruth, the question begging the two obvious alternatives: to have the baby, or to abort.

"You know what I want to do," Ruth said, breaking down in sobs, with tears I could imagine streaming from her cheeks, three thousand miles across the country. There was silence between us, as I grappled with the dilemma, until she asked, her voice full of emotion, "What do you want me to do?"

"You know that I love you, Ruth," I said. "I'll make a way for you to come out here," I said. "I'll get the money and send for you, in the next few months, and you can come to Oakland to have the baby."

In the days that followed, while trying to figure out how to get the money to bring Ruth to Oakland, I began to see disturbing signs in the Party's direction. Instead of sending members back to their home chapters, as had been promised before the campaign, the leadership began calling for more and more comrades to come to Oakland. Among those brought out were Coon, from Winston-Salem, and Hazel, Ruth's sister. At the same time, other longtime members in the Bay Area were leaving the Party. Though I was somewhat isolated in the Ministry of Information, rumors began to filter back to me that some members were being forcibly expelled after being beaten by the security cadre. I also learned that many members were having to endure "physical methods of discipline" by the security squad—beatings and whippings for various and sundry offenses against Party rules. There were also reports that Huey Newton was using cocaine, and that cocaine was being sold from the Party's restaurant and bar, The Lamp Post. Most damning of all was word that some sisters who worked at the Lamp Post were "taking dates" with customers, with the money they got going to feed Huey's cocaine habit.

In January 1974 I ran into a member who had left the Party who told me that the Squad was using its guns and muscle to shake down illegal after-hours bars and gambling joints around town. In response, he said, underworld figures had put out a ten-thousand-dollar contract on Huey Newton. It seemed that Huey's cocaine use had led to carousing in bars and speakeasies, and several altercations where the Squad had intervened with muscle and guns. Huey had become a marked man, the brother told me.

I'd seen signs of all this in the increased paranoia around Newton. This descent into the sort of gangsterism the Party was once sworn to oppose stemmed in part from the rebel/outlaw mentality of the organization's early years, and I suppose that kernel of machismo still existed in most of the male Panthers—including me.

During my community work I encountered a pimp who lived a block from Gina's apartment, where I still spent some nights. His name was Richard, and he lived in a house with two beautiful women who waited on him hand and foot. Richard was a glamorous figure, a handsome brother always nattily dressed, and he loved telling me stories of the Oakland street life. This was during the period when movies like *Superfly* and *The Mack* were glamorizing the fast life of the streets, of living outside the law. Together with the gangster aura of the Squad, like many black youth of the day I was taken by the grand allure of the streets.

I would steal away from Panther duties to drop by Richard's crib, smoke some dope, and soak up the lessons of the outlaw game, which had the basic philosophy that the authentic black man should do whatever he could "to beat the man," to get over without slaving at a nine-to-five.

One day, while smoking dope with Richard, I told him that I badly needed cash to bring my pregnant lady out to Oakland. He said, "If you really need money, I know of a job we could do," then he ran down to me how he had information about a honky-tonk bar in San Jose, about ninety miles south of Oakland, where they cashed payroll checks on Friday. "The manager goes to the bank to pick up the money around eleven o'clock," he said. "It's easy money, if you got the heart to take it." The last statement was posed as a challenge: *If you have the balls to do a real stickup.*

"I'll think about it," I told him. And indeed I did. The idea of crossing the line into crime pressed upon me the rest of the day as I half-heartedly hammered out an article at Central. I thought of the line from Chairman Mao's Red Book, which was also one of the Party's ten cardinal rules: "A Party member will not take anything from the people, not even a needle, or a piece of thread."

That evening at Gina's apartment, I was still pondering the

choice at hand. I thought about the old days of the Party, when Panthers were said to have engaged in armed robbery of white merchants, calling it "reappropriation of the wealth," in order to support Party programs. Would robbing a redneck bar to get money for the family I wanted to form be any different? The thing was, such "private" activity was outlawed by the Party, and if found out, I would face certain expulsion. The fear of being kicked out of the Party loomed in my mind even more than the possibility of being caught and imprisoned.

When Gina and I went to bed, she sensed that something was wrong. I had been playing Marvin Gaye's "Distant Lover" over and over on our little turntable, and she dug that while I had become more and more distant from her, she was not the one on my mind.

"What's wrong, baby?" she asked, and I confessed that I'd learned from Ruth that she was pregnant and I didn't know what to do about it.

"She wants to come out here and work with the Party, and have our child grow up at the Institute," I told Gina. As I lay beside her I realized that she was the one true friend I had in Oakland, by virtue of her being my lover. "Comrades" were supposed to be ruled only by Party discipline, and friendships were said to be bourgeois and were discouraged. But I also knew that, with my revelation about Ruth, our affair would be ending.

I thought Gina would be angry, but instead she said, "You must love her a lot." Then silence, as the Marvin Gaye album ended, and in that silence I understood the meaning of her words: *Your love for her must be greater than your love for me.* Then she said, "Whatever you decide, I'll understand."

The next day I told Richard that I was ready to pull the job with him.

"You sure?" he asked. "'Cause you got to know now, once you get a sense of the power you have when you pull a gun on people—the power of life and death over white folks who done ruled over you all your life—once you taste that power, ain't no turnin' back."

"I'm ready," I said, willing a cold steeliness into my stare that I didn't really feel. He looked at me as if trying to see any weakness in my resolve. Then he took me to the back of his little house and crawled underneath to retrieve something wrapped in oilskin. He opened it to reveal an almost antique pump shotgun, sawed off with barely twelve inches of barrel, a piece so old it still had an external hammer and the bluing had been completely worn away, so all that remained was shiny steel.

I followed him back into the house, where he told me, "You always use a shotgun in sticking up. People might try to buck on you, they see a little pistol. But there's something about seeing that big-ass hole of a twelve-gauge bore—with the power they know will blow them away in an instant—that makes them give it up quick."

Then he basically took me through a class in how to rob. "You break up in the joint, mask on, and scream loud that you don't want no shit, don't want to have to kill nobody. You get to the manager who got the key or the combination to the safe, and if he don't move fast enough you take the stock of the shotgun and hit him up under the jaw, like this—" demonstrating with the piece, coming within inches of my jaw with frightening dexterity. Easing down, he said, "I'm showing you like this so you can *feel* the fear you got to put in their hearts, 'cause anytime you let them sense a weakness—remember that somebody might have a gun up in there—then both of us could end up dead, or having to blow away somebody, which you definitely don't want to do."

No doubt it was all scary for me, but though I was still only nineteen, I wanted to believe that I was a man—*and* a warrior. The thought of criminal action seemed to my mind a rite of passage into total manhood, and was in that sense exhilarating. The power and allure of the gun was already set deep within my psyche, and I longed to give it physical expression.

Richard said he would come up with another shotgun for the

heist, and gave me the job of stealing a car for the stickup from the relatives of one of his women. "They keep the key to this old Pontiac under the floor mat, so all you have to do is grab the car in the morning, go down to San Jose to case the joint, make sure the owner takes the cash to the bank at the same time as usual. We can then catch him the following week in the parking lot, and won't have to bust up in the bar."

But things did not go at all according to Richard's plan. No one emerged through the back door of the bar as I sat in the stolen Pontiac on the street behind the honky-tonk joint, with the hood up, pretending the car had broken down. After an hour a California Highway Patrol car pulled up behind me, red lights flashing, and I knew I was busted.

I quickly pulled out the two sticks of reefer I had in my sock, pushed them into my mouth, and began chewing, as the patrolman approached with his .357 magnum drawn. He ordered me from the car, searched and handcuffed me, and the next thing I knew I was down at the Santa Clara County Jail, being interrogated—not by regular cops, but by two FBI agents.

"What were you doing in that stolen car?" the younger one asked. I gave the story of having had a breakdown and how the car was borrowed and this was all a misunderstanding that would soon be cleared up. But he was not going for it. "Look, we know you're a Black Panther," he said, producing photos of me with Bobby Seale from the campaign. "What are we to make of the fact that you were arrested only a half mile from a power station that was bombed last year, in protest to the war in Vietnam? Since we know you to be an associate of some pretty bad men"—at which point he pulled out the address book taken from me when I was arrested. Leafing through the pages, he said, "Let me see . . . We have Bobby Seale on Santa Rosa Avenue, Huey Newton on Lakeside—what do you think of his snazzy penthouse? And here we have Big Man's number. Now we have on record a lot of violent rhetoric from them. So why don't you tell us what you were really doing in this area?"

I'm up shit creek without a paddle, I thought, with a groggy high from the marijuana in my stomach. Not really knowing what I was saying, just thinking, *How the fuck did you get yourself in* this *situation?* I looked at the silent, older agent and said with a confidence I did not feel, "You're the senior agent here, I take it." His lack of response told me the answer. "Then you know this is bullshit, you know enough about the Party to know we're not into bombing and stuff, we're into politics now." I looked him in the eye and added, "There's no need to waste your time on me. You'll see this will come out as a case of my borrowing a car from a friend who just changed his mind about me taking a trip this far."

And so I spent the night in jail, before my arraignment the next day, getting my first taste of incarceration—a baloney sandwich and soup, which I downed with a degree of hunger born from the long high of ingested marijuana. I was scared, but would not show it, the image of San Quentin looming in my mind, telling me that I needed to steel myself for prison, if it came to that.

The next day, with the help of a court-appointed lawyer, I was cut loose on my own recognizance, until my trial date. While I felt sure that Richard would be able to square away the charge of unauthorized use of a vehicle with his girl's people, on the bus ride back to the Bay Area I wondered just how I was going to explain this shit to the Party.

Upon my return to Oakland I was called before the organization's "Board for Methods of Correction," a quasi-judicial disciplinary board, and my story of a simple mistake did not go over well. At the end of the hearing I was told, "You will be notified of your punishment."

After waiting two days, I was told to report to the basement of the Party's house on Twenty-ninth Avenue, and informed by Lonnie, one of the security cadre, that the board had mandated a "physical method of correction" for me. I was ordered to strip down to the waist. Bracing me against a wall, Lonnie delivered my punishment: five lashes from a bullwhip on my back.

I felt that I was accepting the pain like a man, thinking that it was a lesser punishment than if I'd been kicked out of the Party. I had heard that this sort of "discipline" was being meted out to comrades, but had no idea of the degradation that came from being whipped.

That night, at Gina's, I told her what had happened. She retrieved an ointment and rubbed it into the wounds on my back. Then she confided that the salve was left over from when she, too, had received such punishment, for a relatively minor transgression. She rubbed ointment into the scars on my back with a tenderness that soothed my physical pain. But it would take a long time—if ever—for me to heal from the emotional scar cut deep into my psyche from being lashed like a slave, and knowing that such violence was being visited upon comrades I cared about, like Gina.

The winter of discontent stretched on, with comrades disappearing one by one, their names listed in the weekly inner-party memorandum under the heading MEMBERS EXPELLED, with no differentiation between those who left voluntarily and those who were kicked out, often after suffering a beating in the Squad's reign of terror.

One day I learned that a close comrade had left, after being brutally assaulted by Huey and his bodyguards at The Lamp Post, because she had said that something he had said was disrespectful. I decided that something had to be done to change the Party leadership in order to save the organization I still believed held the key to the liberation of black people. I tried to contact the former comrade who had told me of the contract on Huey, thinking that I might find comrades still within the Party who might want to help depose the despotic leader by any means necessary. But he had moved from the rooming house where he'd been staying, and there was no way to contact him.

With my plan to bring Ruth out to Oakland blown, I began to outline a trip back home to be there when she gave birth to our child, which would also give me a chance to do some soul searching about whether to return to Oakland. I had been attending classes at Laney Community College, and my parents sent me money to enroll in a program at U.C. Berkeley wherein one could obtain college credits and a degree outside of the normal curriculum. But I held back on enrolling, thinking that I might need to use the money for the trip home.

Then Coon was beaten and severely injured by Huey and his Squad, also while working at The Lamp Post. When I went to see him at his apartment, he was wearing a bandage over his eye, his dark brown face swollen to a horrifying black-blue. "The doctors at the emergency room don't know if the sight in my eye can be saved," he told me, a pitiable shell of the hero figure who'd recruited me three years before. "I need to get home, Derrell, get back home to get some treatment," he told me, tears welling up in his one visible eye. "But I don't have the money for a ticket."

The next day I used all the money I had to buy a plane ticket for him, along with a two-hundred-dollar pound of California marijuana, which would easily fetch at four or five hundred on the East Coast. "Take this reefer and sell it as soon as you get back," I instructed Coon, "and send me at least two-fifty, so I can come back to Winston before my son is born." I don't know why I believed the child would be a boy, but I held on to the belief that I'd soon have a man-child to carry on in the world, and that his life would give meaning to the confusion and disillusionment swirling around me.

Over the next weeks, while waiting to hear from Coon, I tried to fight through the welter of conflicting thoughts by throwing myself into what I knew to be righteous and true and just: writing impassioned pieces for the paper about the Vietnam War, the conspiracy surrounding Watergate, and the continuing police brutality in black communities all over the country.

But no word came from Coon, and calls to his home were met only with the message that his phone had been disconnected.

By then I knew that the internal contradictions within the Party were destroying it. But my disillusionment with the organization, and my overall rage against the power structure, began to manifest as a personal hatred for Coon, my dear comrade who was betraying me so, the mentor who I felt was now leaving me stranded in amid increasing turmoil.

By time spring arrived, Ruth had stopped communicating with me, and I was so filled with shame at not getting back to Winston to be with her that I could not bring myself to call her mother to find out how she was doing. Then, one day in early May, as I was running out of Central to catch a bus to go downtown to sell papers and collect donations, Aaron called me back to the desk. "You got a letter here," he said. I grabbed it and ran across the street to hop on the bus before it took off. Once seated, I opened the small white envelope and pulled out a photo of a baby, with the words underneath, *Roderick Anthony Mack, Born April 30th, 1974,* in Ruth's distinctive script.

A surge of pride hit me as I beheld the picture of my son, who favored me, even in infancy with a light complexion and distinctive high forehead. Then the shame followed, that I'd not been there for Ruth, and was still unable to get there anytime soon, because I'd been weak enough to help Coon. My seething resentment for him then began to brew into a murderous rage.

Spring turned to summer, and I still didn't have enough money to get home. The situation in the Party was getting worse, and while angry at the leadership, I still felt love for the organization and the hardworking rank-and-file members. I had sworn to die for the people, for the Party, and somehow I still held out hope that there might somehow be a way to save the organization. I began to think that money was the key to get us back on track. I had watched Omar Barbour, the chief fund-raiser for the Institute I admired so much, and seen how he had been able to raise money for the school with the children's choir he conducted, having black celebrities like

Richard Pryor and Melvin Van Peebles to donate, and getting stars like Abbey Lincoln and Oscar Brown, Jr., to perform benefit concerts for us.

So when a comrade from Detroit told me that Stevie Wonder was his cousin, and that Stevie's mother was going to Los Angeles to visit her son in early August—at the same time my parents were to vacation there—I came up with a grand idea. I would travel to L.A. and somehow hook up with Stevie Wonder through his mother, and persuade him to do a big benefit concert for the Party. I believed that this would solve our money woes and also place me in ascendancy to become part of the Party's leadership, where I could effect real change.

I got my folks to send me money for a ticket to join them in L.A. and then return home. Then I was able to get Stevie's cousin to arrange a meeting for me with Stevie's mother. In L.A., at the hotel where Mrs. Morris was staying, I met with her and his press agent, and then met Stevie himself, when he dropped by to visit his mom.

I had learned from a call back to Oakland that a screening of the film Bert Schneider had shot of Bobby and Elaine's campaign would be held at the American Film Institute up in Laurel Canyon, and that Elaine would be attending. I got Stevie's press agent to agree to bring Stevie to the event, and to have him meet Elaine.

I just *knew* I was making all the right moves, and that my maneuverings would bring about a good result. But another call to Oakland gave me some bad news: Huey Newton was on the run after allegedly shooting a prostitute to death on the streets of Oakland, and a massive manhunt had been mounted. On top of that, I learned that Bobby Seale had been expelled from the Party after being beaten on Huey's orders.

That evening, as I drove a little Pinto I'd rented through the elaborately manicured streets of Beverly Hills and Laurel Canyon, in awe of the opulence with which folks with *real* money lived, I still believed that my efforts could somehow pull the Party out of its present morass. Stevie Wonder would meet with Elaine Brown and do a benefit. Elaine would rise to leadership; the organization would be saved.

Such would not be the case. Stevie Wonder never came, and Elaine's security contingent, on high alert after Huey's flight from Oakland, was suspicious of what I was doing in L.A. Lonnie, the Squad member who had administered the beating to me some months before, grabbed me by the elbow, took me into the AFI cloakroom, and began going through my briefcase to see if I had a weapon.

When I told him that I had informed Michael, the deputy editor of the paper and my immediate superior, of what I was doing, Lonnie ordered me to call him. Michael, true to form, punked out, saying he never gave clearance for me to attend the event.

"I think you need to come back to Oakland with us," Lonnie said with a degree of menace.

Trying to disguise my fear as personal outrage, I told him, "That's fine with me, 'cause I want to get this shit straight with Michael. I've got a rental car outside, so I'll pull around to the front of the building and follow you back to Oakland."

Luckily he agreed to this, and I calmly walked out the door of the American Film Institute. Once I got to the parking lot, however, I began to run. Reaching my rented Pinto, I jumped inside and sped down the winding canyon road, thinking only of escape, fearing that I was being followed.

When I reached Sunset Boulevard, I finally slowed down, and it struck me: *I'd had to run away from the Black Panther Party.* I was fleeing in fear from the organization I loved, that I had dedicated my life to. The open world represented by the glitz of Beverly Hills and Hollywood now seemed totally remote to me. My mission of changing the system, with the Party, was suddenly gone.

I had no idea what to do now, no idea that it would take half my life to recover from this total disillusionment. Only one idea held some hope of salvation for me then: *Make your way home, see your son, find a way to regroup—and continue the struggle.*

CHAPTER FIVE

Post-Party Syndrome

I t was a joyless reunion.

I had called my father from L.A., telling him that I would be arriving at the Greensboro airport the following day and needed a ride home. But the trip back to Danville was an ordeal, for Pop was only too happy to slip "I told you so" into the conversation in not very subtle ways and to ask ribbing questions to which I gave noncommittal answers. Then came blessed periods of silence, yielding brief relief.

Two days ago I had been a Panther, one of the elite, a member of the vanguard party, a dedicated revolutionary ready to give his life for the people. Now I was alone, filled with rage, disillusioned by my dashed belief in the Party, mad at the system, at whites, at the world. I was being driven back to a hometown I loathed, by the father with whom I could barely communicate, who hadn't bothered to question why his usually optimistic son was now brooding.

"It's good you're coming back on the weekend, right after our vacation week," he told me. "You can start to work with me on Monday." No question, just the assumption that his son had come home to work for him. Then, perhaps sensing something in my mood, he added, "That is, if you want to."

I figured I might as well play the game. "Okay, Pop" was my brief answer, using that word now instead of Daddy, thinking the latter too soft for a warrior. Yet, a part of me warmed to the moment, something deep within that still wanted to please my father, though he hadn't a clue about the turmoil of my world. Feigning enthusiasm, I said, "Yes, that would be good. You can teach me the ins and outs of landscaping, and maybe I can go into business with you one day."

"Well, you know that has always been my dream," he responded with a smile.

The rest of the hour's drive was largely silent, my father now reassured that he had his son back under his wing. But I had only three ideas on my mind now: figure out how to continue the revolution against the System; see my son; then find and deal with Coon, whom I still blamed for destroying this phase of my life by fucking up my money and my attempt to get home for my son's birth.

The first week back was one of work: hard days in the sun, my mind raging in the heat of late August, trying to repress seething emotions. I worked silently alongside men who wanted to joke and play, raking dirt and sowing grass, digging holes and planting shrubbery. All the time I felt like a slave for my father, doing all the things I'd tried to escape, for minimum wage (which Pop explained away by saying, "That's what I start all of my men out with"). While I'd told my parents about the birth of my son, he still didn't see the need to help me out with more money.

Evenings I spent talking with Mama, trying to maintain a congenial attitude while discussing the mundane concerns of life. I didn't want her to sense the turmoil I was feeling. Then, later in my room, I had to confront my growing sense of desperation.

At the end of the week my father told me, "You know it's my policy that my men have to work a first week in the hole before getting paid, but I'm willing to loan you half of this week's pay now. You get the other week-and-a-half at the end of the next week." Fuming, but realizing I was the prodigal son and in no position to argue, I accepted the meager sixty bucks as humbly as I could. I immediately mailed fifty off to Ruth with a letter saying that I was back home and would try to get to Winston to visit the following weekend.

That next Friday I took my paycheck, got off an hour early, and went to get a new driver's license, using my California ID, which gave my age as twenty-one, instead of twenty. This enabled me to go to a gun shop with a firing range, where I purchased a .22 semi-automatic Ruger for fifty-two dollars, along with a hip holster. While firing the pistol at the range, I envisioned pumping the full clip into Coon's body, practicing with each pull of the trigger the cold resolve I would need to carry out the execution of the friend and mentor I now saw only as betrayer.

By Sunday I felt I was ready. I would attend church with my parents, borrow one of Pop's trucks, travel to Winston-Salem and see my son, then find and confront Coon.

Pop lent me one of his jackets, along with a shirt and a tie, for my return to High Street Baptist. I carried my pistol in its hip holster, slipping it under the seat as I got out of the car with my mother and father. During the service I felt a twinge of remorse, thinking of my plan to deal with Coon, feeling that my path of violence was at odds with my religious upbringing. But I was an atheist. *There is no God,* I thought, looking at those around me as fools who believed in a false sense of salvation that kept them from confronting the need for revolutionary action in the here and now. Despite my contempt, I felt envious of their belief in the certainty of salvation. Most especially, I envied the warm sense of community they had.

I went back to my folks' car before them in order to retrieve my weapon, telling myself, *I'm only doing what I have to do,* as I slipped the pistol beneath my jacket. Then my father and mother dropped me off at the office to retrieve the truck my father was lending me, and I was off to rendezvous with my past—and my future—in Winston-Salem.

I arrived late that afternoon at the apartment Ruth and Roderick shared with Hazel. After an apprehensive knock, I was admitted by a stern-faced Ruth, who perfunctorily thanked me for the money I had sent, asked me to take a seat on the living room couch, then went into the bedroom to get my son.

Seeing Roderick Anthony Mack for the first time was a revelation, spurring something in me I had not previously felt. Holding the chubby six-month-old, looking into his bright, inquisitive brown eyes, sparked a glow of hope in a spirit that had been devoid of warmth since I'd left California. Roderick had one of those constant grins that certain babies have, and he looked so much like me that I could not help but feel: *This is me. This is my own, my future, my love and dreams become living flesh.*

The visit was not long, as Ruth was still angry that I'd not gotten back in time for Roderick's birth. I gave her some money and said that I'd like to come back to see Rod soon. As she saw me to the door, I said, "I'm sorry, Ruth, that this hasn't worked out any better, that I didn't get back sooner. But I want you to know that I still love you, and I thank you for giving life to our son." I turned and walked away before she could answer; before tears might betray the depth of my feeling.

I then drove to the apartment in the projects where Coon lived with his wife and two sons. I wanted to surprise him, and indeed I did. He answered the door, but showed no fear of me, instead swinging the screen door wide and embracing me with a hug and the words, "Man, am I glad to see you."

This greeting disarmed me, as I'd come with murderous intent. Coon invited me into his home, called out to his wife, Anne, to come and greet me, telling her to break out a bottle of wine in celebration of my homecoming.

When Anne left the room, however, I called upon my wannabe-gangster mood, and told him frankly that I was seriously disturbed at how he had failed to send back the money I'd fronted him for his ticket home—or for the pound of marijuana—and how it had kept me from getting back home to see my son born. I tried to give off all the gangster vibe I could, but I had already begun to see that it was not in my makeup to do this man any harm.

Coon gave me a real sob story: "Derrell, you know how bad they busted up my eye out there. When I got back I had all kinds of medical bills to make sure I could see out of this eye again," he said, pointing to the left eye, which, indeed, still seemed to be not quite right. "The doctor was only able to remove the patch from my eye a month ago," he continued, a pleading tone to his voice. "I'm sorry that I didn't come through for you, man, and I'll make it up to you somehow. I'm making a little money now, painting. I'll see you straight as soon as I get a few jobs under my belt."

While he was talking, I reviewed the scenario I'd rehearsed: get him into the truck on the ruse of going somewhere to make some sort of hookup for more reefer, then leave him on the outskirts of town, dead. But maybe the visit with Ruth and Roderick had changed my vision of the world; or maybe there was still too much pity—or perhaps too much love—for this brother who had first recruited me to the Party.

I ended up making my way back to Danville, leaving Coon alive, taking with me his promise to repay me, which I knew he would not keep. But my heart was lightened by the fact that I was able to replace the intent of deadly vengeance with some semblance of forgiveness.

My dreams of writing were still with me then, along with my dream of hooking up with celebrities and getting them to endorse progressive struggle. I finally hooked up with Stevie Wonder when he came to Greensboro, North Carolina, and did an interview with him there. Soon after, I corralled jazz musician Roy Ayers in Greensboro for an interview, and then followed with Maurice White, leader of Earth, Wind and Fire, in Hampton, Virginia. But I had no idea how to market the interviews, having not yet learned how to make it as a freelance writer.

I continued working for Pop through the fall, warming a little to the manual labor of landscaping, enjoying the camaraderie with the three other employees. I tried to relate better to my father, having lunch with him sometimes, and talking with him and Mama while riding to and from work. But it was hard to talk to him. We were still on totally different wavelengths. Conversations with Mama were better, when I was able to spend a little time in the tiny office where she'd taken over as Pop's secretary. She stayed abreast of current events and watched television with a discriminating eye. But at home I mainly stayed in my room, reading, trying to do a little writing in a journal, but usually just brooding.

I saved a little money from my checks and visited Ruth and Rod on weekends. Pop cosigned a loan for me to purchase a little four-door Fiat, which facilitated my travel to Winston. After regular weekend visits, Ruth and I became lovers once more, and we began talking about a life together as a family, with Rod.

Then, in November 1974, during a weekend visit, Rod began throwing up his food. Ruth and I sped him to the hospital, where doctors discovered his heart was not functioning correctly and immediately put him on life support. Seeing his tiny body hooked up to an IV, with all sorts of wires attached to his chest, his heartbeat registering with that bleep-bleep-bleep sound from the monitor above his bed, was heart-wrenching. Ruth, already a high-strung woman, was thrown into a trembling fit by the sight, and she refused to leave his bedside through the first night.

The next day I persuaded her to go home for some rest. In the parking lot, just as we were getting into my car, she suddenly wheeled about and began running back to the hospital, screaming, "I can't leave my baby, I can't leave my baby!" I backed the car out of the parking space, cutting in front of her while driving in reverse. Jumping out of the car, I grabbed her, clutching her to me as she struggled to run back to the hospital, and was finally able to get her to settle down. "He'll be all right, sweetheart. You just got to believe our baby will be all right."

We went back to her apartment for a few hours, then returned to the hospital, where we learned from the attending cardiologist that Rod had a heart defect and would have to be on a medication called digitalis, with constant monitoring, if he were to go on living.

I realized that I needed to take a new view of my need to be in the life of my son and with his mother. I talked with Ruth about her future, and of my disapproval of her being on welfare. (It was a throwback to the Panther belief that welfare lulls one into an attitude of subservience to the system and should be avoided at all costs.) Ruth then took a typesetting job at a local knitting mill, but she was still living with Hazel, who had returned from Oakland, in a housing authority apartment, and on public assistance. In response to my prodding, she said, almost offhandedly, "Okay, then, so why don't you marry me, and take me away from all of this?"

I told Ruth that we would, indeed, marry soon and begin a new life in Danville. I had fallen in love with her once more and wanted to do whatever was necessary to form a family with her. But the winter was upon us now, and as usual the landscaping work was drying up. My father didn't see the need to help me out financially during the off-season, when he generally laid off most of his help.

Meanwhile, I had hooked up with a friend from childhood—from Sunday school, actually—named Frank, and he introduced me to the dope scene in Danville, and the smaller town of Martinsville, some forty miles away. In trips with him to Martinsville I got my first taste of the fast money that could be had from the dope trade. Frank paid me well just for transporting him from city to city.

He introduced me to snorting heroin, and soon I began accepting heroin for payment instead of money. Heroin was a dreamy sort of high, for a young man given to dreams. At the time it was thought that you couldn't really get a junkie jones from just snorting dope, and I never got enough of it to get strung out physically, in any case. But the serious drugs, along with the reefer, began to change my perception of work, especially since I was still making only minimum wage with my father, and then only on the few days of the week when he had anything to do. I recall Pop waking me up to go to work one morning after I'd been out all night. I told him I was sick and would be coming in late. With words that would remain with me for the rest of my life, he said, "Derrell, maybe you just don't have the daily courage it takes to do this type of work."

Daily courage. While I didn't appreciate his questioning my courage, in years to come I would remember his remark and realize that he intuitively knew what it took to succeed in life.

In November I went to Winston-Salem, and Ruth and I went to the county courthouse to change Rod's name from Mack to Hopkins. Then we drove back to Danville so that my parents could meet their grandchild. They welcomed Ruth and the baby warmly, but I knew they would never fully accept them into the family until we were married.

Ruth and I were wedded in a civil ceremony at the Danville

courthouse, two days after Christmas 1974. I was far from ready for the responsibility of marriage, but I believed that I needed to take the step to make sure Rod would be provided for by my family, should something happen to me. Deep down I knew I was on a wrong track, so I wanted to make things legal, so that Ruth and Rod would be embraced by my middle-class family. While my up-bringing still had me believing that, in the end, family is all we have, there remained in my mind the Party's teaching of the need to view family as a bourgeois constraint upon the revolutionary. I still felt a need to believe that I was a revolutionary, only now I had the half-psychotic view that leading the life of a street gangster was some-how still rebellion against the system—though it was but an excuse to live the life of the streets.

My trips to Martinsville with Frank changed from just providing transportation to providing protection, after some junkies robbed him at gunpoint. I enjoyed having a reputation as an ex-Panther and a gunman, having soaked up gangster movies of the period like *The Godfather* and *Death Wish*. I wanted to believe that I was still prepared to kill, or die, in revolutionary battle. But there was no revolution around me, and my major battle was really with my idea of self, my past in the Party willing me to find some way to prove my manhood through violence.

By February 1975, my hustle with Frank in Martinsville had played out, but Ruth was on me to move Roderick and her to Danville, as I'd promised. By then I was so deep into my gangster mentality that I couldn't see going back to work full-time for my father. I decided that I would get the money by taking it from the power structure: I would rob a bank.

The idea hit me after passing this little branch bank, way out in the county, outside Martinsville. *It's just a little walk-in bank, I can take it off, easy.* My gangster persona mixed with my militant past into a highbrow literary notion that I was some sort of Robin Hood/Jean Valjean character, who would rob from the rich to save his family and ailing child. But, still mindful of the Panther rule that a Party member should not take anything from the people, I rationalized that robbing a bank would actually be stealing from the government, since all banks were federally insured, and the federal government was the main enemy, robbing from the people in every way.

I bought a riot pump shotgun, like the police used, along with a .380 automatic and a shoulder holster. Still thinking of myself as an intellectual in all things, I checked out books from the library on shotgunning and the use of handguns, all the while taking notes of my madness in a journal. I'd practice my quick draw in the mirror in my room, high off reefer, with the music from *Shaft* on my record player. One day, after putting on my coat for a trip to Martinsville, with the cool music playing and half high and thinking to myself *You really are one cool gangster motherfucker,* I decided to practice one more draw in the mirror—forgetting that I had fully loaded my pistol with a round in the chamber. I blasted a hole straight through the mirror, the noise reverberating through the house, leaving me standing there shocked at the hole in the middle of the torso of my reflected image, smoke rising from the barrel of my pistol. I just laughed at my folly—not taking this as a sign that I had truly lost my mind—and taped a few pictures over the hole, so my folks would not know.

One evening soon after, Pop called me into my bedroom and confronted me with the fact that he'd discovered my shotgun in a case under my bed. Thinking quickly, I told him that the gun belonged to a friend who wanted to come out to our farm property to do some hunting, and I was just keeping it for him.

"I looked at that shotgun," he said, "and anybody can see that that gun is made for killin', not for hunting." I assured him that this wasn't the case, and took the weapon out of the house immediately in an effort to keep peace with him.

I knew I needed a partner to watch my back during the robbery, and I thought I had one in a brother named Junior, who seemed to share my philosophy of attacking the system. But when the day came to pull off the job, he didn't show up. I then thought of

Jonathan Jackson, who had gone into the courtroom after others who were supposed to be in on the action didn't show up. So I decided to go it alone.

Things did not go well from the beginning. I pulled up at the bank, got out with my shotgun under a long coat I had borrowed from Frank, and tried to go into the bank through a side door, but it was locked. Having shown up at closing time, I felt like a fool pushing against the door, the barrel of my weapon exposed to all the world: *Was I late as usual? Should I give up on this crazy plan?*

Then I saw someone exit through the front door. Pulling down my ski mask as I passed him, I said, "Get the fuck out of my way," hoping that I looked menacing enough to scare him, but knowing that he would soon be calling the county cops. Since I wasn't able to wear my glasses with a mask on, I couldn't see well as I entered the foyer between the outer and inner doors, which made me feel even more foolish.

I suppose I was still in a postadolescent dream of re-creating Jonathan Jackson's move, as my words when I entered the little two-teller branch were the same as his: "All right, gentlemen, I'm taking over now." Holding the shotgun in one hand and a flight bag in the other, much as Jonathan had done in the courtroom, I was met with bewilderment by the stunned tellers, as well as the lone manager of the rural bank. They all froze, as if they couldn't believe what was happening, and all I could feel was panic and fear, as they weren't reacting like I thought they might. Further complicating the situation, without my glasses I couldn't focus on the man in a green uniform who was sitting in the window of the place, and I had to squint to discern whether he was an armed security guard or just a farmer wearing work clothes.

Swiveling back and forth from the man in the window to the man behind the customer service desk, I told the four people, "Look, I don't want to hurt nobody." I tried to sound menacing, but the echo of my voice made me realize that my demand sounded more like a plea. I saw the manager coolly nod to the tellers, as if he knew he was dealing with a crazy kid. They put the money they had in their drawers into the bag for me, and I made a hasty exit.

I thought I was home free with the four thousand dollars I'd stolen, until later that evening when I was renting an apartment in Danville for Ruth, Rod, and me to live in. I'd asked the apartment manager to let me use his phone to call home, and when Pop answered, his voice was full of alarm. "Where are you, Derrell? The police are out here looking for you, with the FBI. They have helicopters and everything. What have you done?"

I told him not to worry, it was just a mistake, but by the time I hung up and got back to the front of the apartment, the lights of police cars were flashing outside. I fled out of the back of the building, running through woods, falling into a ravine, then emerging at a school building as the searchlights of helicopters swirled from above. I kicked in a window of the school just before a patrol car came past, badly cutting my thigh as I slithered into the building. Once inside, I climbed onto the top of a row of lockers, removed a panel from the ceiling, and crawled onto two water pipes after replacing the ceiling panel.

I remained there for hours, holding my thigh in order to staunch the bleeding. Emerging in the middle of the night, I began searching for a phone to call my friend Isiah, who was working the midnight-to-dawn shift at a nearby radio station. But there were no phones on the wall; I would have to break into the office to get to a phone. I found a child's baseball bat in the back of the stage in the auditorium, and was about to use it to break into the office when a night watchman came around the corner of the hallway and immediately went for the pistol at his side. I struck at his hand, then at his head. Knocking him down, I fled out the front doors and ran across the lawn as he fired several shots at me. Weaving in a zigzag pattern, I could hear his bullets whizzing past my ear.

When I reached the street in front of the school, a patrol car was just approaching. I ran between two houses on the other side, but found myself blocked by an impenetrable row of hedges. "Come out

or I'll have to shoot," came the voice of a policeman from the side
of the building. I realized I was trapped, and surrendered to capture.

I sat on a cot in the isolation cell of the old city jail, looking out at
the A&P parking lot. In the eye of memory I could see the young
Derrell as he looked up at the window in the cell that now imprisoned me on this Sunday, the parking lot now containing only the
cars of visitors to the jail. My visit with my family—my father and
mother, with Ruth and our one-year-old Roderick—had just
ended. It was the first time I'd seen my son walk, so adorable as my
wife held his arms aloft while he ambled into the screened corridor
of the jail's visiting area.

As I played that scene over and over in my mind, they appeared
in the parking lot below, with Ruth holding up Rod to wave his
little arm bye-bye to me, before they all got into my parents' car and
disappeared from view.

I then sat upon my bunk and thought of the meaning of this day,
this visit. I had to repress the shame I felt, for I was still intent upon
maintaining an attitude of resistance, still thinking that it was my
duty to escape the cage my captors had me in, to escape the judgment of my crimes.

In opposition to those thoughts were re-emerging dreams of
writing, of using my life as grist for the mill of literature. And with
my fatherhood I'd begun to have *feeling,* emotion that was beating
down the coldness I'd used as a defense against the shame and despair of my jail identity of bank robber. The artist's compulsion to
create, to dream of worlds where I might subsume emotion into
story, began to grow within me.

And what a story I have to tell, I thought then, recalling the path
that had led me to that place in time, a time when I still thought the
world was mine to engage—having no idea that I'd only begun to
endure. And while the pain of my present fought against the idea of
examining the pain of my young past, at that moment fledgling

thoughts of creating something *literary* from where I'd been began to win out over the madness within my mind, the calculating madness that kept demanding that I somehow find a way to escape.

So I began to imagine a work of my life to be called "Letter of Reparation." It would be a father's apology to a son he might never see again, a father about to escape from prison to go into the revolutionary underground. The protagonist (a word I'd gleaned from my study of the art of fiction) was an embodiment of myself—a man in prison facing years in prison for bank robbery, a young man who still saw himself as a revolutionary and felt compelled to react to capture by breaking out.

At the time I did not realize that my recourse to the world of imagination was the artistic impulse seeking purchase in the world of the real. But luckily, it kept me going, this thought of a literary apologia to my son: for while I'd not given up on my plans to escape, my dream to become a great, revolutionary writer kept the artist within me alive, nourishing me inside my bleak imprisonment—an imprisonment that would form my reality for many years to come.

And so it was that I first began to face up to my past, and retravel the road that had led me to the first of my many jail cells.

In the weeks following that visit I met with the high-powered attorney my father had retained for me, and he told me that if I pleaded guilty to all offenses, he could work out a deal where I'd get a ten-year sentence for the assault on the night watchman and breaking into the school. Then he would get the federal judge to give me a sentence of ten years for the bank robbery, and have it to run at the same time as the state sentence.

It was a sweet deal, I knew, but I thought that pleading guilty would be a capitulation to the System I loathed, and doing ten years of hard time seemed more than I could bear. I still believed myself to be a revolutionary, and that my first duty was to escape from bondage.

But the memory of my recent visit with my parents and Ruth and Rod and was still fresh in my mind. Seeing my son walk, and the dedicated love of my parents and wife—despite the fact that I had messed up so badly—had percolated in my mind along with the idea of escape. Wrestling with it in my fictive "Letter" made me think: What would be the reality of my life, should I actually become a father writing to his son while on the run? Or should I resign myself to one day being a man going home to his family after incarceration, to be there in real life?

So I decided. I would do the time, and then go home and try to make amends.

I pleaded guilty in state court to all charges. But Danville's hard-nosed young prosecutor, William Fuller, didn't make it easy for me, insisting that I give a full accounting of my offenses in public.

After my forced confession, the judge asked me if I had any statement to make before he pronounced sentence. What came into my mind was Fidel Castro's famous words at his trial for the assault upon the police barracks that presaged the Cuban revolution, a statement enshrined in Panther lore: "History will absolve me," I told the court, trying to save a bit of dignity from my surrender.

The judge took a moment and then replied, "Well, Mr. Hopkins, I suppose that history will absolve us all, one day." Then he gave me the ten years.

The following day I was to go on trial in federal court. But before the court session, my lawyer met with me. "Derrell, there's a problem. Commonwealth's Attorney Fuller didn't like your statement to the court, and somehow he got wind of our deal to have your federal time run concurrent to the state," he told me. "It seems that Fuller sent a telegram to the attorney general of the United States yesterday, saying that you were the most arrogant individual he'd ever had in his court, and protesting the deal he'd heard about. The attorney general sent a telegram to our judge this morning, stating, 'It is not the policy of the Department of Justice to run federal sentences concurrent to state verdicts.' "

I was enraged. The idea that the attorney general of the whole fuckin' United States was teaming up with the goddamn Danville prosecutor to double-cross me made me think that they had honed in on the fact that I was an ex-Panther, and were out to get me. Seeing a twenty-five-year sentence before me instead of the ten years I already thought to be too much, I screamed at my lawyer, "What do you mean it's not *policy?* I already made a fuckin' deal with you for ten years!"

"Settle down," he said. "I've talked to the judge, and he's going to stick with the original deal. You'll have to do the ten years for the state, but with good behavior you'll make parole early. But I can only tell you, after this, it might not be a good idea to return to Danville, because that Bill Fuller will have it in for you."

And so I was sent off to state prison with a ten-year sentence, with the hope that, as a first offender, I might be released in two and a half years.

In December 1975 I was transferred from the old jail in Danville to Southampton Correctional Center. The facility was primarily for youthful offenders under the age of twenty-one, and was called the Cotton Farm, as most of the prisoners worked on the surrounding acres, where the main crop was cotton.

The idea of picking cotton didn't sit well with me, and I was glad that the detainer the Feds had on me—because of my concurrent sentences—meant I would have to work inside the compound. The "spread," as it was called, consisted mainly of three redbrick cell houses that dated back to the 1920s, two honor buildings that resembled university dorms, a large cafeteria, and a school and industrial building. With all of them surrounding a central grassy yard, the place resembled a run-down college campus combined with an old prison.

Before you were assigned to a job, you had to go on the "gun gang," where, under the eyes of shotgun-wielding guards, new prisoners had to cut saplings and brush with bush axes and dig up tree stumps—all in the dead of winter. It was largely make-work intended to break the spirit of rebellion, much like the slave-breaking camps of old. Indeed, on the gun gang I felt like a slave, mindful of the fact that the prison was located in Southampton County, where Nat Turner had staged his slave rebellion in 1832. There seemed to remain an atmosphere of us versus them, for the prison's population was predominantly black and the guard force and administration almost all white. There was also tension in the air from an escape attempt and riot by black inmates earlier in the year, during which a white guard had been killed.

After a two-week stint on the gun gang, I was lucky enough to find help from a black counselor whose job was to oversee the I.Q. testing all incoming prisoners had to go through. He was impressed with my high score, and got me a job in the prison library. There I would spend every spare minute on the typewriter, hammering out whatever was on my mind, mainly stories of my Panther past and general diatribes against the powers-that-be.

Working with me in the library was a brother my age named Nathan McCall. We played chess during periods when we weren't busy, and would argue about all sorts of issues, especially religion. Though Nate had a past in the streets of Portsmouth, he had become a devout Christian in prison, and didn't care very much for my assailing his beliefs with my atheist/Marxist doctrine that religion was the "opiate of the masses," a tool used by the white power structure to keep black people subservient.

Still, I liked the brother. He always had probing questions that made me think, showing the sort of inquisitiveness that was altogether rare in prison. Coming up behind me while I was banging away on the library's manual Royal typewriter one afternoon, he asked, "Do you think the way you pound on that thing might be a sign of your anger?" (Didn't appreciate that one.) Another day he happened upon me as I was using colored pencils to draw an abstract painting, causing him to laugh and say, "Don't tell me you're now breaking off from writing to go into visual art?" And when he saw me writing musical notes on a page, he shook his head, smiling, and asked, "Have you ever wondered if having a name like Evans Hopkins has influenced how eccentric you are?" I wasn't sure what he meant by that one, but I did give it some thought. (I had mainly been called Derrell by family and friends up to that point, but had begun being referred to by my first name of Evans by prison authorities—and "Hop" by most prisoners.)

We took college classes together, under a Pell grant program that allowed the local community college to come into the institution with a variety of courses. I recall his getting an A on an English test on poetry, while I only got a B. I wondered, jealously, how this brother had done better than I, a man who considered himself a seasoned writer. At the time I was of the mind that poetry didn't really matter in my world of radical writing, not realizing that, with that class, I was picking up something lifesaving, which would one day mold my style, and provide salvation for my soul.

During the first two years at Southampton I remained hopeful that I'd be able to utilize my intelligence and emerge from prison as a writer. In the library I discovered a Norman Mailer omnibus, and his work became a seminal influence on my development. His ground-breaking essay, "The White Negro," astonished me with Mailer's depth of perception, as well as his ability to identify with the lot of black folk. I had not realized that whites could be so enamored of the plight of my people.

I was also influenced by the work of black writers like James Baldwin, Toni Morrison, and Ralph Ellison, along with black writers from the Harlem Renaissance of the 1920s like Jean Toomer and Claude McKay. I also read every magazine I could get my hands on, and especially studied *American Film,* the periodical of the American Film Institute, which fed my interest in film-making.

I took college classes in philosophy, with one on ethics helping me to develop a moral sense of the world. A class in world literature presented me with the amazing play *Lysistrata,* by the ancient Greek Aristophanes. I marveled that a writer from so many centuries ago could fashion such a sophisticated, hilarious antiwar work, in which the wives of soldiers in the Peloponnesian War decided to withhold sex from their husbands until they refused to fight.

After a year in the library I got a job as a clerk in the institution's chapel, working for a former priest from Illinois named John Alle-mang. He became a counselor and mentor, and helped me to realize that there were whites who understood the plight of black people, and who were willing to lend some degree of caring to me, person-ally. "If I were black, and growing up during your age," the gray-bearded Allemang told me in one of our many confidential sessions, "I would have become a Black Panther, too." Working in the chapel sparked an interest in theology, and I even considered enrolling in divinity school upon my release. I began to realize that I was more of an agnostic than an atheist, and thought that I might someday formulate a theology free of the strictures of the literalist, Anglo-Saxon bent that I felt organized religion had become.

Mama and Pop came to visit me every month, bringing Rod with them during the summers, when he stayed with them. Their continued faith in me gave me strength, especially after my third year, when I was first turned down for parole. I felt totally encaged by the system then, for if I did not make parole, ten years loomed ahead as an interminable amount of time. When I was denied again one year later, my rage began to come to the fore once more.

I also stayed in touch with Ruth, by letter and with phone calls. One day, while talking to her on the phone, she said, "I have some bad news, Derrell. Nelson was shot out in California. They found him in the desert, with three bullets in the back."

"What happened? Who did it?" I asked her.

"He can't talk yet," she replied. "Mama arranged for him to be transported back to Winston-Salem. He's paralyzed, Derrell; but they think he's going to make it."

Later, I learned how Nelson, the co-coordinator of my home chapter and a big brother figure for me, had been called out to the Bay Area to run the Free Ambulance Program he and Hazel had started in Winston-Salem. While working at the Party's health clinic in Berkeley, he'd been called on to treat a member of the Squad who'd been shot in an abortive attempt to kill a witness scheduled to testify in the murder trial of Huey Newton, who had returned to Oakland after several years of exile in Cuba. Two days later Nelson was found in the desert along the California/Nevada border, left for dead half-buried under some rocks. After recovering full consciousness, he still refused to talk about the incident to authorities, or to anyone else.

I shared this news with Mack, a brother who had also become close to Nelson when he briefly worked with the Party in Winston-Salem, and who was now doing time with me at Southampton. "We need to break out of this joint and go out there and kill Huey's goddamn ass," he said, his words giving expression to the latent rage I would continue to harbor against Newton and his squad of thugs. The shooting of Nelson made even more personal the way I felt about how my former leader's excesses were bringing about the demise of the Black Panther Party—which would finally fold completely in 1979.

On my third try, the board granted me parole. First the feds sent a representative to talk to me, and they granted my release. Then the state parole board saw fit to set me free, and set a date for July 14, 1979.

On the fourteenth I packed up all my belongings into a laundry basket on wheels, and pushed it to the administration building, where my mother and father greeted me, there to take me home. Then, the prison's assistant warden came into the room.

"There seems to be a problem, Mr. and Mrs. Hopkins," he said, as if I weren't even in the room. "I'm afraid that the federal authorities have not sent through the paperwork releasing your son from their detainer. I'm sorry, but we can't let him go today. You'll have to come back in a week or so, once we get the situation sorted out."

I was devastated. To have been at the gate of freedom and then be told that I couldn't go was unbelievable—and enraging. My folks were shaken up; Pop was close to tears. I felt the need to step up, comfort them both by saying, "Don't worry about it, they'll get it straightened out, and I'll be home soon."

Pop told me then, "You're a stronger man than I am, son. I just don't know how you can deal with something like this."

With those words from my father, something arose in me, telling me that I had to be strong for him, seeing him brought so close to despair by this senseless bureaucratic fuck-up. I gave my father and mother strong, reassuring hugs, willing them to maintain in the face of this latest injustice. "Don't worry," I told them again—though my blood was boiling, and I could barely contain my rage.

I would be strong, would *have* to be strong, for them. I would emerge from this with the sort of fury my father could never muster. As I stewed in prison for two more weeks, I took this final indignity as a sign that I should never forget the inhumanity of the forces that oppressed my people, that I should never relinquish the fight.

"I advise you not to come back to Danville once you're released," the lawyer had told me after my trial. But I'd forgotten his warning. Nor did I think about the Party teachings that said, "Prison is only maximum security. All black people are prisoners in America, and those of us on the outside only exist out here in a state of minimum security."

Upon my release I attempted to resume a life with my family, to live some semblance of the American dream. I felt I owed it to my parents to try to fit in. I immediately went back to work for my father, telling everybody that I was looking forward to becoming a partner in business with him.

After renewing my driver's license, I traveled to Winston-Salem to visit Ruth and Rod every weekend or so, borrowing a truck from my father. But after a few months things with Ruth didn't gel. I'd always known that she had a fiercely independent personality, which was one of the things that had attracted me to her in the first place. Now she had finished college in my absence, with a degree in education. Having made it on her own while I was gone, she didn't accept the rebellious, at times domineering mood I had after what I felt had been a lengthy imprisonment. This led to more friction during my visits than either of us seemed willing to endure. When the only teaching position she was offered was in Sumter, South Carolina, she decided to take it.

I kept Rod, who was now five, at my parents' home during the first weeks in August, to give Ruth a chance to go to Sumter and get set up. It also gave me a chance to bond with him. But I knew that the separation from Ruth would probably mark the end of our relationship as husband and wife.

My relationship with my father did not go well, either. You're always ten years old to your father, and he still treated me as a menial employee at work. Years of resentment at being treated like a little boy produced almost daily friction. He was used to being the boss, and nothing I had to say, in terms of changing or streamlining the business, had any effect on him. I was able to deal with it for the first several months. And then winter came once more, when the seasonal aspect of landscaping made it apparent that working for him was not for me.

Pop had again cut my pay down to minimum wage, telling me how work was scarce, and that he had given me a bit more during the summer only because I was his son. Now he was just cutting my wage, instead of laying me off, like he did with his other men when he didn't need them—making it seem like he was doing me a favor. This pissed me off to no end.

I began smoking marijuana again, the dreamy highs refueling my dreams of writing. One day in January 1980 I decided to throw away my ex-con fears of going into the job market, where I would have to answer that dreaded question on the application: *Have you ever been convicted of a felony?* I dressed in the sharp herringbone suit I'd bought from my landscaping pay, asked Pop to lend me his prized Mercury Marquis, and set out from my folks' home in the country to go to the office of the *Dunville Register,* even though the paper was known to be notoriously biased. But I would declare that I was a damn fine writer, then humbly ask that they just give me a chance.

I was running late for my appointment as I turned onto the main highway leading to town, so I accelerated to over seventy, only to notice a state police car in my rearview mirror. Trying not to panic, I turned off onto a side road that ran into the back side of the road where I lived. The trooper turned in behind me, and with the sudden irrational fear that a speeding ticket might mean a violation of my parole, I decided to outrun him to the back road to my home before he could get close, zigzagging through sharp turns until I no longer saw him in my mirror. But when I looked at the road in front, there was suddenly a stop sign, something that I'd not remembered from my adolescent days when I drove the road with abandon. I braked hard, and my rear tires hit gravel on the side of the road, causing the car to fishtail into a bank.

So much for my venture into the job market. (I found out later, traveling down the road and passing a state police car parked in front of a home, that the trooper had turned in after me because he *lived* on that side road, not because he was after me.) The damage was done. I had to continue working for Pop throughout the winter in order to repair his car, though I should say that he bought another one while I was getting the Mercury fixed, and then he gave the old car to me.

When spring came I felt increasingly trapped in my job with Pop. But rather than try to find another job, I decided to stay with him and help in his grand project to build a new office. So began my stint as a construction laborer, doing a thing with hammer and nails and electric saw. Then, in midsummer, while trying to extract an errant nail from a metal stanchion while constructing the basement of the building, the hammer slipped from the nail, and my hand slammed into a metal strut, cutting a knuckle to the bone.

Strange, how things can throw you off track, how certain things linger in your memory. Pop dropped me off in front of the hospital, with me holding a blood-soaked handkerchief to my wounded hand, and said, "They'll fix you up in there. But I've got to get back to the work site, to make sure the contractor is finishing up."

The injury was bad enough to keep me from working for several weeks—a tendon had been torn—but not bad enough for me to get disability. It was August, and I was keeping Roderick again for two weeks, so I reveled in the time I had to spend with my precocious six-year-old. We went on forays to the park and library, and spent a memorable day at King's Dominion, on the church's Sunday-school picnic. I would forever remember how, on the bus trip up, Roderick said to me, "This is going to be the best day of my life."

I told him, "It's good that you think that, son, because this feels like a special day to me, too. But you should always remember that you have a lifetime of such days ahead of you."

I decided to go back to school in the fall at Danville Community College, having saved up a little money from working during the summer, with the hope that the college classes would reignite my intellect and love of learning. I took classes in English (the Bible as literature), political science, and even a class in film appreciation, which fired up my latent interest in film.

But, during the same time, I had added another drug to my habit of smoking marijuana: alcohol. And alcohol led to drinking partners. One of them, a man named Jerry, began to tempt me toward breaking the law again.

"Why we sittin' here with no money, when we can go out there and get paid?" Jerry would say after we'd smoked up all our dope and drunk all our liquor. "It ain't like you don't know how to do it," he said. And me, thinking myself the real gangster/criminal, would say, "Fuck it. Let's go!" Half drunk, we'd pull juvenile smash-and-grab jobs at jewelry and gun stores, smashing in windows and grabbing whatever we could run away with. After trading our meager takings for drugs, we'd soon find ourselves broke again, trying to think up another score.

At the same time, I was acing my classes in college, and taking notes for all sorts of essays attacking American capitalism and race relations. Then there was the activity that really gave evidence of my mental state: I would visit bookstores at night, hiding six or seven books at a time under my winter coat, then take them home to read in a drunken stupor.

I was crossing over into some sort of psychosis, to the dark side of my psyche, yet there was a part of me that *realized* what was happening. One day I stole a book from the college library, *On Moral Fiction,* by John Gardner, the renowned novelist and critic, in which he wrote of how the artistic impulse, when repressed, might only find expression in the activity of an overly conscious outlaw.

Soon after reading Gardner's book, as fate would have it, I learned that he would be speaking at Averett, the local liberal-arts college. I showed up midway through his reading, lit to the gills off reefer, alcohol, and speed. When the audience turned around to see who was bursting through the doors, I had the nerve to pause, and take a bow, before taking a seat.

After Gardner's speech, I went up to the stage, pulled him aside, and told him, "I'm a writer, I just got out of prison, but I know they're trying to throw me back in."

"Don't let them lock you up again. You've got to keep your gift alive," he told me, as if he had no doubt that I was for real. "Whatever you do, just keep on writing."

His encouragement reminded me of what I was supposed to be about—for a moment, at least. I then spent feverish nights at home with my notepads, madly scripting ideas for poems, films, novels. But I was too far gone in the street life for salvation.

Soon after that I went out of control. Driving one of Pop's trucks to a nightclub that was just across the county line in North Carolina, I was so intoxicated that I had to close one eye to keep from seeing double. I made it there, only to hit another car while trying to park. Knowing that I was violating parole by being out of state, I took off toward home. I was almost there, doing close to ninety or one hundred, when a county sheriff got behind me with lights flashing. Speeding down the unpaved part of the road where I lived with abandon, the cop lost in my dust, the truck began to skid. Instead of braking, I floored it, and came out of the slide, but the cop car ended up in a ditch.

Weeks later, on New Year's Eve, while stone-blind drunk, I drove my car into a wooded area in the middle of town, making it a total loss. Less than a week after that, I wrecked Pop's main truck while driving home, and was arrested for driving drunk and leaving the scene of an accident. After picking me up, Pop told me how crazy I had been at the jail, telling the cops that I would whip their asses. "I don't know what's wrong with you, boy," he said, "but you got to be crazy to talk to the cops like that."

I reached into my sock to retrieve jewelry I'd stolen during my drunkenness and had managed to keep hidden from them. "Look at this!" I said. "You think these white folks are gods. But look at this! They ain't on top of everything!"

One day soon after, while walking through the heart of the black community during the height of the gas crisis of 1981, I saw an attendant pumping gas who had a little .22 in a holster on his side. *How dare this white motherfucker pump the life out of our community,* I thought, *with that little cap pistol on his side, like it's gonna keep somebody from taking him off.* I told Jerry about it later, told him it was time to do a *real* robbery. "It's time we take some straight-up money from the people who been stealin' it from our people," I said, flashing back to my Panther persona, my rage against the system (and my own hard luck) coming to the fore. I had used the money from our last score to buy a long-barreled magnum, and I was ready to roll.

That evening, as the gas station closed down, we crept from the darkness with dark stockings pulled over our faces, and accosted the attendant. It turned out that he was not the gun-toting man I'd wanted to confront, but an unarmed nineteen-year-old working there for the night. He was scared shitless as we stripped him of the cash he had on hand. Jerry, who had a knife, felt the young man's pockets for more money, and feeling the hardness of the change he had, shouted, "He's got a gun!" and took off running. But I stayed and asked, "Where's the safe?" When the boy told me there wasn't any safe, I told him, "Give me your wallet."

Then, in the moment I was leafing through his wallet, the thought hit me that I was going through the personal effects of a civilian, instead of taking the bounty of the gas station/oil company. The Panther adage, "A Party member shall not take even a needle or a piece of thread from the people," shot through my mind. I tried to wipe my fingerprints from the wallet as I asked the young man, "If I give this back to you, tell me you won't give it to the police!"

"Okay, okay," he said. As I threw the wallet down, my pistol discharged onto the floor, the sound reverberating in the small alcove.

My first thought was, *Goddamn fool, you could have shot yourself.* Then, trying to regain my composure, I told the kid, "That's just a sign of what you'll get if you talk to the police."

A week later, detectives picked up Jerry and charged him with being the gunman in the robbery. I made plans to rob again, to get him out on bond. But before I could, I was arrested and brought before the head prosecutor in a little room in the city jail.

"You don't remember me, Derrell?" the man said, smugly leaning against a desk with his legs crossed. "I'm Bill Fuller. I'm the one who prosecuted you for beating up on the old night watchman six years ago. You mean to say you don't remember me?"

The memory of the enemy who had tried to quash my deal for my first crime came back to me, along with all the hatred I'd felt for him at that time. But I tried to play it off, telling him, "No, can't say that I remember." Fuller asked me to confess, and implicate Jerry. I refused, only to find out later that Jerry had already given a statement implicating me, in return for the promise of a suspended sentence.

The trial, on May 19 (which I remembered as Malcolm X's birthday), was quick. The night before I had scripted an elaborate alibi defense, which I would deliver when I took the stand. I figured that it was Jerry's word against mine, and if I could deliver my lies believably, as if I were a superb actor, then I could come through. But it turned out that I was a terrible actor, made worse by valium prescribed by the jail doctor, which I had hidden in my pocket and would clandestinely pop, with water, during the trial.

When I took the stand, Fuller jammed me with questions so relentlessly that I blew up at him, becoming the image of black anger to the all-white jury. Standing before them as I awaited their judgment, I could not help but think of the Party's demand that black people be tried by a jury of their peers. The foreman, a man with a particularly red face already scorched by the suns of late May, made the pronouncement: "We find the defendant guilty of robbery and the use of a firearm in the commission of a felony, and recommend the punishment of life and one year in the state penitentiary."

I was stunned. I had expected a long sentence, but life, for a robbery in which no one was injured?

"I want the jury polled," I told my lawyer. I watched each white face mouth consent to my condemnation. *They would have given me the death penalty had they been able,* I thought. *I am a black man, the object of their collective fear and loathing, to be sent far away, for as long as possible.*

My attorney, perhaps slightly embarrassed at his part in helping to get me the max, leaned over and whispered to me, "Don't worry. Life is only twelve and a half years in Virginia."

Twelve and a half years. A life sentence. It all seemed unfathomable to me. While I was still trying to grasp the concept, the judge asked me if I had anything to say to the court before he pronounced the sentence. This caught me by surprise, even though the same thing had happened at my first trial.

I would have liked to sound defiant, but could think of but one response: "The sentence is extreme and beyond the mercy of a so-called Christian nation."

As soon as I uttered those words, I realized that they betrayed too much pain—not only the personal pain of being punished so cruelly, but what you might call a *political* pain, the pain born of learning that twelve of my countrymen could condemn me so. I did not want to feel such hurt, much less reveal it before my oppressors. Though I could not understand it then, my pain was also born of the deep and somehow still abiding Christian ideals at the foundation of my being, a foundation formed before the rage and rebellion had set in, and enduring despite the heartbreaking disillusionment I was suffering.

"You are to be remanded to the Virginia State Penitentiary," came the judge's pronouncement, "there to remain for the rest of your natural life."

And at that moment, as surely as I was ashamed of myself, I was also ashamed of my country. Even though I believed that the system was evil, and that whites hated me more than I could ever hate them, I still found it incredible that every one of those jurors had acceded to such obvious injustice. I had hoped that there was still some redeeming concept of justice, even in the hearts of those who despised me. Somehow, I still believed that these people could hardly be as bad as I'd made them out to be, in my desperate need to rationalize my criminality. They would prove me wrong, I thought. Show me how wrong I was to rebel so senselessly, and thereby point the way back toward what was good and true and just.

The fact that they were, to my mind, so lacking in Christian justice dashed my belief in the possibility of my own redemption. They would never change, so why should I? The life sentence was their way of declaring me worthless—which I interpreted as a declaration of war. And since I'd been cast on the wrong side, I determined then that I would continue to rage on, with all my might. . . .

PART TWO · DOING LIFE

CHAPTER SIX

Days in the Life Sentence

I was being held in the new Danville jail, the old one having been torn down some five years before. Security was much tighter than in the old facility, as the new jail was housed in the basement of the new courthouse. There were no windows, only concrete walls and steel bars. The only time one saw daylight was when the men in one's cellblock went to the roof of the three-story building for recreation, where there was a small basketball court surrounded by barbed wire. Since the area was monitored by a security camera, there was no guard present during recreation times. George Jackson's mantra that "the revolutionary prisoner's first duty is to escape" resounded in my mind after I'd heard the judge pronounce my sentence, and I made up my mind to do just that, despite the odds against me.

I'd been in the jail for a month waiting to be tried, and had heard prisoners speak of a young man named Jericho who had jumped from the roof in an attempt at freedom, only to break both ankles. I would do better than that. I developed a plan to climb the fence of the recreation area atop the jail, just out of view of the camera. Tying a rope made from sheets to a ventilator shaft, I'd scale down the wall to freedom. After making it to the street I would run to the river, wade along the banks to throw off dogs that might follow, then make my way to my father's office, where I would break in and get the keys to one of his trucks.

The night after my trial I began cutting three-inch-wide strips from two extra sheets I had secreted under my mattress, braiding them into strong lengths. On laundry days I ordered an extra-large jumpsuit, and practiced looping my lengthening rope over the shoulders beneath it.

It took two weeks to complete the rope, as I had to go through two sheet exchanges, holding back one sheet each time, in order to have enough strips for my rope. I would tie each length from the top of my cell door and test it with my full weight. And I worked out hard, doing push-ups to increase arm strength, and practicing karate katas to develop my fighting ability. I would lie on my back in my meditative pose, hands crossed upon my chest like a mummy, and envision my getaway. My cellblock was given recreation on Thursdays, and I worked to build up my courage until my rope was completed.

Two days before the Thursday I had decided would be the date of my flight, a fight occurred in cellblock D, where inmates who had been sentenced to state prison were housed. That night, guards brought in the inmate who had been stabbed in D block, after he'd been treated at the hospital. They told me that I would be moving to his former cell, since I was sentenced to a long prison term, and therefore more suited to this block where the jail's "hardcore" were housed.

The move took me by surprise, and I was not able to take my escape rope with me. Further enraged that fate had thwarted my plans, I conspired with other prisoners in the cellblock to try another route. I would fake a suicide attempt, and while on the way to the hospital, supposedly unconscious, I would make my move. I quickly befriended a dreadlocked brother from New York named I. Sparks (who, ironically, was the one who had attacked the man whose cell I now occupied) and a radical white guy named Bobby. I would make superficial cuts on my arm to bleed enough to make it look like I was trying to kill myself, and Bobby and Sparks would tell the guards that I had been depressed and had hoarded enough of the Valium I was taking to try an overdose.

The plan seemed to be working, but I didn't have one critical bit of information: The day before my attempt, a shakedown had been called, and the rope that I'd left in the other cellblock had been discovered. While being wheeled out on a gurney by the rescue squad, I heard the sheriff order, "Don't take any chances with him. Keep him shackled to the gurney, and call Danville police for backup. If he tries anything at all, shoot him."

At the hospital, they pumped my stomach while armed guards stood by. The next thing I knew I was nearly naked, dressed only in undershorts and the gauze on my cut arm, freezing in the air conditioning of the "strip cell" on suicide watch, monitored by cameras. The next day they had me in a sheriff's car and on my way to state prison, perhaps to remain there for the rest of my life—if I could not find a way out.

Powhatan Correctional Center, also known as the State Farm, was a prison complex housing more than a thousand men, most of whom worked as virtually slave labor tending the cattle and crops on the hundreds of acres that surrounded the prison.

I was housed in a unit expressly for parole violators. As soon as I arrived I began to examine the fifteen-foot brick walls topped with razor wire for a means of escape. I began pumping iron, trying to strengthen myself either for escape or for fighting off any assailants in prison. But after being classified to go to the State Penitentiary in Richmond, where most of the long-term prisoners were kept, I gave up on the weight lifting. I'd talked to men who had been at The Wall, as it was called, and they told me of the violence at the state's oldest and toughest prison. I realized that any fighting that I'd have to do would likely be with the homemade knives said to abound there.

I filled my days with reading from the meager library, using a notebook to take down any words I did not know, still intent on developing as a writer. I also played chess with an intelligent Vietnam veteran named Gerald Stovall, who was in for robbery, as well. He considered himself a communist, so we connected there. He was also bent on escaping. "There ain't no way out of here," he told me. "But wait till we get to the Penitentiary. I did eight years there on my first bit, and I know we can find a way of breaking out."

I didn't want to wait. I'd heard of a successful escape by a prisoner from the corrections department unit at the Medical College of Virginia, which was located in the heart of downtown Richmond. So I devised a ruse in order to be taken there for an examination, telling prison doctors that I felt I had a lump in my throat, and that I also had trouble breathing at night. I smuggled wax from Gouda cheese my parents had brought me during a visit, and took impressions of the locks on the ground-level windows of the MCV holding cell, with the fantastic thought that I might be able to fashion an instrument to pick the simple locks. After getting the doctors at MCV to sign off on a nose operation to relieve my nasal congestion, I made a handcuff key from the ink refill of a ballpoint pen, so that I'd be prepared for any opportunity to make a run for it.

My face was on fire, pain flaming from my nose, blasting through my eyes and mouth and head. I opened my eyes, and closed them immediately, the light seeming to suffuse my skull from the inside. I imagined the front of my face glowing like a jack-o'-lantern. When the waves of pain shortened and subsided, I dared to open my eyes once more.

I was in the hospital, the prison ward on the sixth floor MCV, in the heart of downtown Richmond—the result, it took a moment to remember, of the "minor" nose operation I had engineered. But damn, it was supposed to be a simple procedure to straighten out that deviated septum that caused my allergic congestion, little more than plastic surgery, the Chinese doctor had said. But he hadn't said shit about this kind of pain.

I pressed the nurse's button to get more pain medication, then drifted in and out of sleep, drugged dreams mixing in with fantasies of escape. When I awoke during the night I was still determined to get away, to try to climb into the ceiling as the man I had heard about had done.

I struggled to the bathroom with the IV caddy still attached to me, wearing only a hospital gown in midwinter. Seeing no way to climb to the ceiling from the bathroom, I had to give up for the night. I would be stronger the next day, and I'd try again.

I never got that chance. The next day I was shipped out to a holding cell in the basement of the State Penitentiary, a place that was for all the world like a medieval dungeon. It was freezing, as several windows were broken out, and I was given only a woolen blanket for warmth and an iron cot with no mattress. To make matters worse, I was highly allergic to wool, and had been told that the allergy medicine that had been prescribed for me hadn't been sent from the hospital. I knew I was in for a cold, sleepless night, with an inflamed and bleeding nose.

The mental patients at the Pen were housed in this basement, which I learned from one of them who stopped in front of my cell. He was picking up cigarette butts on his way back with a dozen others from receiving their psychotropic medications. He seemed such an object of pity that I offered him a whole cigarette. His almost dead eyes brightened to reveal what might have once been an active intelligence.

Almost drooling from the effects of his Thorazine, the haggard, disheveled man told me with slurred speech that this was the section of the prison that had once housed the state's death-row inmates. "They ghost-es keep us company down here, though." He looked up and around, eyes blinking from his medication, and said, "Can't you feel them all around? It's warmer down here, with they spirits all around."

I had no response for that and was glad to see him move on. After he left, I looked out the half-basement window, at the long twenty-foot-high brick wall that would mark the circumference of my home for many, many years. I now had an early glimpse of what happened to those who were not strong enough to take the punishment meted out by the system.

When the nurse came along to give me the pain pill from MCV, and the antidepressant I had gotten prescribed for me at the State Farm, I threw them both into the toilet. I resolved then never to use the crutch of drugs, never to give my captors the purchase to kill me mentally. *They won't break me,* I vowed. *If I have to do hard time, I'll get hard with it.* My rage would be the fuel to keep me alive.

I was transferred to A-building at the State Pen, which had been reconstructed at the turn of the century from whitewashed brick taken from the original postcolonial prison that had been designed and founded by Thomas Jefferson in 1789, making it the oldest penal institution in America. Along with added cell houses and factory buildings, the institution rose as an ugly walled fortress in the heart of Richmond, scant miles from downtown and the state capitol building.

My first view of my cell in A-building was forbidding. The walls were like something out of a cowboy movie. Made of boilerplate steel with giant bolts riveted to four-inch seams, during the winter you could feel the cold actually *radiate* from them. The windows fronting the structure, which rose five tiers, had panes missing like in B-basement, allowing the wind in off the James River. The cell's floor was cement, with a ceiling so low I could stand and place the palm of my hand flat against it. The steel cot had a torn plastic mattress on it, and it could contain my six-foot-two frame only if my feet hung off the end. There was only cold water coming from the twelve-by-eight-inch ceramic sink, which separated the bunk from the toilet by less than two feet.

The cell doors worked on a medieval winding system, and the cranking sound of the door of my cell being wound closed—and then slamming shut with finality—on that first day after my transfer from the medical unit would remain in my mind, and be repeated over and over for thousands of days and nights.

The day after my release into the general population of the State Pen, I went out to the ballpark for recreation. The ballpark was like a tiny Roman coliseum, made of red brick "bleachers" descending to the two-acre expanse of grass that served as a ball field, surrounded by a looming brick wall that rose some thirty feet. There were three guard towers atop the wall, and the guards in them carried high-powered M-14 carbines.

From the top steps you could see into the city, watch people walking along the streets, a freeway with zooming cars just beyond the wall. After being at rural prisons, it was mind-bending being so close to the freedom you longed for, yet so far away.

Looking out over that wall, I heard a familiar voice behind me saying "Hey, brother man. What's happening?" I turned to see Gerald, who had been sent to the Pen just before my trip to MCV.

"Glad to see you made it out of the hospital—though it wasn't the way you had planned, huh?" he said to me in greeting, ever with the broad smile he liked to use to bring me out of my customary serious mood. He'd known about my plan to escape from MCV, but he played my failure off like it was no real loss.

His lightheartedness didn't produce a corresponding smile from me, as I was intent on presenting the coldest demeanor I could, to make sure everyone in the population of one thousand hardened cons would know I was not to be fucked with. Maybe he sensed that I needed some help in my transition to doing hard time, and said, "Come on, man, go with me to a meeting of the Creative Workshop. I'll introduce you to some brothers, and show you how to program while you're here."

Programming was the word for getting into the rehabilitation aspects of incarceration, of which the Penitentiary offered more than any other institution in the state. Because of its long history in the heart of Richmond, volunteers from the community came into The Wall regularly, sponsoring programs like Homestretch Drug Program, Family Life Counseling, Alcoholics Anonymous, and the Creative Workshop, an inmate-coordinated program offering outlets for drama, creative writing, music, and the visual arts. And unlike any other institution in the country, the prisoners were allowed to actually run the programs, independent of the administration, thus increasing the sense of responsibility of those taking part.

At the Creative Workshop meeting, Gerald introduced me to Charles Satchell, the organization's leader, who was a gifted poet. I told Satch, as he was called, that I wasn't interested in being part of an organization at that time. He responded, "How you not gonna be interested in organization, brother, with you being with the Panther Party?" When I told him that I was shy about sharing my work with others, but that I had brought along something someone else could read, he said, "That's bullshit, my brother. Who ever heard of a shy Black Panther?"

He then turned to the assembled group of fifteen and told them that I was a brother who had been a Panther on the West Coast, and had written for the Party paper—which was highly regarded in penal systems across the country, as the paper had been sent to prisoners for many years until the Party's demise. Then, during an open session when brothers were giving up verses they had written, he put me on the spot by calling on me to read something.

I read "Soul Trained," a poem I'd written while at the State Farm in an effort to deal with the promiscuity of the street I'd just left, and to exorcise the images of sex and of the loose women I'd been relating to:

> *I watch the Soul Train.*
> *Chic women wiggle and pump,*
> *Grind and bump*
> *Like Hoo-doo of old, but*
> *Sassy and bold,*

Cool and sexy
With dudes who dance so slickly,
They pose and primp
And style like pimps,
All jamming with dedication
To sensual gratification . . .
That somehow almost seems spiritual
And linked to ancient ritual.
But the thought behind the sound
Is only of bourgeois love, and sleeping around
Trying to be the sleekest freak
In a moral landscape, depressingly bleak.
If only those dudes' grins weren't so ludicrous
And that joy of living, still within us
Was in celebration of victory's sweeping tide—
But what have we won, people?
Why have we such pride?

My poem was greeted with strong applause by the group, the first applause I'd ever received for my writing. Indeed, it was the first time I had shared my artistic side in public.

Being around Gerald and the brothers in the workshop was good for me, but it soon became evident that Gerald, having spent eight years at The Wall on his previous bit, was in the programming mode, and planned to do his time and try to make parole in eight or ten years. I could tell that he felt at home at the State Pen. He actually confided in me that he believed so many Vietnam vets who had once done time returned to prison because "they miss the camaraderie, the sense of community they felt in the 'Nam."

"Might be that the same is true with you," he said. "You're like a war vet, too, being from the Panthers, and maybe you also missed the brotherhood of your first bit in prison." I did not want to believe this, but would later come to wonder if there might be some unconscious truth to his view.

Hanging with Gerald and Satch gave me a certain standing in the prison. They were good-hearted brothers with reputations as serious men, worthy of respect; but with their heavy sentences (Gerald had forty years, Satch had life on a murder beef), they were also known as men you'd best not cross.

One day, Gerald warned me, "Hop, you just too much of a nice guy. You want to think everybody black is your brother, but that ain't the case, especially in here. You're the kind of brother who needs to make sure you always got someone to watch your back."

Indeed, I had found the world of the State Pen to be rife with violence. Stabbings occurred regularly, often resulting in deaths. I would see men smuggling homemade knives ("shanks," in prison parlance) on their persons, slipping them under doors, bringing them out of the school and factory complex in their sleeves. Some of the hardcore used paperback books to make protective vests against stab wounds, before venturing into battle. (One year, there were so many killings at The Wall that authorities locked down the institution at year's end, for fear that any more deaths would push the city's already high homicide rate to a new record.) Being around an abundance of such lethal men threatened my determination to view life with a degree of optimism. "It's hard keeping a balanced view of life," Gerald told me, in one of our intellectual conversations, "when you see the worst of humanity all around. It kind of gives you a raw view of humankind in general."

One man I knew was burned to death inside his cell, after someone jammed closed his cell door and threw in a Molotov cocktail made from lighter fluid. This killing caused me some concern. Since I stayed up well into the night reading or writing, and slept when I could during the day, the idea of sudden attack while sleeping during the day was a source of real apprehension. I developed a habit of dozing lightly, with at least one ear open, in order to be able to respond should my cell door suddenly be thrown open by an assailant—since cells were unlocked during the hours from breakfast to 11:30 P.M. lockdown.

Perhaps to hook me up with someone who could help ensure my safety, one day Gerald introduced me to Jericho, the young brother I'd heard about in Danville who had tried to escape by jumping off the roof of the jail, and who also enjoyed a reputation as a tough con.

"I heard about the moves you tried to get away at the city jail," he said to me, with obvious respect. "I also heard you play a little chess. Why don't you come check out our chess club, and we can talk some more." He and I became fast friends when we found out that we both still shared the dream of escape. Jericho had two life sentences for a double killing. His codefendant had committed suicide in jail, leaving Jericho holding the bag. He was deep into the chess, and got me to join the prison's chess club, which had some renown in Richmond, with players coming in from the community every month for tournaments.

Jericho was a big-boned young man with a baby face. Standing six-foot-three and weighing close to two hundred, he had the appearance of a giant teenager, though he was twenty-two. He also had the gift of gab, and was always animated, talking beaucoup shit, as we liked to say. One day I accompanied him to the weight room in the basement of the recreation building. When I told him that I wasn't into lifting weights, he told me point-blank, "You can't be a trooper, brother, if you don't train."

The first chance I got I checked out the prison's library, which was located on the fourth floor in a complex of rooms above the industrial metal and print shops, where the school was located. The library's collection came from the discarded books of libraries around the state, going back some sixty years or more. I was thrilled to discover John Dos Passos and find new volumes by James Baldwin. Then there were Hemingway and Faulkner, along with James Joyce and Kafka, classics I had long wanted to read. I also found collections of poetry that contained newer lights like Alice Walker, Sonia Sanchez, and Nikki Giovanni. Library call found me at the cage (the central control room of the cellblock) most every day, getting a pass to go to the fourth floor. Once more, the library would become my refuge.

I also began to spend time in the law library, a small room located at the back of the recreation building. I had my legal avenues to push, with the hope of getting my unjust sentence reversed somehow. My appeal was based primarily on how I'd received what amounted to cruel and unusual punishment, with a life sentence for a robbery in which no one had been injured.

I worked with an inmate paralegal named Pete, who had a reputation as the consummate jailhouse lawyer, having gotten the cases of many men sent back to court. He looked at my cases, going back to my conviction for bank robbery, and told me what I didn't want to hear. "Bank robbery, when committed by middle-class men, is largely seen as social suicide," he said. "Bank robbers get caught most of the time, and if you're not of the regular criminal milieu, criminologists have written that, more often than not, it boils down to a middle-class man attempting to escape the constrictions of his life—for deep down he knows that he'll probably be caught."

But Pete was willing to work for me, thinking that I might get some play because my sentence was excessive. He said that I needed to work on my own legal research, if my appeal were to be expedited. But I couldn't deal with the idea of immersing myself in legal reading. I knew that my brain could only take but so much input, and that the sort of thinking needed for legal work was at odds with that of the imaginative writer. I had to choose one, and decided to follow my heart, to go wholeheartedly with my writing, with the faith that it would somehow pull me through while I delegated my legal hopes to paralegals. Maybe, by some miracle, I'd attract the attention of some dynamite lawyer through my writing.

When I told Satch of my decision, he said, "You got to go for what you know, lil' brother. But the system is getting tougher, and while I hate to say it—being a writer myself—things have changed since Jack Henry Abbott wrote *In the Belly of the Beast* and had Norman Mailer get him out. Since Abbott went back in for killing a dude, people now think of inmate writers as just being smart cons, and all the more dangerous for being so smart. You got a hard row to hoe if you think you can write your way out of prison."

I waited to be called for my visit, sitting on my bunk in starched jeans and shirt, street clothes sent to me by my parents so that I would not have to wear the degrading prison-issue rough denim. Mama and Pop were coming to see me for the first time since my transfer to The Wall. They were bringing Roderick with them, and delivering the gift of a typewriter—evidence of their continued belief in me. I had the nervous expectancy of a proud father seeing his newborn, though in this instance the pride was mixed with shame, since my son would once again be seeing me in a prison's visiting room.

It wasn't as bad as I'd envisioned. The room was divided into two sides, with one reserved for visitors with children. It was like a lunchroom at a factory, with a dozen or so Formica tables and plastic chairs, and rows of vending machines. The reunion was joyous, with Roderick rushing to jump into my arms as I emerged through the doorway. My shame melted away as I carried my six-year-old to the table where my father and mother rose to greet me. Remembering visits at Southampton where I would give him change and hoist him up to get drinks out of the vending machines, Rod said with great relish, "Let's go get some sodas!"

"You're such a big boy now," I told him, standing before the bank of soda machines. "Here's the money, you can get what you want without me holding you up now." And mixed with the pride of his adroitly filling the orders of what he, and Grams and Poppa, wanted, I fought back the guilt of my son's having to go through all of this again.

While we were at the vending machines, an inmate taking pictures with a Polaroid for the prison's Jaycees came up and asked if we wanted a photo. I'd tape the photograph he took that day to the wall of my cell, and I'd take it with me whenever I was moved. It showed Rod standing on my toes for extra height, his arms raised like a weight lifter's to display imaginary muscles, his joy infectious enough to infuse me with a dedication to somehow find a way to join him, once more, in freedom.

In August 1982, an ex-cop named Frank Coppola who was on death row for the murder of a lady during a robbery suddenly dropped all of his appeals. He was immediately scheduled for execution and transferred to the holding cell adjacent to the death chamber that housed the state's electric chair—in the basement of A-building, almost immediately below my cell.

I would catch glimpses of Coppola in the fenced-in exercise area just outside the death chamber: a tall white man with shaved head and Fu Manchu mustache, an image of defiance of the death penalty, which I felt to be no more than state-sanctioned murder. His execution was to be the first in Virginia since 1962, and only the second in the country since the end of the Supreme Court's moratorium that had judged all of the states' death-penalty statutes unconstitutional.

I could not help but feel a personal sense of violation: These sanctimonious motherfuckers were going to take the life of another human being, here in the place they were forcing us to live—despoiling our *home.*

I began a journal that night, feeling a need to vent my rage. But I also had the instinctive feel of a trained reporter, sensing the dramatic possibilities in chronicling events filled with drama: the anti-death-penalty attorneys had filed a petition to block the execution (claiming that Coppola was not in his right mind, and therefore shouldn't be allowed to drop his appeals), and the Supreme Court had yet to rule on their claims.

Aug. 9, 1 A.M.

There are few ends worse than being fried in an electric chair, but perhaps living without parole in prison is an even more ignoble and hellish path to oblivion. It doesn't strike me as strange that a white ex-cop might be less fearful of two 55-second cycles of high voltage, than of being dogged for years in captivity by a vindictive adminis- tration and an inimical population—especially since he would still probably have to suffer in solitary confinement, with death-row doubt, for an extensive period.

He won't even feel the second surge of juice, and very little of the first. So why would he care, anyway? Who's really afraid of the elec- tric chair?

As soon as the cell doors were unlocked after breakfast, I went to Gerald's cell to show him the first serious words of prose I'd written in years. "Hop," he said, "you always told me you could write, and it looks like you won't just talkin' shit. Keep it goin', brother man."

Encouraged, each night I wrote more about the mood of the prison, as Coppola's execution loomed:

. . . An older con mentioned that Coppola probably didn't want to go through the hell of prison, stating that growth is a necessity for a human being and how that's impossible under present prison condi- tions . . . Another black prisoner expressed the widely held view that the execution of this white man who wishes to die will lead the way for killing all the black men on death row the state really wants to do away with. "Look at it this way," he said, "the death penalty is just an extension of the days of lynchings."

Many of the prisoners viewed Coppola's declining to appeal his sentence further as indicative of a resoluteness bordering on courage. Others questioned his sanity. "If he wants to die, give him a syringe and let him take his damn self out."

Word got around the prison that I was writing about the death penalty, and a prisoner I didn't know approached me and gave me a copy of the procedure manual for executions, which he'd picked up while cleaning the death chamber. It was chilling in its detail.

As I wrote each night, I could not help but hope that the methodical killing outlined in the manual's pages would not take place below my cell. I tried to joke about it, telling Gerald, "I hope there won't be an earthquake if this shit jumps off, 'cause if the floor to my cell gives way, my ass will land smack-dab in that goddamn chair."

One man bet me that they wouldn't go through with the execution, and I took him up on that, betting a pack of smokes. Then a news flash came the next day, saying that Coppola had been given a stay of execution. I never thought that I'd be glad to lose a bet.

However, on August 15, the prison was locked down early, at 9 P.M. Two hours later, I recorded the following:

They're killing him now. Three guards go to his cell and escort him to the chair a short distance away. He is strapped into the chair, and guards secure the head and leg pieces, which have been immersed in a saline solution. They then place a leather mask over the upper part of his face. I wonder what he is thinking.

The generator is activated, giving off an eerie, whining noise. When the first 55-second cycle of 2,500 volts of raw electric power hit his brain, all thought and feeling must cease. But this does not stop his body from surging violently in a vertical jerk.

He doesn't feel the drop in voltage after the first cycle, doesn't know that his body is going limp. At the next thump, announcing the second 55-second cycle, his muscles vibrate and twitch involuntarily.

I wonder what he would think of the indignity of this death if he could see through the death mask. I wonder if he has bitten his tongue, if the blood of this deed is flowing from below the mask onto his shirt.

I picture the guards picking up the stiff form from the chair, the body cruelly contorted. The guards place sandbags on the arms and legs to keep them flat before the body is taken out to a waiting hearse.

I wonder how the crowd outside feels at catching sight of the body. I wonder if the men now locked in their cells on the street side of the

building can see what's happening out there. I wonder if they care.
And I wonder, who's really afraid of Virginia's chair?

The following day I typed up my account, with a title drawn from the last sentence of my piece. That evening I went to a Creative Workshop meeting conducted by a sister who wrote for the Richmond paper, the *Times-Dispatch.* She took the piece to her editor, and sent word to me later in the week that her paper would print it, but only parts of it as a letter to the editor. Angry, I told her, "They can kiss my ass if they think I'm going to give it to them for free, to dissect the parts they see fit to print."

Then I caught myself, and apologized to the sister for my fit of rage. She offered to give it to the local black paper, the *Richmond Afro-American.* "They only pay twenty-five dollars or so," she told me.

I told her, "I'll accept only *one* dollar, before I give away my work."

The next day, a Thursday, I had an appointment to see the coun selor I'd been assigned when I got to the prison, a demure black woman named Lois, who had seemed to take a special interest in my writing. I showed her a carbon copy of the piece, just to let her know that I had begun to write again.

Lois took the time to read it. Then, looking up, she said, "This is good. Very, very good," her words giving me all the gratification I figured I'd get from the piece, having become reconciled that it might never see print. Then she said, "Why don't you send it to *The Washington Post?*"

I almost laughed at the notion. But, being in a cocky mood, I said, "That's a good idea. Get them on the phone for me." I was only joking, since counselors weren't really supposed to make outside calls for prisoners. But, to my surprise, she picked up the phone, called Information, got the number to *The Post,* and dialed it. Then she handed the phone to me.

The receptionist on the other end connected me with *The Post's* op-ed section, OUTLOOK. "It sounds interesting," a woman's voice told me. "Go ahead and send it to us, and we'll take a look at it." I put my carbon copy of the article in the mail the next day, and more or less forgot about it.

Sunday came, and I stood in line outside the phone kiosk for my weekly call home. Gerald was behind me, and we talked about the fact that little had been written about the execution, how it was almost like it hadn't happened. "Well, maybe the *Afro* will print my article, and a little something will get out," I told him.

When I finally got through to Mama, she said, "People are talking about your article in the paper."

"Oh, you must have picked up the *Afro* on your way home," I said.

"The *Afro?* No, your uncle Carroll called us this morning before we left for church, telling us that you had this big article in *The Washington Post*. So we picked it up at the newsstand after church. Everybody up there is talking about it," she said, her pride coming through with her voice.

In *The Washington Post!* I could hardly believe it. Mama went on, "Your uncle Carroll says that it's good you're writing again, but that maybe you should tone down what you write. But I told him, 'That boy is never going to change, so you can forget that,' " she said with her musical laugh. It was a moment to savor, the rebel writer being validated in the Establishment press, of all places, reaching millions of people, and getting my family to really believe in me again.

And so it was that I began to believe in myself once more.

At the end of the week I received an envelope from *The Post* containing the OUTLOOK section with my piece: my first view of my words in print, under my by-line. I was on the front page of the section, with a prominent photo of Coppola and the caption, "NOTES FROM A PRISON CELL ON THE COPPOLA EXECUTION." Then, on the inside turn, there was the bold headline, WHO'S AFRAID OF VIRGINIA'S CHAIR? To see words I'd written from inside prison, to know that they had been seen by millions around the world in an Establishment newspaper, filled me with a sense of power. I felt a validation from the world at large, knowing that I'd done what few incarcerated men had ever done before. It filled me with a new sense of responsibility to find ways to continue to be read by the millions I believed I could now reach.

My friend Jericho really got off on my success. He walked around introducing me as "Evans—'Who's Afraid of Virginia's Chair?'—Hopkins," telling everyone that he was my business manager. When we walked together on the yard, if someone approached me, he loved putting up his palm and telling them, "You got to talk to me first, 'fore you can talk to him." To others he'd whisper conspiratorially, "You know he used to be a Black Panther," and then he'd smile, knowing it was hard for the hardest of men to believe that the bespectacled, skinny me was once a bad-ass Panther.

Jericho became my "stick man" (prison parlance for one who sticks with you no matter what—also called a "walking partner," as convicts tended to walk in pairs, in case trouble arose). Walking with tough brothers like Jericho lent an amount of protection in a world of cutthroats, and gave me a certain amount of freedom to get down with my writing. I began to look at myself as a freelance writer—or "an unfree-lancer," I used to tell people jokingly, especially volunteers who came to the programs I attended.

I became close to one volunteer in particular, a talented freelance writer named Ben Cleary, who brought a variety of Richmond officials and personalities to the creative writing class he taught every week. He introduced me to many Richmond writers, editors, and civic leaders, and he and I became close friends, exchanging letters about books and writing, and talking often over the phone.

I learned to write query letters to any magazine or newspaper I thought might publish an article by a writer behind bars, and though I garnered a lot of rejection slips, I refused to let it deter me. I sent in pieces cold (or "over the transom," as it is called) to various publications, including *The New Republic*. I was surprised when the editor, Hendrik Hertzberg, wrote back and said he had taken note of my piece in *The Post*. While he wasn't interested in the article I'd sent, he said he'd like me to do a back-page piece for them about prison life, thus giving me my first professional assignment.

While the piece never ran (my tone, it seemed, was still a bit too militant for the mainstream media), I kept pushing on, getting things published here and there, even writing a piece for *Chess Life* magazine about our unusual club at the Pen, and how we had players from the community coming in to play tournaments sanctioned by the United States Chess Federation. The article was read by a Russian émigré grandmaster living in Canada named Ivan Ivanov, who wrote to the club and offered to come in and play ten of our members at the same time, in what is called a simultaneous exhibition. I covered the event for *Chess Life* as well, a fun piece in which I was able to write about my own match with him and pretend that I'd actually had a chance of winning.

My cell became a cave of creativity, with me staying up well into the night, reading and writing about whatever moved my spirit. On the steel walls I taped photos to inspire me: Nelson Mandela, Malcolm X, visiting-room shots of my parents and Rod. A lone bare bulb above the barred door provided light for my forays into literature during the wee hours. Sometimes I would listen to the radio or to cassette tapes of jazz. I decided to do without a television during this period, fearing it would distract me from my thoughts. More often than not I would vibe to the silence of late night, my only comfort the *shlict-tick, shlict-tick* of my wind-up clock—which was at once a method of discipline, marking out the hours, and a demon of sound, counting away my days.

As well as being my artistic haven, my cell was also a dungeon, in which to reflect upon my misdeeds. How had my fervor for the struggle, for freedom, been so corrupted, leading to my descent into criminality? How had a young man, now so enthralled with the idea of poetry and beauty—of sharing with the world—how had he once been so enraged as to resort to common brigandry?

My reading gave some clues. In John Gardner's *On Moral Fiction,* I was able to connect with his analysis of the relationship between the artistic impulse and insanity, with his view that the alienated artist might emerge as a self-conscious criminal. I studied the Russian great Fyodor Dostoyevsky, whose existentialist *Notes from the Underground* seemed to speak directly to me, and whose letters regarding his *Crime and Punishment* postulated that the deep-seated Christian morality within a criminal might cause him to do things to ensure his being caught, and punished. Had I been just an unfulfilled artist, sidetracked into violence by revolution, then cast adrift to engage in a banal criminality that was sure to bring about my incarceration? Was my imprisonment—and my writing—returning me to sanity, to the young man of moral purpose I'd been raised to become? Was my life now being saved by a belief in my artistry, redemption now to be won at the expense of my freedom?

I would contemplate such thoughts in the crucible of my cell, taking notes well into the morning in my journals, and on any scrap of paper I could get my hands on: paper towels, the backs of envelopes—even napkins and toilet paper, when there was nothing else. I developed a sort of note mania, believing that any thought that seemed worthy of preserving had to go on paper, as if putting down my ideas made them valuable, gave them birth and purpose in the world.

Taking notes about any and everything made me feel that I was alive, that every moment was pregnant with meaning, somehow conjoining with a future in which I would be fully able to share my thoughts, my feelings. Writing about my world gave me the sensation of being truly alive and connected to the world, words that would someday yield the acceptance and approval I needed so badly. If nothing else, I came to believe that even if never reviewed, every word I wrote would become part of my subconscious, and might someday be resurrected in my work.

· · ·

I began a serious study of poetry during this period, and came to believe that writing verse was my primary duty. My love of words was a comfort; the ability to lend beauty to my beauty-less existence gave meaning to my plight. To discipline myself as a poet, I dedicated every Sunday afternoon to creating a poem—inspired, somewhat, by Wallace Stevens's poem "Sunday Morning." I began the series thusly:

> *Sunday afternoons I write verse.*
> *It is my work for the week, my*
> *Worship for the day . . .*

Poetry gave me the fullest freedom of expression, just as the reading of poetry had allowed me to commune with masters past and present, to exult in the beauty of the wedding of word and idea, image and emotion, all tied to the musicality of language.

One poem I wrote in the spring of 1984, "Warehoused," was published in the journal *Southern Exposure,* in which I used the warehouses along the banks of the James River (which I was able to view through the bars of my cell and the windows of A-building) as a metaphor for the penitentiary:

> *Hard Times is now a nightclub*
> *In The Streets and an old song*
> *On my new radio*
> *As I notice my view*
> *For the first time this year:*
> *It is nearly Spring, March blowing winter away*
> *In blustery wisps discernible on threadbare branch.*
>
> *Under the bridge are centuries-old warehouses*
> *Where slaves or Union soldiers and spies*
> *Were perhaps once housed with the tobacco.*
>
> *I realize anew the wide river that is there*
> *Still for me to marvel at the motion*
> *Of simple brown currents crested with*

Shallow white water going—which way?
I know, but still there seems to be
Some rolling, raging force in its midst,
Drawn strongly upstream.
I look away quickly, eyes resting on
The blue flag of this fortress prison,
And notice the flesh tones of the antagonists
On the seal. Pale cousin conquering cousin, in color . . .

On the far bridge a yellow bus is out early,
And I remember the gauntlet I braved
To reach the sanctuary
Of the back of the bus, pushed there
By the overwhelming might
Of Majority.

A pioneer in pride, certain my desegregation mattered,
I am shamed by capture before being humbled by servitude.

> *My warehousing evinces such a design*
> *As to put you in mind*
> *Of the mouth of this James*
> *Where we were first swallowed,*
> *Way down-river from these warehouses*
> *On the bank, here.*

Excerpts from this poem were reprinted in a long article written about me in my hometown newspaper, the *Danville Register*. Encouraged, I began to concentrate on poetry. Much of my verse dealt with the existential loneliness and alienation I was feeling, with titles like "Self Doubt," "Self Pity," and "Remorse":

> *Remorse is a renegade DNA molecule.*
> *Its serpentine tentacles*
> *Entwine the heart*
> *And asphyxiate the spirit.*

Sinking,
Remorse dwells as tarnished jade,
Encrusted in atrophied loins,
Longing for exorcism
At one's own expense.

One Sunday, after reading in *The New York Review of Books* a poem by Nobel laureate Derek Walcott called "Elsewhere" (a verse about the atrocities going on around the world, which we pay little heed to), I wrote a poem to express what was happening daily inside our penal institutions, but hidden from the world.

Herein

Herein lies a man who is
To die, yet cannot confess;
He has not lain down at their behest.

Herein are untouched traces of men
Who are not yet without love or mercy
Though loathed and tormented daily

For it is 1984, and in ten days
Fascists everywhere will celebrate the assassination
Of Comrade George who?, lite champagne chilled by gluttons
For thirteen years, as African babies extend famine-rounded bellies
And their best smiles to cameras-not-from-CARE.

Herein are eight XL-100's by RCA Victor with flesh tones so real
You could almost feel, were it not that a narcissism has been sown
So deep within your woman that she looks down and behind
at herself as she dances, looking back at a primordial past that
Just ain't you, Man . . .

Herein a writer pens verse but cannot rhyme
As well as his son, who has not had to
Awaken within walls but an armspan apart,

While one's heart slumbers on, for no joy is promised
Or expected.

Salvation comes some Sundays from a
Perversion of poetry, written down for good,
But somehow still hidden,
Somewhere, herein.

During this time when I was trying to define myself as an artist, I met Carole Kass, Richmond's preeminent movie reviewer, who came in every week to teach her Cineastes Film Class. She'd begun the group a decade before, naming it with the French term for "lover of film." I had seen her walking through the prison with a sassy New York switch to her hips, still vivacious at sixty.

I visited a session of the group just to check it out, and dug the way she spoke about the elements of film. She talked about how emotion was the essential element of communication in film. It was little one of those epiphany moments I'd encountered in my study of James Joyce. I realized I hadn't given much thought to the need to elicit emotion from readers, wanting mainly to reach their minds. This was the omission of thought by the extreme rationalist, an indication, in some respects, of just how cold I was. It was a condition I would have to overcome, were I to become the writer I wanted to be. I knew then that the study of film would be instrumental in my development as a writer.

Carole wanted to talk to me after the class, and told me that she was impressed with my intellect. She asked that I join her group, pledging to help me in any way she could.

I became part of the Cineastes, and Carole and I were soon steadfast friends, with her adopting me as something of a protégé. She gave me her phone number—something not normally done by volunteers—and we talked often. She encouraged me to study writing for film and theater, bringing me books on the subjects, and lending a fellow writer's ear whenever I called. I reciprocated by breathing new life and leadership into her film class, writing a proposal and short film on literacy, which garnered enough funding to do three public-service announcements on the subject.

The attainment of literacy moved me because of the job I had taken in the prison school as a teacher's aide, tutoring semiliterate men in reading. I found the work both rewarding and dispiriting, as I encountered so many prisoners who had never gotten any semblance of a proper start in school, and were so far behind that there was little I could do to help them.

One student in particular filled me with pity. He was a bedraggled brother, ill kempt with a long beard, very bad teeth, and a body odor so bad that I found it a challenge to sit next to his desk. I tried to learn more about his life and the circumstances that had led him to such an existence. He had a view of the world that seemed to epitomize that of many men who came from extreme poverty. One day, while we were reviewing a book of photographs I was using to try to spur him to use words to describe various scenes, he tried to express the way he felt.

"Look at those people," he said, pointing to a picture of a family of whites in a park, having a picnic. "They so happy, they *all* smiling. White people act like they own the world." He paused, flipped a couple of pages, and then said, "Well, I guess they do. Must be nice," he added with a wistful air, "to own your own world."

My friendship with Carole and other volunteers, along with writing and my reading, helped me feel that I was still part of a wider world, reigniting my love for people of all races—which proved to be essential to the reformation I was going through. My friendship with Ben Cleary grew stronger. In addition to his writing class, he also taught the college English course at the prison that I took. I also became close friends with Greg Donovan, a professor at Virginia Commonwealth University, who volunteered his time with the Creative Workshop. Donovan and I became "literary correspondents," as he termed it, and as it turned out his former teacher had been John Gardner, whose work had influenced me so much. We formed a lasting bond based upon shared sensibilities, and he helped me to understand how my work could aspire to the highest ranks of artistry.

Other white people who read my work in *The Washington Post* wrote to me, some of them becoming supporters who sent money on occasion. Because of these whites befriending and helping me, I began to reexamine my views regarding race, realizing that the white world was not necessarily inimical to my personal development, and that I need not feel ashamed for wanting to fit into the world of American letters. I also began to understand that it was all right to feel genuine affection for them, and love for a general audience of all people; that it was all right to have a desire to create art and beauty for the world, that writing needn't be only a form of protest.

I was reading everything I could get my hands on—*The Nation, The New Republic, The Catholic Century, Poetry Magazine, American Film, The Atlantic, Harper's*. I filled out subscription forms for every magazine I could find with a form that said "bill me later." And I stole shamelessly from the library, emerging from weekly visits with books stuffed down my pants, or under my arms in the sleeves of my jacket, even though one could be charged with stealing or possession of contraband for taking books and magazines out of the library without checking them out. I became enamored with Faulkner's prose, and got deeply into Hemingway for a period, only to find his phrasing too short for my taste. I found Norman Mailer again, and reread an old copy of *Invisible Man,* Ralph Ellison's masterpiece, the prose of which would forever influence my own. I discovered a collection of Chekov's plays, which ignited a spark for dramaturgy, causing me to delve into Tennessee Williams, and to fall in love with the work of the late black playwright Lorraine Hansberry.

A friend sent me a copy of John Edgar Wideman's *Brothers and Keepers,* an incredible nonfiction work by the man I considered the foremost black novelist of our day. In the book he examined the plight of his brother, who had received a life sentence for a robbery that had gone bad and resulted in a man's death. Wideman's book became a beacon of how life—even in its harshest terms—could become literature if put on page with passion.

It became a running joke in my cellblock that "Hop got more books in his cell than they got left in the library." It was half true: I had books lining the wall of my little cell from top to bottom. I would collect plastic milk crates from the chow hall, sneak them into the building, and stack them into makeshift bookshelves along all sides of the cell, with papers, file folders, and magazines in piles on the floor.

When the time came for a shakedown search, I would quake in fear that I might get charged with two hundred counts of possession of contraband. But generally the guards would just throw the books into a box out on the tier, and send them back to the library, where I could once more smuggle favorites back to my cell.

I was already known throughout the prison as a writer whom people "out in the free world" were noticing, who wasn't afraid to give up the real deal from the perspective of the prisoner. But I became notorious for my "intellectual debris" (as I privately called it) when, during one shakedown, guards took out some twenty milk crates filled with books from my cell. The supervising sergeant became so incensed that he called the institution's fire marshal to videotape the cell, in case they needed it for evidence. There was so much junk piled on my bed by the time the guards left, I just pushed it to the side, and lay down exhausted, for a nap.

I should never have let Jericho see that, when he came by later to walk with me to chow. "Hop so into his writing thang," he joked to those at our table, "he be sleeping in bed with papers and books and shit. He one crazy, dedicated muhthafuckuh. Y'all need to get ready, 'cause soon they gonna be doin' 'Hop—The Movie.'"

CHAPTER SEVEN

Turbulent Time

Gerald was shaking my cell door, yelling, "Wake up, Hop. Now! Six dudes escaped from Mecklenburg last night— off of death row! It's all over the news. You don't want to miss a minute of this story, man."

It was nationwide news that June 1984, the biggest escape from any death row in history, sparking the largest manhunt the country had ever seen. The leaders of the escape were said to be the notorious Briley brothers, killers from Richmond convicted of murdering an entire family, and blamed for more than a dozen killings.

Everyone was glued to the communal TVs in the cellblock, watching the developments, fascinated as it came out that the six men had captured several guards at knifepoint, taken their uniforms, then used the ruse of finding a bomb to walk through the gates into a waiting van.

I took the pulse of prisoners at the Penitentiary, many of whom knew Linwood and James Briley, as had I, during my first bit. The escapees were hailed as heroes who dared to do what every man with long time thought of doing: stage a daring getaway. But when all of the condemned men were captured without violence and within a month, they quickly became subjects of scorn. "I don't have no sympathy for Lin," one man told me. "Even though I used to hustle with him and we did time together, I can't believe he didn't hold court out in the street when they rolled up on him. But the nigguh didn't even have a gun."

The escape caused security to tighten up all over the Virginia penal system, especially at The Wall, where Linwood Briley was transferred for execution a few months following the escape, to await execution. I paid attention to who visited him in the basement below A-building, taking particular note of a tall, very thin woman who came to see him almost every day.

One day I approached her as she was leaving and asked if she was an attorney. She told me no, she was a paralegal for Briley. I introduced myself by giving her a copy of my *Post* article on the Coppola execution, telling her that I would like to interview her if she could arrange it. The next day she made arrangements with the administration for us to meet.

Her name was Marie Deans, a former board member of Amnesty International who had come to Virginia to found the anti-death penalty Southern Coalition on Jails and Prisons. We connected from the beginning, as she was a former short-story writer and it seemed we shared a common aesthetic, as well as similar politics.

Marie had an interesting life story. The daughter of affluent white Charlestonians, she became a civil rights activist at the age of fourteen when she took part in her first sit-in. When her mother-in-law was killed by an escaped convict, she gave up her literary career in South Carolina and founded an organization called Murder Victims Families for Reconciliation. As an Amnesty International official she became a national figure, keynoting national conferences, appearing on regional and national television, and publishing extensively in newspapers and journals. She had counseled more than two hundred men condemned to death, all across the country, helping to get more than fifty of them off death row.

Marie and I became "fellow travelers," talking on the phone for hours. She saw herself as a radical Christian, and taught me all about the legal intricacies and politics of the death penalty. It's the "vortex of evil in America, as it allows us to believe that certain lives aren't worthy of living," she said.

My friendship with Marie fed into my passion for justice. The death penalty became a surrogate issue for the personal injustice I felt I was facing. Indeed, it represented a microcosmic example of the plight of black men in general. Through research I learned that of the 240 men executed in Virginia's electric chair, 204 of them had been black, with one having been only sixteen years old. I also learned of the notorious case of the Martinsville Seven: in 1949, Virginia had executed seven black men accused of raping a white woman—four on a Friday, the remaining three the following Monday—despite international protests.

Seething from the denial of my first appeal, I identified with the men on death row, for most of them were also black, had been underrepresented in court and received the maximum sentence, and had to deal with the heartbreak of appeals being shot down by a legal system in which racism was not only systemic but *institutionalized.* (Statistics showed that not only were black men and women more likely to be arrested, tried, and convicted than whites, but that they were denied parole more often, as well.)

Fighting with my words against the death penalty became a fight against the system that imprisoned not only me but more than a million of my fellow inmates. (Indeed, during the mid-1980s, the prison population nationwide had begun to explode exponentially, doubling to more than two million by the twenty-first century.) More than half of that number were black. The prison system became the symbol of the greater oppression that people of color had to endure in America.

At the same time, my association with Marie helped me to begin seeing human nature in a different light. If Marie could forgive the man who had killed her mother-in-law, and if I could join in calling for forgiveness of those on death row, should I not also contemplate forgiving the surly and abusive turnkeys, or the court system that had condemned me to this hell? And should I not begin trying to forgive myself, for having screwed up my life so badly?

When the day of Linwood Briley's execution arrived, the Penitentiary was in a state of agitation. In the mess hall at lunch, the tension in the warehouse-like room was palpable, with many more guards than usual. Many of the six hundred men in the building were wearing black armbands. Several men stood at the stage at the front of the hall, in quiet protest.

Those of us going through the chow line were served fish fillets upon stainless steel trays dented from time and use. For a change there was no limit on the amount of food. During the meal a prisoner climbed the stage and, gaining the attention of the assembled, said, "We'd like to ask all of you for a minute of silent prayer for our brother and comrade Linwood Briley." Then the Protestant chaplain got on the stage and said a few words of Scripture, causing one man at my table to get up and walk out with the words, "This is bullshit. You want to stop somethin', you got to be ready to do more than this!"

The strong feeling among the men in the prison had much to do with many of them having known both Briley brothers, and being close to the younger brother, who had been serving time with us at The Wall until the Mecklenburg escape. (More than a quarter of the population was from Richmond.) Some saw Linwood as a hero for leading the escape from Mecklenburg. And there was a general feeling against the death penalty in the prison population, which was three-quarters black, for this was the first execution of a black man since the death penalty was reinstated in 1976.

At 11:00 P.M., the appointed hour, I was in my cell looking out at the media show in front of the Penitentiary, and simultaneously watching what they were showing on my small black-and-white television. It was somewhat surreal, seeing the cameramen and re-porters scrambling about through two sets of bars and grimy win-dows, then watching the scene of the building I was in, from the reverse angle, through *their* lenses.

I kept looking at the bare bulb in my cell to see if it would dim as the switch was thrown, but realized that was something that only happened in the movies.

The prisoners began beating on their bars in anger after seeing the prison spokesman come out to announce that the execution had been carried out. Then followed anguished and vehement curses of men watching the guards carry out Briley's remains: a macabre scene, six men bearing the covered form, rising up the steps from the darkness of the dungeonlike basement.

The anger at Briley's execution seemed to increase after his death. Some men told me that they felt more should have been done in protest. Many told me of feeling powerless in the face of what they saw as state-sanctioned murder. I dealt with my anger by writing a piece on the execution for *Commonwealth,* at that time Virginia's premier magazine, and began to feel an even greater obli-gation to attack the system on behalf of prisoners in Virginia.

When the editor and publisher of a new Richmond paper called *STYLE Weekly* came in to speak to Ben Cleary's group, she was im-pressed enough with my writing to provide me with a forum for my attack journalism. I decided to go after the governor, Chuck Robb, with a piece I called "Robb's Prison Thriller in Virginia." With a lead that made fun of his telling an interviewer that his fa-vorite video was Michael Jackson's *Thriller,* I wrote that perhaps the governor identified with Jackson's song because he'd been facing his own version of a thriller with all the turmoil in the state's prison system.

First, there had been the death-row breakout from Mecklen-burg—the state's most sinister prison, a modern Orwellian institution under legal attack by the ACLU for its behavior-modification tactics. This was followed with an escape by two men on a work detail outside of the Penitentiary. Next, there were two violent altercations between prisoners and guards at Mecklenburg, followed by a nineteen-hour hostage crisis that captured headlines. In short order there was an escape of five men from Nottoway, the state's newest prison; then finally there came a Houdini-like escape from The Wall by Pie-Man (who just happened to be a member of my chess club), who seemed to have disappeared into thin air after shipping himself out of the State Pen in a box.

Pie-Man's escape was the stuff of prison legend, and I wrote jokingly that someone had heard him say, "Beam me up, Scottie," just before he disappeared. I ended the piece with these words:

> There is an unreal perception of all men behind bars as vile and inhuman beings, unworthy of anything but the harshest possible treatment . . . thereby allowing public officials to take "get tough" stands and increase multimillion-dollar budgets for security with no thought of the rehabilitative treatment and training of men within prison. The continuation of this characterization and the medieval punishment it fosters has a great deal to do with sensationalist press coverage. The dramatization of evil is seen daily on television and film. Our inhumane prisons are regarded as fitting places for such villainous evildoers as those depicted on innumerable police and private detective shows. Politicians play to the very real fears of the populace by continuing to assert the myth that crime can be eliminated by locking up more and more people for longer and longer terms.
>
> But the prisoner is a human being, and the spirit of man cannot be controlled by bars, razor wire, or the sensory-deprivation torture of solitary confinement, for it is the nature of man to seek freedom, and to fight injustice. . . .

After the publication of that piece, Gerald told me, "Little brother, you got a lot of heart to be attacking the fuckin' governor.

You better be ready, they might scoop you up at any time and throw you in the hole, or transfer you to get you out of their hair."

Ironically, Gerald, Satchell, and several others were soon shipped out to other prisons for having voiced opposition to certain policies the prison was implementing. I had to wonder why I hadn't been in the group. When I told Jericho about it, he said, "Hop, you too strong for them to fuck with like that. You internationally known, Bruh. Better get used to it."

It might have been that in shipping out the known prison leaders, the administration had sensed how tense things were, for all hell broke loose in April 1985, on the scheduled day of James Briley's execution. Walking between buildings after breakfast, I saw a sudden gathering of men around B-building. Over their heads I caught glimpses of men in guard-blue uniforms being knocked down by prisoners with hoods on, then knives flashing in the early morning sun. The prison went on immediate lockdown, and we were all herded back into our cells. I learned later that there had been a rebellion against the guard force, led by friends of Briley, in protest to his impending execution. Nine officers had been stabbed, some injured critically. While Briley was still put to death that night, from that point on, the Penitentiary would never be the same.

My outrage against the death penalty culminated with the execution of Morris Odell Mason, a man so retarded that he asked his lawyer, before his execution, "What should I wear to my funeral?"

I recorded my feelings in my journal that night:

June 25, 1985
In the basement below me Morris Mason's head and calf are being carefully shaved by men who will, with the same strange care, soon attach to the bared patches of skin electrodes that will kill him. They

then give him a shirt and pants that have Velcro fasteners that will not conduct electricity, or retain heat and burn the hands of the doctor who will check the silenced heart.

I imagine Mason being moved to the holding pen, where he watches as guards pack the personal effects in his death row cell, and take them away with a ritual air of finality.

Members of the same guard force are now winding the barred doors shut on the 300-odd men of A-building. We are locked in an hour early to make sure we can't interfere with the justice below. We have been on modified lockdown since authorities claimed to have heard rumors of a repeat of the bloody uprising that saw nine guards hospitalized on the day of the last execution.

With Mason now is Marie, his paralegal adviser and about the closest thing to family that he has. She has told me that Mason has asked her to walk to the door of the death chamber with him. I know it is going to be rough on her, for she has told me just how childlike the man is. "It will be just like killing an eight-year-old," she said.

It has been established that Mason is clearly classified as mentally retarded, with an I.Q. of 66, and suffering from schizophrenia. He has been in and out of mental institutions, and is said by neighbors to have been a fire starter as a child.

Discharged from the service for mental incapacity, he was paroled by the Department of Corrections shortly before raping and killing two elderly women and sexually assaulting and maiming two girls. He had called his parole officer days before the incidents and asked to be taken off parole and put into a halfway house, but his request was ignored.

Mason pleaded guilty to all charges and proudly proclaimed himself to be "the killer of the Eastern Shore" upon conviction of the crimes. And although his acts are thought to be reprehensible by the men here, his case has elicited rare sympathy, "'cause it's evident the man ain't responsible," as one prisoner who knew Mason during his first incarceration put it. "He was one of those dudes who couldn't stand to be by himself," the man told me. "He would pay other pris-

oners with the money he got from the Veterans Administration just to keep him company, write letters for him and stuff."

It seems like Mason is still freehearted. It was reported that he ordered four Big Macs, two large orders of fries, two ice cream sundaes, and a couple of large grape sodas as his last meal, and shared it all with two guards, perhaps the same ones who are by now strapping him into the old oaken chair, for it is 11 P.M., the time of the death chair.

I turn on the news, and cynically wonder if the execution time was chosen to coincide with the late-night newscast. I listen to the hush of expectation in the cell house as the men await word of Mason's death, via the press.

I imagine what is happening below as 2,500 volts of electricity are diverted from the dwellings of Richmonders and sent slamming into Mason's body for 55 seconds. There is a pause, and the buttons are simultaneously pressed again by three guards who have volunteered for this duty for a bit of extra pay. (Only one of the three buttons is actually hooked up to the juice, so that no one manning the switchbox will feel ultimate responsibility for the prisoner's death.)

I turn back to my small black-and-white portable to exorcise this gruesome imagery with a montage of scenes from the three local stations.

There is an interview with Mason taped just after his conviction in 1978. He is shown grinning like an imbecile, saying of his death sentence, "It don't worry me none. I did wrong, so I get 'lexecuted, right?" Poor dumb bastard, I think—can't even say the word right. . . .

On another channel, the head of the corrections department tells a reporter that "carrying out the execution in the place that is also the home of people is difficult."

No kidding. The next channel has scenes of a prayer service held by death penalty opponents at a nearby church, and of the hundred or so gathered up the street from the prison in a candlelight vigil. The camera then cuts to the other side of the street, where redneck support-

ers of the death penalty are seen guzzling beer, hollering "It's Miller time!" and carrying "Fry the Coon" signs. There is a shot of an old woman dancing a jig in joy of the occasion.

The Penitentiary's young spokeswoman finally comes out of the prison entrance and announces with perfect composure, "The order of the court has been dutifully carried out in the manner prescribed by law." We are told that the last statement Mason made was to tell one of the witnesses, the warden of death row at Mecklenburg prison, that he would "go out strong, just like I promised you." A minister is then asked for his opinion, and he likens Mason's last words to a child's being anxious to please a parent by acting grown-up. It is a sickening bit of irony: the poor fool actually looked upon his killers as his friends.

When the men in the cell house see the body borne up the basement steps by the six-man death squad, curses are hurled at the keepers in sporadic bursts throughout the building: "Y'all the killers now, you freak motherfuckers!" Reporters walk in front of the building after rushing to get pictures of the departing ambulance, and someone screams out at them, "Y'all just ought to drink his goddamn blood!"

I now engage in something of a ritual of my own, one that began with Frank Coppola's execution three years ago, staying up all night writing and in thought. If the rituals of death—the funeral, the burial, the memorial—are actually the means the living use to mark, measure, and give meaning to life, then maybe I use these death sentences to impart some sort of meaning to my own life sentence.

Writing until it is nearly dawn, and I wonder if there are other men still up, unable to sleep. I think of what one man said to me, that he can smell the death after each electrocution, and that he believes the spirits of slain men continue to inhabit the dwellings wherein they meet their deaths. I suppose he may still be awake, looking out of his fourth-tier cell at the rolls of concertina razor wire hanging from the ceiling, thinking of the 243 souls locked forever in this hundred-year-old building.

As the sun begins to rise, a solitary bird begins chirping outside, its lonely, slow one-note complaint coming in clear through the open windows with the cool morning air. I cut out the light in my cell and watch the natural light grow, an orange glow seeping through the bars and grimy Plexiglas, playing upon the steel walls of my abode, mixing with and then overcoming and extinguishing the harsh glare of the street lamp Virginia Power erected for the press gathered for executions.

Life imprisonment, it seems to me, is a sort of death sentence where one is simply buried alive in places like these, hope in resurrection through the distant dream of parole. But living above the electric chair has a way of giving new meaning to clichés about the joy of beholding the natural beauty of a sun rising.

I expanded the journal entry and sent it to *The Washington Post,* and they printed it on the front page of their *OUTLOOK* section, as well as in a national edition of the paper they'd just begun to publish. I received a dozen letters in response from readers, and from editors around the country who were interested in having me write for them. When my parents visited (as they'd continued to do every month), they told me how thrilled all the family was that my work had hit the national stage again. I was riding high, believing that my career had reached a new level.

Meanwhile, I was still trying to get back in court on appeal. Marie had introduced me to the foremost appellate attorney in the state, Lloyd Snook. "We're going to get you out," she had said optimistically in her little-girl voice, giving me new hope that I'd find a legal avenue to get my life sentence overturned. However, after reviewing my case, Snook told me over the phone, "I hate to tell a client that he will have to spend the rest of his life in prison, but to challenge a conviction in Virginia because of inadequate counsel—or for a cruel and unusual sentence—is almost impossible. The standard of legal representation in this state is so low that a lawyer has to be really bad to be judged incompetent. And unfortunately it's been ruled that a life sentence for robbery is not altogether unusual in Virginia."

This news was daunting, to say the least, and would have been completely devastating were it not for my increasing success as a writer. I tried to maintain the view that life was still worth living, as long as I could keep my imagination alive. My writing gave me hope, and I believed that somehow it would deliver me from my cage. But the rage at the injustice of my sentence continued to seethe within me. Sometimes I'd stew in my cell and wonder if the judge's condemnation "to remain in prison for the rest of your natural life" would actually come to mean that I would never get out, that I would never be free. I couldn't accept that idea, or accept the notion that I would have to wait until 1994—when I'd be forty—to even be *eligible* for parole.

With the trend toward an increasingly punitive justice system, I wondered if believing that I might one day make parole was realistic. These were the Reagan years, and it seemed to have become what George Jackson had predicted: One day fascism would, indeed, be in power and secure in America, offering the illusion of freedom while steadily oppressing the masses. While I gave full energy to my writing, I continued to harbor the dream of escape.

And my dreams—while awake or in slumber—were my escape, *the only freedom that I knew,* I would often think, remembering the seventies song *Wildflower.* My practice of daytime sleeping with one eye open to the possibilities of the danger around me elicited a strange sort of dreaming: I seemed able to hear all the activity in the cellblock even as I slept, and sounds of things occurring around me would blend into my dreams. Sometime they were nightmares of having to fend off assault, or of being rousted by guards engaged in sudden shakedowns—searches wherein I would be stripped of all my books pilfered from the library, my treasured papers thrown away as if they were so much chaff. I'd dream of a world beyond the bars and wall encasing me; I'd dream whole movies in which I was the hero fighting against some injustice or making love to some beautiful woman, cinematic dreams that seemed to develop with my love and study of story and film. I would lie in bed and meditate on one of my film or fiction stories, and envision it unfolding before me on an imagined movie screen—only to doze off and *enter* the film/dream, becoming a character or even merging with another character already in the dream. I could awaken from a dream and doze again, then *resume* the thread of that very same dream. But dreams of women would always seem to end abruptly, because as soon as I began making love I'd have the thought, *This must be a dream, I'm in prison, I can't have a woman in here*—and I'd wake up.

I had dreams of being Superman, flying and fighting evil; dreams of old England complete with Shakespearean dialogue in rhyme and couplet, though I'd never seen one of Shakespeare's plays, only read them in school. Such dreams enabled me to believe in the breadth and power of the human mind and of my own imagination. But most of my slumber was filled with strife, reflections of inner turmoil. My journal gave private voice to my pain:

> *In my dreams I'm always fighting against some authoritarian figure, in danger of being caught, engaged in some subterfuge, or locked inside some sort of prison. The one I just awoke from had me in a library, watching television in secret in the prison school, discovered and then "playing con" as if I were one of the staff—then going after a woman who appeared, a woman I could not have. The library transformed into a home or college dorm, where I listened to my sister's stereo, read her advanced books, all the while being spied upon by a father figure of some sort.*
>
> *I love to dream, but remember none of them as pleasant. I am always involved in struggle. My earliest remembered dream from childhood is of hiding out with my gang in the bushes behind my house after pulling a robbery, my earliest memory of falling from my sister's tricycle after daring a downhill run in our cinder-and-ashes covered driveway.*

Then even my writing dreams were threatened, on two fronts. A clerk who worked in the treatment center, where the offices of the prison administration were, came to me one day with serious news. "They're talking about you, Hop, saying that maybe they should lock you up. They think they can use the fact that you get paid for writing to say you're operating a business without permission." While this news was alarming, I made up my mind that I would not—and indeed, *could not*—stop what I was doing, for anyone or anything.

Next I got word that the men on death row had somehow taken offense at my writing about them after hearing a false rumor that I was going to write about their women visitors. A messenger was sent, a man with a double life sentence and a reputation for viciousness, rumored to have been one of the participants in the uprising and known for his lethality. He approached me on the ballpark one day, while I stood on the brick bleacher steps, looking out over the wall at the Richmond streets. "Brother Hop," he said, "word is on the Row at Mecklenburg that your writing about them can hurt what they're trying to do there. Maybe you want to chill for a bit."

I gave the man my hardest look, and told him, "Look, I haven't backed down from writing about the system, though the administration has threatened me. Whatever stories they've been hearing on the Row, you can send word to them that they're bullshit. But you can also tell them this: I won't stop writing the truth for *any-body*—especially when what I write is *against* the death penalty, and all I'm doing is trying to help them."

When I told Jericho about the threat, he said, "Well, you know we're in a dangerous place, and ain't much we can do about that, except be on guard. But if some kinda way they do get to you, you have my word as bond that I'll get to them, and they'll be dealt with." Pausing to look me in the eye, he added, "And I expect you to do the same, if one of these fools gets past me and my bone knife and takes me out." (Jericho loved talking about his bone knife—a piece, as prison knives were called, with a special blade he claimed "could cut through bone.")

While it was chilling to hear him talk about the possibility that we could be killed, I was actually touched by his devotion to me. I told him, "Can't nobody get to you, Bruh, but if they do, you know I got your back."

He and I became even tighter after that. He was at once like the little brother I'd always wanted, and the big brother I'd never had. We would walk to meals together, play chess during the day, and spend early evenings in the chess club after we finished our jobs. Once a week we'd attend Ben Cleary's forum, which met on the fourth floor of the building where the school was located.

On these occasions Jericho always seemed to have a couple of joints. We would slip away from the class to the bathroom area, which was between the classroom and the guards' station at the entrance. There, above the urinals, were windows without bars, and he and I would talk about escaping. While breaking out had once been part of my imagined revolutionary impulse, the thought of escaping now was part of my dream to create, not destroy: to get away to somewhere like Mexico or Cuba, where I could become, in the words of the Russian playwright Anton Chekov, "a free artist, that's all."

But, for Jericho, escape was all he could hope for. He had *two* life sentences, and would have to pull more than twenty years to be eligible for parole, with little chance of ever making it.

After months of such talk, when Jericho presented me with serious plans for escape in 1985, I was divided. He had a woman whom he'd persuaded to help him escape. She visited him every visiting day, bringing him lavishly cooked meals, along with narcotic painkillers called T's (for Talwin) that he was able to sell to the many intravenous drug users inside. This provided him with ready cash, though cash was outlawed inside the prison. He had also made contact with someone on the outside who would have a jeweler's string—a long wire encrusted with small diamonds, used to saw precious metals and stone, easily smuggled and able to cut through bars in seconds—smuggled in to him. The only problem was that Jericho could not get a transfer to the front side of A-building, where I was housed, and where the barred windows actually opened out onto the street, with no fences to climb. He also talked about stealing an oxygen tank for an acetylene torch from the metal shop, where he worked, and finding a way to detonate it beside the ballpark wall to blow a hole in it.

But finally he believed he'd come up with the surest means of escape: climb out of the unbarred bathroom window on the fourth floor while a writing class was going on, using a rope of sheets and a grappling hook (which he'd fashioned in the metal shop) to climb down to an unguarded piece of ground, and from there climb up to a building level to the great brick wall. Then we could use the rope to hook on to the wall, and climb over and down onto the highway off-ramp. He told me his girlfriend would be waiting there to pick us up.

I would lie in bed and try to envision such a bold escape. Jericho worked out daily to be strong enough to handle the ropes, and he urged me to begin doing the same. So I began doing a few pushups and pull-ups, thinking about the possibility of seeing my son and parents again in freedom, though this thought gave me some pause. I would only be able to see them while on the run, or when they might find a way to visit me in some foreign land, if that were possible at all.

Then two things happened. I received a letter from an editor at a publishing house in New England named George Gibson, who had read my piece on the Mason execution in *The Washington Post*. He said that his firm would offer a modest book deal if I wanted to write at length about my prison experiences. He had also included a letter he'd written to Governor Robb, a copy of which he'd also sent to *The Post*. In it he called upon Robb to exercise executive clemency in my case: "Mr. Hopkins' writing is of great public value and I urge you to utilize all means at your disposal to see that he is free to give of his talent to the world."

The second thing was that Jericho had added something to the plan. He'd noted that the place where we wanted to breach the wall was perilously close to the ballpark guard tower. "We got to be able to take him out, if he sees us," he said, and then produced what looked like a large vitamin, wrapped up in cellophane. Tearing away the wrapping, he let two .22-shot shells fall into his hand. "I can make a long, thin shotgun from pipe in the metal shop," he whispered to me at the fourth-floor window that had come to represent the portal to our freedom. "We have to be ready to deal with that guard, if it comes to that."

I wasn't exactly thrilled by the possibility of having to kill a guard. In addition to my reluctance to take a life, I definitely didn't like the idea of having the police forces of the entire United States of American looking for us—with sure death sentences waiting if we were to be captured. I asked Mack, the young brother who had been with me at Southampton and was once affiliated with the Party in Winston-Salem, about the wisdom of maybe having to use deadly force while escaping. What he said rammed through all of the revolutionary illusions I still had.

"You know me," he said. "I like that kind of action. And I'd go with you, 'cept I ain't got but two years left in this joint. But you got a life sentence, so you got to at least think about it. All I can tell you is, you go out there and get caught, they ain't *never* gonna give you parole anyway. You goin' out there to die, so you got to be ready to kill."

With Jericho pressing me, I had to make a decision. I had to confront the image of myself as a stone revolutionary warrior, or come to grips with the more realistic self-image of a radical artist fallen into a most precarious situation.

By then Jericho had ascended to president of the chess club, grandly calling himself President for Life, like he was Idi Amin. He managed to arrange a meeting with me during the day, where we played what I somehow felt might be our last game of chess.

Along with his customary reefer, he had a quart of the wine we called mash, as it was made from mashed fruit and juice, along with sugar and yeast stolen from the kitchen. "I got us a little faucet wine," Jericho said, as he poured a dark purple liquid from a plastic bag, as evenly as if he were drawing it from a real spigot, into cups for us.

"Why do you call it faucet wine?" I asked him, getting ready for his jest.

"'Cause it's so strong you have to faucet-it down," he said, grinning.

Midway into our game, he laid the question on me. "So how you gonna do this thing, or do I need to find me another partner?" He paused to execute one of those exquisite knight maneuvers that made me wonder, *How can a man so unlettered, in so many ways smarter than I, become doomed to two life sentences at the age of sixteen?* With the brilliance he exhibited on the chessboard, and his innate intelligence, he might have become a tremendous businessman had he not been born into poverty and a crime-ridden adolescence.

"Jericho," I said, "you know we tight. I feel like you're the brother I never had. But some things are opening up for me." I showed him the letters from the publisher, and he read them silently, and made a couple of moves before he spoke again.

"Hop," he said, "in this life you play the hand that's dealt to you. And at this stage in the game you just play the pieces on the board you got left."

I made a move, he made another move. "This way out for me might not be the way out for you. As your agent"—he smiled here, laughing at the absurdity of his being the controller of my career— "I got to say that you need to see if the writing thang works out for you. But as your stick man I got to warn you—you liable to end up sixteen, maybe even twenty years deep into your life sentence, with no book or nothin', still wondering if they gonna let you out. I'm tryin' to give you a way out here. The system has dealt me double life, so I got to go with what I know."

He must have been concentrating too hard on what he was saying, because he made a bad move. With my knight I took his queen, and backed his king into a corner. He looked down at the board and said, "Damn, you gettin' better, my brother," and knocked his king over in resignation. Then he raised his head, looked me in the eye, and said, "You gotta do what you gotta do, man, and I gotta do what I *have* to do."

CHAPTER EIGHT

A Season of Loss

Showtime—that's what I used to say to myself when going into the visiting room. With that breath I'd emerge into a different world, a world of street people, as those of us on the inside called them. And while most of my visits had been from my parents, today I had a woman coming to see me—and you wanted to be really on top of your game if you had a woman visitor.

I was still shy, to the point of being damned near scared, sometimes. While it was so hard to be around people who were happy, the visiting room was a chance to shed one's blues. It was the closest thing to freedom we could savor, and seeing a woman, on a romantic basis, was the closest thing to fun the lucky few of us could find.

On this day in early July 1986, I walked into the room with my best swagger, had on pressed street jeans, my sharp-toed suede shoes, and my best shirt. This new girl, one of the African dancers who annually came into the institution to perform, was coming to see me. Her name was Denise, and she had the exotic face of an African doll, and an out-of-this-world body, which, dressed in the tank top and short skirt she wore on that first visit, seemed to just ooze with lusciousness.

I had gotten her interest after seeing her with her dance troupe perform at a prison function. I pulled up on her afterward, telling her I'd written a short story called "The Artist and the Dancer," in which I'd imagined her as a character remembered from the group's performance the previous year. She'd heard me recite some poetry earlier in the program, and was impressed enough with my line to give me her address. That was all I needed. I serenaded her by mail for two weeks with the loveliest prose and poetry I could muster, and she had responded by consenting to visit.

We hit it off well, that first visit, and our kiss at the doorway as she was leaving was like something out of a high school dream, for I'd been deprived of affection for a very long time. And oh how I dreamed of her that night, fantasizing with her perfume-laced letters beside my pillow. I relived each moment of Denise's visit, from the waiting at the table and then the light touch of a hand on my shoulder when she appeared at my side, looking up from those thighs and then at that bosom, all that soft flesh for the eye followed by the real touch and dearness of an opening hug—with a mere taste of cheek, smooth tender young cheek—as my hand dared the slope along the curve of back swooping out to the merest beginning of that awesome posterior.

The next day, a Sunday, brought more joy, when my parents and Rod came to visit. He had been staying with them for a couple of weeks at the end of the summer, while Ruth got situated back at her mother's home in Winston-Salem. She had moved back from South Carolina, after getting a new teaching position near her hometown.

At twelve years old, Roderick was a tall boy, promising to take after me in that regard. He reminded me of the time when he was an infant, and looked so much like me that Ruth would refer to him as "the little replica." It seemed that he was also taking after me in school, having tested in the top 98th percentile in the nation, and

winning several awards in science competitions. He was highly regarded at the school he'd attended in South Carolina, where his
mother had taught. Having also gone to a school where my mom
taught, I identified with what he'd been going through. One of the
first things he told me was how happy he was to be "going to school
on my own now," since Ruth would be teaching in a nearby town.

"What good movies have you seen lately?" was the first question
he asked, almost as taken with movies as his old man. "You got it
made, Dad, you get to see free movies," he said, impressed by the
fact that we got to see the latest films on a regular basis.

Mama and Pop doted on their grandson, making me proud that
I'd brought something other than sadness and shame to them.
Mama said, "He does like movies, but spends most of his time
reading."

"He's real smart, just like you," Pop added. "He showed me how
to work that VCR we just got, took him no time to do it."

Rod and I went up to the vending machines to get popcorn for
the microwave, giving me a chance to talk to him alone. I wanted to
know how he felt about moving back to Winston-Salem.

"Though I'm happy to be back in Winston with Grandma and
the family, and closer to you, I know my friends are going to miss
me down there in Sumpter, like I'll miss them. Dad, is it wrong to
be happy, and sad, at the same time?"

I felt pride in Rod's being able to express his feelings so, and
tried to assuage his worries as best I could. "No, son," I told him,
"we all feel different things at different times. And sometimes we
feel different things at the same time. It's just a part of life. But you
can give me a hug, because I'm proud of you, facing this change
with such feeling. You just have to be glad for the happy days; and
remember, there's always more of them ahead."

Back in my cell, Jericho stopped by to ask how my visit went.
"Man, you're lucky to have dedicated parents," he said, "people

who keep visiting you every month, rain or shine, for all these years. Most dudes' folks stop coming after a year or so—if they come at all." He didn't need to add the fact that he very rarely received a visit from his family.

After Jericho left, I looked at the Polaroids we'd taken in the visiting room. Having such parents to continue to support me, despite my earlier misdeeds, was indeed inspiring, and certainly one of the reasons I continued to write, in an attempt to make them proud. But especially inspiring was having such a great son. I taped the photos we took that day on my cell wall, beside the poem Rod had sent to me a few weeks before, for Father's Day:

I've always been able to talk to you,
You've always been there through and through,
I've always loved and been proud of you,
That's why I hope you feel the same way too.

You are a great fighter,
You are a great writer,
That's why on this day I would like to say,
Happy Father's Day, Dad, with no more delay.

The following Tuesday I was still in a pretty good mood. I awoke to put finishing touches on the literacy script I'd written for the film class, happy that my proposal had netted five thousand dollars in funding to do the project. I was looking forward to the evening, when Denise would once again come to see me, with a promised meal of chicken wings and rice (she'd asked me what was my favorite), along with the promise of real love.

Then, after lunch, a call came over the intercom: "E. Hopkins, number 10-68-24, report to the treatment center immediately." I wondered what the deal was, as I had no appointment with my counselor for today. I figured it must have something to do with all of the paperwork for my film class, and all the red tape to make a movie inside prison. I was surprised at being met by the treatment program supervisor. "Mr. Hopkins, your wife has called to speak to you," he said. "Your counselor is waiting in her office to facilitate your returning that call."

The manner of the man struck me as portentous, as did the fact that he had personally received me, rather than the counselor herself. The counselor, a short, chunky black girl who was usually all business, had a softer manner for some reason as she put through the call for me. Handing me the phone, she rose to leave, saying, "I'll leave you alone. Take as much time as you need."

Ruth came on the line, and her voice immediately gave way to sobbing. "Derrell, Rod had a mini-heart attack last night," she began. "He stopped breathing, and I couldn't do anything to help him." She broke down and began to sob again. "I tried giving him CPR and called the ambulance, then tried the mouth-to-mouth again. Oh God, Derrell, I couldn't save him. Our baby's gone. Oh my God, our baby's gone. . . ."

By then she had gone into near-hysterics. Perhaps it was this—the need to bring her back from a place from which she might not escape—that kept me from going off there in that office, my head bowed nearly between my legs, left hand squeezing my brow in an attempt to squelch the pain bursting like a fireball in my forehead. I knew I had to try to be of some comfort. "I know you did all you could do, Ruth," I told her, even as my mind reeled. She continued to wail, "Derrell, I tried, I tried, but I could feel him limp in my arms, he was gone, he was gone. . . ."

Then her sister Hazel came on the phone, while others in the family attended to Ruth. "I've already called your parents, Derrell. It took us a few hours to get in touch with you." I was just trying to hold on, at that point. But then Hazel, now an attorney, told me, "We're doing all we can to get you down here for the funeral, but the people I've talked to say we're going to have to go through the governor to get it done, since you're out of state. But we're working on it, so try to get your counselor to call me tomorrow."

I knew what that meant. I wouldn't even be allowed to go to the funeral. Sensing the anguish coming through in my silence, as I repressed my tears, Hazel added, my former Panther comrade now, "Be strong, my brother. Stay strong and take care of yourself on that end, and we'll deal with things here. Just keep it together so you can come home to us."

Her words helped me to come up with some Panther courage, to make it back to my cell without breaking down. But once in the privacy of my steel cubicle, I let loose with a wail of despair, and was only able to muffle it with my pillow. I lay on my bunk and wept for hours, wondering if I might ever stop crying. My son, my Roderick, was gone. And I'd not been there, I was not there, would not even be able to get there for the funeral, to help comfort Ruth—and my mother and father. *Oh my God! What are they going through now?* I thought.

Then, just after seven o'clock, the call came: "E. Hopkins, number 10-68-24, report to the visiting room. You have a visit."

I don't know how I changed into my visiting-room clothes, but I did, and made it through the preliminary shakedown and through the doors into the visiting room. And there was Denise, the girl who might dare to love me, in a lovely magenta cling-pleat skirt and a demure purple blouse, with a beauty that might have been inspiring on another occasion.

I knew I had to find a way to hold it together, but I had no idea how I had even made it to this point, here in public, where I might break down at any moment.

Giving her a quick kiss, I said, "It's good to see you," and asked if she minded that I get something to drink right away. I grabbed up some of the change she had brought in and went straight to the Coke machine. When I returned to the table and sat down, she looked at me with concern. She took my hands, looked at me, and asked, "Evans, are you all right?"

I pulled my hands away, gave her a look I feared might be a little too cold, maybe in an effort to scare her away from seeking into the source of my pain. "I'll be all right, if you don't ask me that again." Then I sat back, sipped on my Coke, and tried to act as if I were the calmest man on earth.

Denise could not help but see that I wasn't acting normally. "Come on, Evans," she said, "tell me about it—if you want to," giving me the strength to open up.

"I got a call today from my wife," I said, working hard to keep from choking up. "She told me that our son passed away last night, that he—he died from his heart condition—in her arms."

The awful reality of it all hit me again as I told her, and all at once I deflated, my head sinking to my chest. Denise slowly pulled my chin up, pressed her forehead to mine, then took me into a long embrace, willing strength into me with a lifesaving tenderness, overcoming the feverish chill I was using to hold my resolve together.

During the following days I lived in a blur, going out to get enough nourishment to get back to the cell, to weep, once more. I would come out for a phone call to Mama and Pop, or to take the one from Hazel, telling me that attempts to get an interstate compact for me to attend the funeral had failed. Then I'd go into my cell and cry again. I thought the tears would never stop.

During one of those days, I remember sitting in the waiting room of the treatment center to make a call home, and being asked by an inmate, "What story are you working on now?" My reply, without thinking, was, "There's only one story now." I realized that whatever I would write from now on would, in some way, embody the story of my son.

The period after Rod's death was a time of near madness. My only salvation seemed to lie in my visits with Denise. She helped to draw me out of the shell I had retreated into, helped me to see love and life and hope as alternatives to my despair.

After a visit where she was introduced to my parents, she asked me, "Why don't you kiss your parents as they leave? Do you ever tell them you love them?"

She lent laughter to my existence, along with hope. On a lark, after talking about Spike Lee's debut film, *She's Gotta Have It,* I asked her to send a letter from me to Lee. When he responded with a postcard from Atlanta, where he was filming his second project, Denise asked me if I wanted her to frame it. "Shit, he ain't *that* important," I told her, having come to believe in the possibility that my writing would soon bring about my freedom, and that I would soon be making movies just like Spike.

But Denise had also become something of a dangerous sexual obsession. The smell and taste of her perfume during visits, the warm feel of her body, would stay with me after leaving the visiting room, promise and dream melding into fantasy, then leaving me ever more alone in my cell.

One morning after the breakfast call I'd slept through, as usual, a brother came by my cell and hollered, "Hey, Hop, wake up." Pulling myself up in my bunk, he laid it on me, point-blank. "Man, they just found your stick man Jericho dead in his cell, with a plastic bag over his head. Stiff as a board. The talk is that his neck was broke. They gettin' ready to take him out now."

I lay back down, hoping this was just another one of my crazy dreams, hoping for all the world that I might ease back into sleep and wake to find that this report was not true. Then I jumped up and threw on jeans and shoes. Brushing past the guard at the gate to my section of the building, I dared to push past the guard at Jericho's section—a sure charge and immediate lockup in solitary if caught. The warden was there, personally overseeing the extraction of the body. Standing next to him, I watched the lifeless form of my brother, encased in a black body bag, being carted out by two guards.

I approached the warden as if I had some semblance of authority, telling him that I was close to Jericho's family and would like to know what had happened, so that I could relay it to them. "We don't know," he said at first, looking somewhat shaken himself. Then he added, "He had a trash bag over his head, and an extension cord around his neck."

Rumors immediately began to fly around the prison. Jericho's enemies in the dope business had killed him just before lockdown and robbed him of his drugs and money. The guards didn't like him and they went in during the night and killed him. No one wanted to believe that this larger-than-life figure of a man had taken himself out. I felt obliged to try to find out the truth, though I was fearful that it might mean I'd have to fulfill my promise to Jericho to avenge his death.

I talked to a doctor friend, telling him that it seemed unlikely that a man could commit suicide by tying a bag over his head. "Surely the involuntary impulse to live would cause him to tear the bag away," I reasoned. But the doctor told me that such suicides were not uncommon.

The man who held Jericho's pills for him, a fellow member of our chess club, told me that Jericho had come and gotten them all just before lockdown, after having an argument with his woman over the phone. "You know how pissed off at the world and everybody Jericho could get. He probably got fed up with it all. Maybe he just saw how little hope he had with double life, and shot up enough dope to put him to sleep, before he put that bag over his head and tied the cord around his neck. I mean, he had his headphones on over the bag, going out the coolest way he could figure. Does that sound like Jericho, or what?"

I spoke with Jericho's sister in Danville by phone, trying to mitigate his family's sense of loss. I could not help but wonder if my backing out of the escape plan had played a part in his decision to take his own life. Hearing the anguish and bewilderment that his family was going through, I realized that thoughts of suicide had also been on my mind after Rod's death, which had been only two months before. I knew then that, come what may, I didn't have the heart to put my family through what Jericho's people were enduring. My friend had always seemed so strong, but now I had to think of him as tragically callous. So, if perhaps I had taken away Jericho's dream of escaping prison—the dream we had shared together—in ending his life he had taken away the latent idea of my escaping my own pain through suicide.

I had too much to live for, his death made me realize. Unlike Jericho, I still had hope. Though I felt abandoned by my best friend, the man I'd loved like a brother, Jericho had actually left me a gift: He'd made me realize that death was not the escape from my hell of imprisonment, that I wasn't really about all of the hardcore convict/gangster stuff the rage within had wanted me to believe. I would have to endure, for somehow my heart still contained more hope than pain.

The stage was set for the big scene: B-building at night, brilliant arc lamps illuminating five tiers of cell. With the command of "lights-action-speed" my cameraman pans from the top tier to the ground floor, capturing a dozen or so prisoner extras leaning over the railings, the shot landing upon a cell with a prisoner-character I have created. He is puzzling over a letter from a girlfriend.

The young man goes next door to the cell of an older prisoner, interrupting him as he plays the theme music of the film on a portable keyboard. He asks timidly if the older man might help him "with a couple of hard words in this letter." The older con reads the letter aloud: ". . . You don't answer my letters, which makes me think that there is something wrong. So I don't think I can be your girl anymore." The older man realizes the younger inmate has gotten a Dear John letter that he cannot read. He tells the man, "I'm a tutor up at the school, and I can help you with your reading, Bruh."

"I don't need help from nobody," comes the explosive retort. Balling up the letter and throwing it away, the young man storms back to his cell.

• • •

This was the climactic scene of the film I'd written on the subject of literacy. The scene was drawn from an event that had happened with a man I'd tried to help with his reading, while working as a tutor at the prison's school. The film, which I'd entitled *A Time to Learn*, was the culmination of the work I'd allowed to consume me following the deaths of Rod and Jericho.

Writing and then making the film came as something of a salvation in my life. I was still filled with turmoil, for it had only been weeks since the deaths of my son and my best friend. Seeing my words, ideas, and images made real with actors, and recorded on film, filled me with the hope that as long as I could keep on writing, my dreams could become realities.

I had assumed leadership of the film class, and had recruited I. Sparks, whom I'd met in the Danville jail, as my vice president. Jerry Williams, the director hired by Carole, knew his stuff, and I learned a lot from him. It was an unprecedented effort, making a film within a penal institution, with a crew of twenty-five prisoners and actors who began work just after breakfast, and continued into the evenings, for ten days. And to top it all off, we had a reporter and photographer from *Life* magazine covering the shoot.

The story I'd written went like this: A high school basketball star with his leg in a cast is called into the principal's office and chewed out about his grades. He blows up at the principal, gets expelled, then gets caught up with gambling in a pool hall, and after losing he agrees to carry drugs to pay off his debt, only to get busted. In prison he's back to gambling, using his basketball skills to get him over, until he ends up in isolation, where he gets the Dear John and meets the tutor who tells him that his main problem is that he cannot read. The film ends with his going up to the prison school with the older prisoner, getting into the reading program, and finally being able to write a letter to his girlfriend.

Released in January 1987, the videotaped film premiered with an introduction by Jeannie Baliles, the governor's wife, in prime time on a local television station, and then was distributed nationwide. The administration allowed us to have a special gathering to view the film as it was aired. Together with Carole Kass and the other members of the film class, I saw the scenes I'd written appearing as if in real life, the words of the theme song I wrote being sung, all being broadcast out into the world, perhaps to do some good. I felt a sense of artistic gratification I hadn't had before.

But my writing was only helping to keep my head just above the surface, for I was still in a terrible depression. I'd lost my son, my stick man was dead, and I was beginning to see signs of trouble with my precious dancer, as her visits became more sporadic. I got the prison shrink to prescribe some tranquilizers for me, and would sleep fitfully through the day, listening to jazz on the cassette player I had at the head of my bunk, and arising only for meals.

In the evenings, when sleep could no longer provide an escape, I tried to write as best I could, concentrating on finishing a stage work I called "Chair Play—or, Who's Afraid of Virginia's Chair?" which I'd begun when my opposition to the death penalty was at its zenith. I'd grandiosely told Marie Deans that I was creating a work that "would bring about a crisis of conscience about the death penalty in America." But in my sorry state I could get only a few words down before feeling defeated.

I began to have nightmares in which I found *myself* on death row. In one dream, guards actually strapped me into the electric chair and placed the hood over my head. I awoke in the middle of the night with a scream, in a horror of sweat, light bursting through my brain like electric voltage. I realized then that I had to give up writing about the electric chair.

But such was not to be. I had met Earl Clanton, one of the Mecklenburg escapees, who had been sent to the Penitentiary after an appeals court had reversed his death sentence. A young boxer of some renown in the New Jersey prison system, Clanton had gotten caught up in a robbery gone bad after moving to Virginia, and had received a death sentence for murder. A tall, athletic, and exceptionally good-looking brother known as Goldie for his complexion, he had a great deal of charisma and was a natural actor. I'd recruited him for my film class, and had cast him in "A Time to Learn." He and I became friends, and one day he told me he was willing to share his written account of the notorious escape.

I was still housed in A-building, and had to dare slipping past the guard at the doors of B-building in order to talk to him in his cell. He gave me a sheaf of papers and said, "This is the real deal of what happened, Hop. I want you to keep it, and get it out to the public if things don't go right for me with my appeal.

"You also get in here what happened with my crime, 'cause I want people to know that I didn't want to kill the person I robbed—it just went bad on me, man."

I stood up to leave, wanting to get the hell out of the building before I got jammed up for the serious charge of "being in an unauthorized area." But Goldie said, "Stay a bit longer, Bruh. I've got a quart of mash we can share."

Well, of course, the rarity of wine made me sit back down. While we sipped on orange-juice mash, he said, "I've got something I need to tell you, Hop. You've been a good friend to me, bringing me into the Film Class and your movie, making my time here have some meaning. My lawyer says things don't look too good for me with my appeal, and I don't want you to leave here without telling you this."

Oh fuck, I thought, *I really don't need any more heavy shit in my life right now.* But I listened, as though a priest to a dying man's confession.

"When I left death row," Goldie said, "there was a lot of talk about you and your writing about the brothers there. They thought you were going to write about how women were smuggling things in to us, that you were putting too much of a spotlight on them."

He then told me that the men had been concerned because some of the women who had been coming to visit them had actually helped them in their escape. He said that he'd had a female guard smuggle a derringer in to him, and that a gun being involved in the escape had been withheld from the press.

"When I was about to leave the Row, the brothers asked me to take a contract on you, to take you out once I got here. And not knowing the righteous brother you are, Hop, I agreed. When you pulled up trying to help me, I had been squatting on you all the time."

I was shocked, thinking of how I'd ignored the threats against me, and realizing that Goldie could easily have poisoned me there, with his wine, or stabbed me to death on any number of occasions when we'd been isolated together.

"But don't worry, Bruh," he said, "I sent word back that you're thorough, and wouldn't do nothin' to hurt us. I just hope you can forgive me for holding this back on you, knowing that you helped change me, man—made me see that I was not just the fighter and killer I thought I was." As I stood up to leave, he reached out and took my hand in a soul handshake, and pulled me into a long hug. "You don't know how much knowing you has meant to me, brother, at this stage in my life."

Within weeks Goldie was back on death row, the reversal of his sentence having been overturned by an appeals court. He was soon given a date of execution, and I felt compelled to write one more death penalty article, this time in an attempt to save a friend.

Alas, I was not able to get the piece I wrote published, though I was successful in getting my friend Ben Cleary to do a cover story on him for *STYLE*. Nevertheless, Goldie would be put to death early in 1987, and it would take months for me to dislodge from my mind the image of a friend being electrocuted in that death chamber below me, a man whose face I'd seen, whose voice I had heard, and whose life might have continued with meaning in the world.

I often thought of what it took for Goldie to share a bit of his soul with me on that last day I saw him. I realized how tenuous are the bonds made between men, but with such bonds even the most callous of us can find some semblance of redemption.

My season of loss had not ended. My beautiful dancer abruptly stopped coming to see me, then sent a Dear John letter stating that she could no longer deal with coming into the prison for visits, seeing no hope of a future with me.

I began to spiral further into the dark cavern of depression, wondering if I'd ever emerge. I got the prison doctor to increase the tranquilizers I was taking, not wanting to risk a mind-destroying antidepressant or to succumb to taking the hard drugs that were readily available in the prison. I tried to sleep through days, through weeks, and my nightmares were terrible, filled with violence and despair. I couldn't concentrate enough to write anything at night, but could muster just enough energy to read a little, trying to heal my mind and spirit with books on the chemistry of love, and the psychology of mourning, along with a bit of poetry to keep my spirit alive.

It was poetry—lifesaving poetry—that finally pulled me through. I came across a verse in a book given to me by my poet friend Greg Donovan, called "Dawn and a Woman." The scene was of a naked man squatting before a campfire, thinking of a woman who would soon come to him—a woman who would never be able to really comfort him, "for she has never known the loss of a son." The poem helped me get over Denise's departure, and indeed to realize that, as a man, I could not expect to continue trying to escape my mourning with the evanescent affections of a woman.

Then I read Robert Frost's famous "Out, Out—" which described a farm boy losing his arm to a buzz saw, his life ebbing away before family and friends, with the closing line: "And they/not being the one dead/turned to go about their affairs."

The coldness of the line took my breath away, and moved me to tears I had feared letting flow for months. I realized that I'd been mourning *my* loss of Rod, not the tragedy of his having lost *his* life. But I was not the one who was gone; it was time to return to the affairs of the world of the living.

That night I had a dream of salvation. I was on my bunk, crying, in a fetal position, and Rod appeared at my bedside. "Don't cry, Dad, it's going to be all right," he said, and his spirit separated from his body, got into the bed to hold and comfort me, then merged into my being. Awakening, I realized that his spirit would have to live on in me—and that I would have to live on, for him.

CHAPTER NINE

Not-a-Way . . .

The ride to Nottoway Correctional Center was not long, only forty minutes or so, but it seemed I was being shipped hundreds of miles into the country, far away from the city of Richmond and the friends who had nurtured my rebirth as a new man. I had fourteen boxes filled with my books and papers stacked in the back of the van, more than the eleven other men being shipped with me had altogether.

My first view of the prison: coil after coil of gleaming rolls of razor wire stacked from top to bottom on each fence, a daunting sight. The buildings were all of the same slate-gray concrete, and the place looked like some sort of Machiavellian, postmodernist fortress keep. This would be the place where I would live for the foreseeable future—if not for the rest of my life.

The prison, located in Nottoway County, had been built in 1984 to hold five hundred men. Now, in late August 1988, it was pressed to the gills with one thousand—with two hundred more of us to come from The Wall, which the state had decided to tear down after selling the land to Ethyl Corporation. Upon arrival we were given an orientation tour. The cells were larger than those at the Penitentiary, with hot-water taps in the sinks, no less. However, most contained two bunks, and it would take several months to qualify for a single cell, and a year or more with a pristine record to get to the honor buildings, where many more privileges were to be had.

While the deal with the double cells was bad news for the nocturnal writer needing solitude, the place was pristine compared to the State Pen. The cells surrounded a central bulletproof-glassed control booth in an octagonal pattern. All the cells had cable hookups, with movies piped in and repeated throughout the day, so I could watch over and over, a wonderful boost to my study of film. The day areas in each pod were clean and freshly painted, with four steel tables for games and general recreation. Decks of cards and board games could be checked out from the booth. There were two telephones in each pod, and amazingly, microwave ovens, where one could heat food bought from the canteen—or smuggled back from the dining hall, as had been my practice at The Wall, except here I would be risking a write-up, since everyone was frisked at each building's entrance.

We were then shown the modern gym, complete with hardwood floor and fiberglass backboards, a weight room, punching bags, Ping Pong tables, and a room with two pool tables. Outside the gym was an outdoor patio with weight-lifting equipment, and a gigantic recreation field of more than five acres, surrounded by menacing thirty-foot guard towers manned by marksmen with high-powered rifles.

There were also horseshoe pits, a handball wall, and, to my great pleasure, two asphalt tennis courts. At last, I thought, I would be able to play my beloved sport again.

While I was gawking at the court from the fence, none other than my old friend Gerald appeared beside me. "Hey, Hop," he said, giving me his broad grin and a quick my-man hug. "I heard you were here. Welcome to Nottoway—which, in case you don't know, stands for 'Not-a-way to get out of this damn place.'" He let out a big laugh, ever able to joke about what seemed to me dire circumstances, and I had to laugh with him.

I said, "All this time I've done, lookin' at what they got for me here—shee-it—I guess I ain't got nothin' left to do *but* angle on parole, now." I knew then that I'd passed another threshold, that after six years of incarceration any last illusions of escaping were now totally gone. While one could always fantasize about escape from the Pen, where there were so many holes in the security and the tantalizing sight of downtown Richmond, way out here in the boondocks all you could see, looking out over all the razor wire, insurmountable fences, and even higher guard towers, was a wilderness of woods.

I didn't let Gerald know how intimidated I was by my relocation, and said to him, "Well, since I was just lookin' for a place to get my tennis game together, I decided to come out here to Nottoway and check you out," letting him know I could still talk a little junk, that I still had a bit of bravado left in me. (The first thing real cons do, when checking out someone they've not seen in a while, is try to gauge whether his spirit has been broken.)

I suppose it was with that thought in mind that Gerald said, "I heard about your son passing away. I'm real sorry, man—I know it had to hurt, to have to go through something like that from in here."

"Thanks, brother man, I really appreciate that," I said, grabbing his extended hand in the solidarity handshake, and pulling his chest to mine once more in a heartfelt hug.

It had taken more than a year for me to recover from the depression of mourning the deaths of Rod and Jericho, to emerge from my season of loss and begin writing and publishing again. The strength I gained from writing had given me the courage to attempt another relationship in my personal life. Two months before my transfer I read a personal ad in *STYLE,* the Richmond paper I was writing for, that read: "In a New York state of mind. Single white female and mother looking for black or Hispanic father-figure for my biracial son. . . ."

I was touched by the writer's frankness, and wrote to her. Her name was Nancy, and her three-year-old son was named Ben. They began coming to see me regularly.

Nancy took up the cause of getting me out, and her dedication made me look past the heartache I'd endured, and entertain the possibility of developing a long-term relationship with her, though I knew it would be difficult, with her being white.

I also knew that my transfer to Nottoway would be a hardship on Nancy, and told her that I'd understand if she stopped visiting. She refused to be put off, and drove the fifty miles from Richmond each week for two months, until her car broke down on the highway while returning from a visit.

In the meantime, Nancy wrote and encouraged me not to let the transfer set me back, to keep on writing. And keep on writing I did. The 1988 race for president was in full swing, and the main issue of George Bush's campaign centered around a black prisoner named Willie Horton, who had raped and killed a woman while on furlough from a Massachusetts prison during the period when Bush's opponent, Michael Dukakis, had been governor of the state. It became a hot-button issue that I knew would affect prison-release programs nationwide, and I decided to take Bush to task for his inflammatory use of race and criminal justice.

I blasted him with a piece that would be published in *The Washington Post* the Sunday before the election, a high point in my career—a prisoner making a strong comment in one of the nation's foremost political forums, and perhaps even affecting a presidential election.

On the Friday before the election I learned that the piece was going to run, and let Gerald see my manuscript, just as I had my first article for *The Washington Post* six years before. "Hop, you still got it, Bruh," he said after reading it. "You're definitely back on top of your game. I'm proud of you, brother."

I couldn't wait to see Nancy that Saturday, to share the good news with her. She hadn't visited in a couple of weeks, having been unable to get her car fixed. So she had decided to catch a ride on one of two vans belonging to an organization called the Prison Visitation Project, which transported the loved ones of prisoners from Richmond to Nottoway every week.

I awoke early that Saturday, cooking up a cup of oatmeal in the microwave for breakfast as usual, then ironing my visiting-room jeans and shirt and shaving for the visit that would be the highlight of my week. I lay back upon my bunk and dozed, waiting for the loudspeaker to blare out a call for my visit. But lunchtime came around, and still no call. I didn't bother to go to lunch, not wanting to brave the hard rain that had begun earlier that morning, and was still coming down. I dozed through the afternoon, half waking with each call on the loudspeaker. But it was always someone else's name that was called. When I came fully awake just before the three-thirty count, I realized that Nancy and Ben hadn't made it.

A man I knew stopped by my cell on his way in from a visit. "Hey, Hop, you better check on things when you come out," he said. "One of the visitation vans had a wreck on the way here, and they say everybody got hurt."

I rushed out after count, and learned from the guard in the booth that the van had spun out on one of Highway 360's rough curves, during a sudden downpour. All of the twenty-one people aboard were taken to the hospital, and three people were believed to be dead. That was all he knew, but he would let me know more after chow.

I went to the mess hall for the evening meal, hoping to learn more about the situation. Halfway through my meal a man I knew from The Wall came to my table and said, "Yo, Hop, my woman was riding in the other van, the one that didn't crash. She say your woman dead, was dead at the scene. And they think that the little boy stopped breathin' before they took him to the hospital. You better go check on it, man."

I tried to absorb what I'd been told. Maybe the dude had been wrong. I sat there a moment considering this, drank down the rest of my tea in an effort to fortify myself, and walked back to the building.

The six o'clock news was on as I walked up to the communal TV set in the dayroom. There was news footage of the accident scene, ambulances along the median strip of the highway, a long white van lying across the center ditch, crushed and turned on its side.

Then there was a shot of attendants carrying a sheet-covered form to the back of an ambulance, with a reporter's voiceover saying, "Two women were pronounced dead at the scene, with nineteen others taken to area hospitals, some in what is said to be very critical condition." As the camera zoomed in on the body being loaded into the ambulance, I recognized Nancy's suede boots, sticking out from under the sheet.

In a daze, realizing that Nancy was gone, I made my way to the phone booth and called my friend Greg Donovan. I asked him to locate the hospital where the survivors had been taken, hoping to find out that Nancy's son, Ben, had pulled through. Before I could call him back, I was summoned to the watch commander's office, where a state trooper waited to give me the official news: Nancy had perished, and emergency workers at the hospital had not been able to revive Ben.

As I left the central command office, the amber lights seemed to form a halo around pansies planted on the border of the concrete steps, flowers daring to bloom in the cold air of the early November evening, amid all the captivity and death. The image would stay with me that night, as I fought back tears, fearing a descent into sorrow from which I might not emerge. I used that image to write a poem, my "Elegy for Nancy and Ben," which would be read at a memorial held at the Episcopal church that sponsored the visitation project, a service that I would not be allowed to attend.

Following their deaths, I stayed in my cell, grieving. For many days I didn't even go into the chow hall. Gerald brought a bag of munchies he'd bought for me at the commissary, offering solace by saying, "Hop, I feel for you. All this after what you went through with your son. You just got to stay strong, brother."

I shut down for a while. I would not allow myself to cry, shoring up my resolve with the thought that this latest loss could in no way compare to Roderick's death. I could not cry, I *would* not cry. I felt bad that I was damming up the tears, for certainly Nancy and Ben deserved at least my tears. Had it not been for their devotion to me, they would still be alive. But I had begun to doubt my ability to hold onto my sanity, to wonder just how much I could really take. I began to wonder if there might really be a God somewhere, and maybe he was punishing me, doubly, for all my sins and crimes.

I went to see the prison psychologist, and got him to order my transfer from a double cell to a single cell in N-building, which was called "The Nut Ward," because "patients" taking psychotropic medications were housed there. Being there gave me the solitude to think, but being around men with severely damaged psyches was depressing, as well. I was reminded of the night I spent in B-basement at the Penitentiary after getting out of the hospital. When I was offered medication for my emotional pain, I refused. Shouldering up my resolve, I told myself: *You've come too far. Don't let them destroy you now.*

After two months on the Nut Ward, I pulled myself out of my funk with my writing. I wrote a piece about Douglas Wilder's campaign to become the first elected black governor in American history. Entitled, "Could Wilder's Critics Be Racist?" I again went after outgoing Governor Robb, who was publicly criticizing Wilder. The piece was a little too hot to get published in-state, so I sent it to *The Atlanta Journal-Constitution,* where Andrew Young was also facing tough opposition as he ran for the Georgia governorship, and they ran it.

After being transferred back to the general population, I got a job in the prison library, and the library once more became my refuge. I searched the shelves for books that might give inspiration or light to my condition, and once again poetry helped bring me through. I discovered a volume by the German poet Rainer Maria Rilke, whose tragic sense seemed to speak to me; and a friend sent me a book by South African poet Dennis Brutus, who had been imprisoned with Nelson Mandela at one time, and whom I met at the Penitentiary when he came in to read from his verse.

Once more I tried writing poems, but the poetry didn't seem to flow. An idea would turn into a first line, and then—nothing. When I sought the counsel of my friend Greg Donovan, he told me, "Just keep reading. Sooner or later you'll find yourself feeling the kindred spirits of other writers, and begin to feel you owe it to them to add something to the canon of literature."

"In the meantime," he added, "don't be too down on yourself. Realize you've given yourself the equivalent of a master's degree in creative writing, that you've produced superior work in a crucible of despair. So don't worry about the poetry not coming right now. Poetry is based upon beauty, and you've precious little of that right now, in there." His words brought to mind a song by my favorite R&B group, Earth, Wind and Fire, called "All About Love," which said that when there is no beauty, you're got to *create* some beauty.

And so, during that winter of sorrow and woe, I determined that I would find a way to keep myself sane by creating beautiful worlds in my imagination. I returned to a fictional project I'd begun some years before, which centered around the story of Maggie Walker, who had overcome crippling disease to save the bank she had founded at the turn of the century in Richmond. This effort took me out of the cloistered cells of my imprisonment and reopened my imagination to the joys of writing fiction.

And then there was tennis. After more than sixteen years, wonderful, glorious, *real* tennis. With the coming of spring in 1989, I began spending hours every day regaining my form by hitting alone on the Plexiglas wall of the handball court. Finally feeling confident, I took to the court with the several decent players at Nottoway. With my polished strokes I was welcomed into their number, and quickly rose to the top of their ranks. The joy of competition revitalized my body, while the camaraderie replenished my spirit.

Tennis lent laughter and joy to my life once more. (The hardest thing after the loss of those dear to you is to find a way to feel joy again, for survivor's guilt brings on the question: How dare you be happy, when your loved one is in the grave?) With my tennis I became known as "the best on the spread," winning the tournaments held by the recreation department, my prowess so highly regarded that men would often line the fences around the court to watch me play.

I became a much better player than I'd been in my teens. With a professional-level serve well in excess of 100 miles per hour, I was given the nickname Hammer—in part from the name of the racket I used, and in part from the popularity of rapper M.C. Hammer.

While playing doubles one evening as dusk descended just before the end of evening recreation, I blasted a serve down the middle that happened to strike a pebble on the court, causing sparks to fly that were visible in the grayness of twilight.

"You see that?" came the cry from an onlooker. "Hop just knocked *fire* from the court." A chorus rang out among the laughing players: "Go Hammer, go Hammer, go Hammer, go Hammer," as I mimicked the rapper in a moonwalk to the other side of the court—and then launched another ace.

And so it was that the court became a place where I could escape the bounds of my prison existence, where I could experience laughter, vent anger, and exhibit the beauty of form that was at the heart of my game. On the court I could display a certain mastery—the same ideal I sought in my writing. On any given day I could be king of a smaller world, if only for a couple of hours.

•   •   •

Tennis helped bring me out of my depression, but by the winter of 1990, I was back in the rut of just doing time, and getting very little writing done, for I was back in a double cell. My cell partner was a young heroin dealer everyone called Tee. He was also a chess player, but after a while our chess matches would cease, for as often as not they would end in argument. He was a smart player, but did not take well to losing.

I did learn a bit about what was happening out in the streets from him, however. He loved to watch horror movies on my television, telling me, "You need to get used to the sight of blood, 'cause you're bound to see it out in the street." He told me how he would tell members of his crew, "It's time to go see some brains," meaning that they would be going out with the intention of shooting a rival dealer—or someone late on paying up—in the head. He also had a particularly warped view of women, choosing those in their mid-teens. "You don't want to have to send your girl out for Geritol for you, and have to tell her to bring back a bottle for herself, too." Being in a cell with Tee made me realize that I had no inkling of the treacherous shit that was happening out there in the streets since I'd been gone.

With no tennis during the winter, I found myself spending days playing Scrabble and bid whist, after working my new job as a tutor in the prison school. Gerald had been transferred, so I had no close friends. I hadn't really tried to make any, having learned the lesson from previous years of doing time that it's best not to get too close to anyone, for, as in slavery days, those for whom you might develop affection can be shipped off at any moment.

Still, I found that I needed social activity during this period when I was still trying to heal, and I became fairly tight with Johnnie G., a heavy-set dude I had taught to play tennis. He locked down in the same pod as I did, and since the prison was divided in small sections, you more or less had to spend your time with those in your pod, except for periods when you were allowed out on the recreation yard.

Johnnie was something of a Scrabble whiz, as was I, and we played most every evening. I used such occasions to cry to him about what all I was going through, especially the problem I was experiencing with writer's block. One night he had had his fill of my woes.

"Hop," he said, "what you're saying is bullshit. Compared to me, with your family support, you got it made. I got a marginal education, and if I don't get help from my family all I can look forward to when I *do* get back out in the street is sellin' dope—'stead of stickin' up like I used to do."

He paused to think about his next play, but he'd gotten so worked up that he threw in his tiles, folded up the Scrabble board, and said, "You can have this fuckin' game, 'cause you need to listen to what I got to tell you.

"Stop feeling sorry for yourself and look at all you got goin' for you. You got family comin' to see you every month, got a God-given talent for writing, with people writin' back to you from all over the country. But your problem is that you feel you haven't been treated fairly in life, so you don't feel like you need to treat others fairly. You thinkin' it's all about you—but deep down inside, you just mad with God."

I tried to interrupt him, to tell him he had me all wrong, but he put up his hand and said, "Just hear me out, brother man," getting up from the table. "Hell, you used to be a Panther. You been writing about the system, and brothers all over look up to you for the way you been carryin' it for them. You got to use that same fire to find a way to give some of that love you used to have *back* to the world again."

His use of the word *love* struck me, for it wasn't a word that cons used often. "You just down on yourself 'cause your son died, and then your people got killed in that wreck. But you got to get over that shit. Either you keep on doin' this time, or you let the time do you." And with that, he stormed off.

When I went back to my cell, I waited until my cell partner was asleep before I tried to iron out my feelings about what Johnnie had said. I stood before the tin-plate mirror riveted above the sink by the cell door, conversing silently with my distorted image in the blue-tinged glow filtering through the bars from the dimmed fluorescent lights out in the pod, smoking cigarette after cigarette. Then, I wrote in my journal:

> *Blasted by J.G. tonight about my block, my overall attitude. Some truth to what he said. Have I started to just feel sorry for myself? How do I regain my fighting spirit—and the love he mentioned— when I don't feel anything for anyone right now, much less myself? Maybe it was the Panther spirit that sustained me, early on in this bit. But where is that courage now, when I need it most? Can I salvage it from strong brothers like Johnnie? I've tried to transcend the wall and fences that have circumscribed my life. But I feel tired—way too tired to reclaim the mental toughness of my past lives. What will it take to bring me out of this funk?*

During this down period I received a call for a visit, though I wasn't expecting anyone. When I got to the visiting room, my old Panther comrade Bernard Patterson came to the door to greet me with a handshake and a hug. He had been back in Danville for many years, and was working for my father then, giving me an occasion to talk to him once or twice when I'd called the office. He'd told me he would try to get to Nottoway to see me, but I was surprised nevertheless.

"I brought Nelson with me," he said, "and we're at a table back here in the corner."

While I'd known that Nelson had been left paralyzed after being shot by a member of the Panther Squad back in the late seventies, I was hardly prepared to see him in a wheelchair. He grasped my hand with both of his, the weak curl of their deformity providing a shock, reminding me of the cruel injustice of his having been shot in the back by comrades he'd trusted, this strong leader reduced to near helplessness by the criminal mentality Huey Newton had fostered as he destroyed the Party from within.

But Nelson's broad grin gave evidence that he was still strong. "How you been doin', comrade brother?" he asked, expressing his concern for my well-being in an effort to put me at ease with the paraplegia he'd been dealing with for many years. Indeed, Nelson was still a leader, for he'd been elected to the city council in Winston-Salem, and militantly represented the city's poorest district.

As we talked, he complimented me on my pieces that he'd read in *The Washington Post*. "You're a strong brother," he said, "to keep carrying on for the Cause while under the gun like this." Then he gave evidence that his sense of humor was still intact when he told me with a grin, "I guess you did what you said you wanted to do— go to prison so you'd have time to become a great writer. I've got to say, you have gotten pretty good."

I'd forgotten about my statement after the grand opening of our Party headquarters, so many years ago. But now I could only smile at the sad irony, as I good-naturedly argued by saying, "Now, brother-man, you *know* I never said that's what I *wanted* to do."

Reflecting on the visit once I was back in my cell, I felt deeply moved. I knew Bernard was going through hard times, working as a laborer; and seeing Nelson was positively inspiring. *If he could carry on the Struggle in his condition, how could I succumb to self-pity now?*

Soon after that visit came more encouragement. I received a notice from the personal-property office saying that I had a package waiting to be picked up, from my cousin Monifa Love, a poet who had often said that she believed that she and I were twins separated at birth. I hadn't heard from her since I was at The Wall, when she had come down to visit me from Washington, only to be turned back because she wasn't wearing a bra under her already restricting garb. She hadn't written to me after that, and I figured that she was just another well-meaning member of the family, like my sister, who had trouble dealing with the fact of my being locked up.

As it turned out, the parcel she had sent was the manuscript of a novel she'd written, inspired by the devastation she had felt in being turned away at the State Pen the night she'd tried to visit. In her note she told me that it would soon be published under the title *Freedom in the Dismal*. I was moved that she had taken my plight into her heart so dearly, and inspired to know that I had a cousin so much on the same wavelength as I, in terms of artistry. She was finishing her doctorate at Florida State University, where she was also teaching. We resumed a correspondence that she would collect and have published in a volume of essays called *Genre and Writing*—a welcome indication that my work was worthy of publication in a book.

Soon after, Carole Kass came to visit. She urged me to restart the film class at Nottoway, saying, "Evans, you can't let yourself die here. You've touched so many people with your voice. Think of the film we made at the Penitentiary, reaching thousands even now. You've got to build upon what you've done, Evans. You have the gift to reach millions."

Her faith reenergized me. Along with the help of my Rasta friend I. Sparks, who had been with the film class at the Penitentiary, I founded the Film and Media Organization at Nottoway. We developed a current affairs program that we videotaped and piped into the prison's closed-circuit system every week. I dubbed the show FM-TV, and we provided a forum for musicians, poets, and rappers from the prisoner population. I also wrote commentary for every program (reminding me of the imperative of deadline, and that I could produce good stuff at will, even a half hour before showtime). I was able to do things like interview the warden, and confront him about issues affecting the inmate population. During one session with him I found myself asking one question while formulating two follow-up questions to be broached in the wake of his response, all the while writing down a *fourth* question to get at the point I was really interested in. *Damn,* I said to myself, *maybe I really do have the mind for this sort of thing.*

I helped a producer from the Norfolk PBS affiliate, Chris

Dickon, do a statewide program on public television called *Virginia Behind Bars*. My folks at home got to see me on television, and men I knew began to joke me out by saying things like, "Hey, TV star, can I be on your next show?"

One day while I was in the prison barbershop, a brother in an adjacent chair asked me, "Hop, you gonna get you one of them television talk shows when you get out?" I had to laugh, but couldn't help but notice that the other men in the shop took his question seriously, and looked expectantly at me for a reply. Knowing what it took to do that sort of thing, I simply said, "Maybe—if I have the time between writing my books."

After finally making it into a single cell, late in 1990, I tried to foster an environment in which I could create. I put handmade posters on the walls with sayings like "Be Strong," "Fight the Power," and "Daily Courage"—a reference to what my father had admonished me for lacking. While he had been referring to landscaping, I applied his words to my writing, and it helped me get through many a day in the joint.

I'd gotten a job in the prison library and resumed sending out pieces to various publications. One day I caught a television program featuring Hendrick Hertzberg, the editor at *The New Republic* who had given me my first assignment. The program revealed that he was now executive editor at *The New Yorker*, so I sent a query to him. He sent an encouraging response that said he'd be happy to look at whatever I might send. I showed the letter to the prison librarian, who told me, "Keep at it, Evans. Once someone is published by *The New Yorker*, he has it made as a writer."

Soon after, upon submitting a piece to *The Washington Post*, I was talking over the phone with the editor of the OUTLOOK section, Jodie Allen. She mentioned that they had another writer at *The Post* who had been in prison like me, and had a story they were about to run. "His name is Nathan McCall," she said.

"Nathan McCall?" I repeated. "You mean *Nate* McCall? I know him! We did time at Southampton together."

She then transferred me to Nate's desk, and we had something of a reunion by phone. "Man, it's good to talk to you again," he said, "but I'm sorry to hear that you're back inside." He told me how he'd gotten a degree in journalism after prison, worked as a reporter for a while in Norfolk and Atlanta, then landed a job at *The Post*. He also told me, with a degree of sadness I could hear in his voice, how so many of the brothers we'd done time with had been locked up again.

Soon after the publication of his piece in OUTLOOK, which recounted his journey from prison to reporter at one of the nation's premier newspapers, Nate wrote to me about the book deal he'd gotten to tell his story, encouraging me to think about telling mine. (His book, *Makes Me Wanna Holler,* would go on to become a best seller.) I contacted George Gibson, the editor who had first approached me several years before. Now heading his own publishing house, he encouraged me to again think about writing a book.

Then a new threat arose. A man who had been writing a column for the local paper, and who worked in the administration office, told me that he been warned by a prison official that he'd better stop, or he might be thrown into the hole—the old catch of writing for pay being a form of operating a business. "And I've heard your name mentioned, too, though you haven't published anything recently that they know of. But I'm just telling you this so you can be careful, 'cause you know they can always just ship you out to get rid of you."

I realized that the authorities would be more concerned about me, writing in national forums that could embarrass them, than this dude working for a local rag. I wasn't fearful of what might happen, but for a while I was content just doing time—marking time, in a sense, just wanting each day to end, hoping tomorrow I'd find myself in another month or year, that somehow I might wake up in freedom. On good days I'd get a few words written, with letters to friends being the main thing that kept me going. On other days I was content to play tennis or Scrabble, or just read. It was probably the reading that sustained my spirit the most, sharing the works of other writers who had struggled to get their words on page, as I was trying to do.

By late fall of 1993, state politics woke me out of my writing block. George Allen, the ultraconservative Republican son of the owner of the Washington Redskins, seemed destined to win the Virginia governorship that year, and succeed Doug Wilder. To my dismay, his chief issue was the abolition of parole. I felt called upon to attack his plan, and did so in *The Washington Post*. I began the piece with a very public confession, recounting how I'd received a life sentence for a robbery in which no one was hurt, and how my lawyer had told me that life meant only twelve and a half years in Virginia.

"But it has been more than twelve and a half years," I wrote, "and I've yet to go up for parole." Friends told me that it was fool-hardy to attack the man who would likely be the next governor, in a paper like *The Post*. But I felt that I had to. If I didn't do it, no one would.

After Allen was elected governor in 1994, I suddenly felt an urgency to try to make parole the first time up, though I knew it was next to impossible. But after Allen had a chance to swear in a new parole board, I knew I'd be lost, for years. I began gathering letters from all my supporters, compiling a strong dossier for the board to consider. I accumulated letters from my author friends like Marita Golden and Patrice Gaines, and from correspondents from all over the country. The letters helped me view myself in a new light. Many of them were so glowing in their praise of how I'd overcome the obstacles of my incarceration that I had to wonder if I was the one they were really talking about. Letting Johnnie G. see the letters, he told me, "Hop, you one bad dude, to get all these folk willing to take a stand with the parole board for you."

Nevertheless, I was denied parole after my initial interview. But as a result of *The Washington Post* piece, I was contacted by a producer from the Discovery Channel program *The Justice Files,* who wanted to feature my case in a program on parole. She sought permission to film my second parole hearing in 1995. I laughed at the suggestion, as the new mad-dog department of corrections chief had already barred television cameras from Virginia prisons. Thinking they had a snowball's chance in hell of getting the system's chief critic on camera, I told them to go ahead and try, and on a lark tossed in a requirement that they make a tape of the hearing available to me, should they be able to film it.

To my astonishment, they were able to get permission. "Them white folks gonna be mad with you about this," a friend of mine named Rasta-Man told me, when I related to him what was going on. He knew instinctively what every black man in the South knew: If you got too high a profile, you were branded as an "uppity nigger," who needed to be put back in his place.

Thinking I now had nothing to lose, I decided to make a major move. I contacted Carole Kass and ran down the situation to her, asking if she could get a reporter from her paper to interview me, and run a story on my case.

The reporter got permission to come in, with a photographer, just prior to my parole hearing. My thinking was that they'd run a small piece that might help mobilize more support for my release.

On the Sunday after my interview, I was awakened at count time by a tobacco-chewing guard "friend," who said, "You better get up, Mr. Celebrity."

Wiping sleep from my eyes I asked, "Oh, so they did run the piece on me?"

"You got that right," he said. "On the front page!"

I went to the control booth and retrieved the Sunday paper, taking it back to my cell. There on the front page was a large color photo of me, under the headline, "SECOND CHANCE AT A SECOND CHANCE: Can Virginia Writer Write His Way Out of Prison?"

This was more than I'd hoped for, and perhaps more than I'd wanted, for the headline seemed to pose a challenge to the parole board: Are you going to let this criminal write his way out?

The article was long, going from the front page, where my supporters praised me, to the second page, which featured quotes from none other than my old nemesis, Danville's commonwealth's attorney William Fuller. Fuller had gained notoriety as one of the country's most hard-nosed prosecutors, having placed more men on death row in Virginia than any other prosecutor in the state. He defended his having asked for a life sentence in my case by pointing out that I'd been convicted of bank robbery before my trial in his court in 1981. But on a positive note, the owner of the gas station I'd robbed was quoted as saying that he thought I'd done enough time, more than many who had committed murder.

While I was first angered by Fuller's statements, the forgiveness offered by the station owner made me think about the after-effects of my crime. I realized that the enormity of my sentence had kept me from thinking about the effect my crime had had on the community of Danville. I decided that it was time to take full responsibility for my actions, and seek some sort of reconciliation with those I had wronged. I sought out Dr. Miller Ryans, a noted African-American psychiatrist who sometimes worked at Nottoway, and asked him to send Fuller a videotape of my parole hearing, along with a letter from me. In that letter I asked him to look at the tape and judge for himself if I had changed, and was deserving of parole.

To my surprise, Fuller asked to come to the prison for a meeting with Dr. Ryans and me. At that meeting he asked questions about my transformation in prison, and pointed out to me how the nineteen-year-old attendant at the filling station I'd robbed had told him of the nightmares he'd had for weeks after the crime, and how the young man had had to go to counseling afterward.

It hit me then. My feeling of injustice had kept me from feeling empathy for the victim of my crime. But my writer's brain now embraced his pain, imagining the country boy's sessions with a psychologist, then wondering about the other victims of my crimes: the old night watchman suddenly assaulted during a routine night at the junior high, and the people in the bank who had been confronted with the big-bore shotgun in their faces.

I asked Fuller if he'd be the conduit for letters of apology to the gas station attendant and the owner of the station. He agreed, and and was impressed so much by my transformation that, in March 1996 when I went up for parole for the third time, he traveled to Richmond with my father and met with the board on my behalf.

It was unprecedented to have a state prosecutor intervene personally in the case of a man he'd convicted. It gave me hope, in addition to providing a sense of closure with those I had wronged. But despite the influence Fuller was said to have in the state, in May I received the same letter I'd gotten the two previous years: "Application for parole is denied, due to the serious nature of the offense."

Mama and Pop came to visit one Saturday with my uncle Carroll and his wife, Jeanne, who had traveled from Washington. Carroll, six-four and well built despite being in his late sixties, drew me to the side and said, "Your mother seems to be slowing down a lot, and has a tremor of the hands that needs to be checked out." Carroll was on guard for neurological dysfunction, as his wife had been showing signs of early-onset dementia. Taking his advice, I urged my father to take Mama to a neurologist when they returned to Danville.

When I called a few weeks later, Mama told me, "The doctor says that I have some kind of disease, which is causing me to slow down."

"What did he say the name of it was?" I asked.

"I can't seem to remember," she said, and told me to wait while she found the paper with the doctor's diagnosis on it. "Parkinson's disease," she said.

Parkinson's disease. I was devastated, thinking that was the deadly, mind-destroying disease that my uncle Carroll feared his wife had, the affliction that destroyed the memories of its victims, before rendering them comatose. I stumbled back to my cell to cry. My bright mother had been hit with the most dreaded of fatal diseases, one that would reduce her to a vegetable shell of herself.

Then, I realized that maybe I was getting it wrong, and was all mixed up on this. I went to the cell of a man I knew who had once been a nurse, and asked him what having Parkinson's meant.

"Parkinson's is a disease that slowly destroys parts of the brain that control movement," he said, "but is not as quickly devastating as Alzheimer's disease, which destroys the brain's ability to remember and think. People with Parkinson's can live many years, but still, it's pretty heavy."

I felt somewhat relieved, since I had confused Parkinson's with Alzheimer's, though I still felt pretty bad, for there was no telling what the affliction would do to Mama.

By the fall, when she visited with Pop, she had to use the prison's wheelchair to make it from the front gate to the visiting room.

"I don't know if I'll be able to come visit you again," she told me, "but I'm going to try to hold on for you, Derrell, until you come home. I just want to live to see you come home."

I knew then that my only focus would be on staying alive—and sane—until I could return home.

CHAPTER TEN

The Waiting Game

After three turndowns, 1996 brought on another low period in my life. Even though I now had a single cell in the honor building, I still didn't seem to be able to get it together. The years had taken a toll on my enthusiasm, and with the bleak outlook for parole, I found it hard to come up with the sense of purpose to work on the writing that had been my escape.

One day I gained new fuel from the unlikeliest of sources: a prison guard.

"Seems like every week now you hear about somebody getting out, after it's been found out that they've had the wrong man locked up," the tobacco-chewing officer I sometimes talked to said while he frisked me as I was going into the honor building. "Used to be, when inmates told me they were in here for something they didn't do, I never believed them. But after two of 'em I *personally* knew got out—from this prison alone, in less than two years—well, makes me wonder how many more like them are in here."

The guard, a ten-year veteran of the prison system, was known as a hard-nosed type, the kind referred to by prisoners as "stone police." That's why his comments gave me pause.

"Why, just last week," he continued, in his classic southern-sheriff drawl, "I had a man tell me how he was doing time for the murder this other man—who I knew when he was locked up here before he died—how he was doing time for a murder the man who died had done. I thought he was just another inmate full of it, till he pulled out an affidavit where the other man had actually confessed, and admitted how he'd lied in court to keep from goin' to the electric chair."

The guard paused to spit out a brown stream of tobacco juice, and wipe his stained mustache. "Now, something's wrong, somewhere, when you keep running into cases like that," he said.

Back in my cell, I recorded the conversation in my notebook. This was a *big* subject, I thought, and I hadn't written a word about it. Here I was crying about my own personal plight, while this revolution brought about by DNA evidence was hitting home all over the country. Like the guard, I also knew the two men who had been cut loose from this one prison alone. I could not help but feel like I'd dropped the ball on this one.

I began collecting information on the subject, the headlines leaping from the news reports:

- **FOUR MEN FREED WHEN STUDENTS DISCOVER INNOCENCE**
- **MAN RELEASED FROM DEATH ROW, OFFICIALS WITHHELD EVIDENCE**
- **HALF-MILLION AWARDED TO MAN IMPRISONED UNJUSTLY**
- **DNA TEST FREES ANOTHER INNOCENT MAN**

Dozens of men were being proved innocent and released from death row and prison, for reasons ranging from police and prosecutorial misconduct, to plain perjury and honest mistakes. The majority of the cases that were winning reversals were rape cases, wherein DNA evidence had played a crucial role. It struck me that if the DNA testing had revealed such a high number of mistaken prosecutions in rape cases—in which a victim usually *sees* her assailant up close—what about the much greater number of serious crimes, judged upon eyewitness testimony, wherein innocence is professed but in which DNA evidence could play no part?

For all the hell I had gone through in doing so much time for a crime I had committed, I could only imagine the anguish an innocent man would be enduring. I suddenly had a new cause to fire my passion for justice. Inspired by the Innocence Project begun by famed attorney Barry Scheck, I decided to begin an innocence project of my own. I would seek out men who had claims of innocence, and I would write their stories.

It is often said that everyone in prison claims he's innocent, but this is far from true. Though such a façade may be presented to those on the outside, to claim you're innocent *within* prison is usually seen as a sign of weakness, something "real convicts" don't do. "You got the time, buddy, just do yours, like I gotta do mine," is the thinking of most inmates, since, by and large, most of them are indeed guilty. In fact, most men don't like to talk about their cases, period. Just asking, "What are you in for?" can lead to serious friction, since for most prisoners the answer would be, in actuality, a small confession. Nevertheless, men inside the prison environment soon come to know who the innocent ones are: they don't talk about it much, but you see it in the time they spend in the law library, in fighting to get back into court long after it seems hopeless.

In all my years of doing time I'd heard all sorts of stories in private conversations, some men confessing to horrific, bloody crimes, while others would lament, with obvious equivocation, "They got me wrong," or "They didn't have any real evidence on me," dancing around the facts of their cases in ways I developed the savvy to see through. I'd also had men to tell me their stories, and say forthrightly, "I didn't do it"—and I had to believe them, for there was that special ring of truth in what they said.

One such man was Frank DuBose, an old-school hustler who had come to adulthood in New York City. Though barely literate, he had worked with others to write a short book about his case. Frank had let me read his story while I was tutoring him at the State Penitentiary. It seems Frank had gotten jammed up while trying to buy a gun on a trip to Virginia, having made the mistake of driving two men to a gun store in Portsmouth. Instead of purchasing the weapon for him, the men had tried to rob the store, and had ended up killing the store clerk. The triggerman in the robbery had implicated Frank as the killer in order to escape the death penalty. As it happened, Frank was housed in the honor building with me, so I started my search with him.

It turned out that Frank was the man the guard had been talking about. He'd gotten a statement from the triggerman confessing to the fact that he had been the actual killer. Unfortunately, the man had passed away from cancer before Frank could get the statement back into court.

Talking with Frank only increased my fervor to find other innocent men. Since he belonged to the small fraternity of men who were fighting their convictions at the prison, he was able to introduce me to Vernon Joe, a tall, quiet, studious inmate housed but a few cells from me. He was known as the Birdman of Nottoway, due to his habit of feeding breadcrumbs to the gulls that swarmed over the compound every day on his way back from the chow hall. As fate would have it, I had heard about Joe's case during my stint at Southampton some twenty years earlier. He'd been the third teen convicted of the death of a prison guard in the abortive escape attempt that had taken place just before my arrival there. There had been no real evidence against him, only the testimony of two jailhouse snitches who had been promised leniency for their testimony. But Joe had changed his name to Jawwaad Bilal, in accordance with his Muslim faith, so I had never realized that the man we called Joe Bilal was the same man.

Joe had the most compelling case of innocence I encountered, perhaps the most egregious case of a miscarriage of justice in the state. He had simply been in the first isolation cell, at the back of the cell house where the teens who'd initiated the escape decided to place the two guards they'd overpowered. When one of the guards succumbed to injuries suffered from being beaten by inmates involved in the escape, authorities figured Joe was involved—though he had not tried to escape—and they offered deals to two other inmates who testified about the beating of the guard who died. Two years prior to my interviews with Joe, the surviving guard gave a statement clearing Joe of the crime. Yet, he continued to languish in prison.

During my search for innocents I was also told about a man named Mike Billington, a white guy who, it was said, had gotten railroaded on a political charge, his primary offense being that he had been an associate of the political maverick Lyndon LaRouche. LaRouche was arrested in 1989, following his second run for the President of the United States, purportedly for fraudulent campaign fund-raising. Billington and several others had also been arrested and charged with similar offenses. When he was transferred to the honor building, I was able to spend some time talking to him. It seemed that we had met during my time in Oakland, when he worked at a radical bookstore, and as he was also a tennis enthusiast, as well as a writer, we became friends.

Mike introduced me to the ideas of LaRouche and his organization, and I found a commonality of spirit in talking to him. In addition to playing tennis (I more or less became his instructor), we played Scrabble whenever we found the time. Mike never shied from talking about the philosophical background of his organization, and the need to fight, nonviolently, against the powers-that-be, just as Martin Luther King had done. He told me that the organization Lyndon LaRouche had founded still had several hundred members, and published a newspaper and two magazines, which he wrote for. Their philosophy was grounded in what he called the Science of Christian Economy, which stressed the need to understand the history of the world in order to change it.

He introduced me to friends of his who came to visit, most notably Marianna Wertz, the vice president of the Schiller Institute, a cultural organization that stressed the need for the study of Classical European art and philosophy. Marianna began writing to me, and challenging me on many of my set beliefs. When I wrote to her about how I felt that Christian religion had been used to keep black people down, she countered with the fact that the founder of Catholicism was an African, Saint Augustine. She sent me his *Confessions,* and enlightened me about *agape,* the Classical Greek and Christian concept of love of beauty, love of justice, and love of humanity. She sent books from the nineteenth-century German philosopher Gottfried Leibniz and the German writer Friedrich Schiller. They both stressed the idea that beauty was a necessary condition of man, that in order to survive and flourish we had to maintain a sense of optimism. "We must believe that the world is unfolding as it should," Marianna wrote, "and we should relish our roles in bringing about a more perfect world."

These concepts were very much in line with my own, and it was good to know that they had been analyzed and studied and embraced by others, even if the others were people of European descent.

Marianna helped me develop a different spiritual view of the world. I learned of the concept of *imago Dei,* of man being created in the image of God—not because we were supposed to *look* like the white bearded figure supposedly up in heaven looking down upon us, but because we were created in the Creator's *intellectual likeness,* and endowed with the power of creativity by virtue of the divine power of reason. I began to see the power of this divine creative force as something that worked *within,* and came to see the power that meditation and personal prayer could have in reaching that sacred spirit we all possess. I was now able to look upon the world as a beneficent place, discarding my long-held view that everything around me was inimical to my existence.

Further, these new ideas brought to light for me the relationship of beauty to human existence, and thus, the relationship of my role as an artist. The purpose of bringing beauty to the world I had developed during my long incarceration was not in isolation, but was part of the historical role of the artist in human endeavor. Pleased that the more progressive currents of European art and philosophy included my views of human existence, I no longer felt that white society was antithetical to my life. This was a transformation of spiritual and aesthetic faith for me, for now I could believe that my work as a writer wasn't just to fight the powers-that-be, but could be firmly grounded in *agape,* a redemptive love for all humanity. And it was personally redeeming, for, with a new sense of the relationship of God to the spirit within us all, I began to pray, once more.

I'd gone to bed early one August evening, with plans to awaken very early to get some writing done before the prison clamor began. I knew something serious had happened when I woke, well before dawn, to discover two guards wearing armored vests and riot helmets taking count. It was then apparent that the prison was on full lockdown status, and that, at a minimum, we would be locked in our cells twenty-four hours a day for the next several days.

Lockdowns were never announced in advance, so I wasn't really surprised by this one, since the buzz among the prison population had said that a lockdown was imminent. The experienced prisoner knows to be prepared for what is normally one or two weeks of complete isolation. But I was hardly prepared for the news I received later in the day from the TV: two corrections officers and two nurses had been taken hostage by three prisoners, following what authorities were calling "a terribly botched escape attempt" that had included a fourth man. The incident was ended around

5:30 A.M. by a department of corrections strike-force team, with the hostages unharmed. However, according to authorities, eight of the rescuers, including the warden, were slightly wounded when a shotgun was discharged accidentally.

Oh, God, I thought. *I might as well forget this only lasting a few weeks.* It was the worst-case scenario, and there was no telling how long we would be on lock. I tried to take heart, telling myself, *It's nothing you haven't seen before, so you might as well take the opportunity to get the old typewriter pumpin'.*

By day nine of the lockdown, things had really gotten bad. One of our hot meals had been replaced with a bag lunch—four slices of bread, two slices of either cheese or a luncheon meat, and a small piece of plain cake, or more rarely, fruit. Since counselors and administrative personnel had to do the cooking that inmates normally did, the lockdown meals were pared down to those that required a minimum of culinary skill. Today we had chili-mac (an ungodly concoction of macaroni and ground beef), along with three tablespoons of anemic mixed vegetables and a small square of plain cake, all served on a disposable aluminum tray the size of a hardcover book.

We had not yet been allowed out to shower, so I laid newspaper on the concrete floor and bathed at the sink. I thought back on lockdowns I'd endured at the State Pen, often during winters with little or no heat. During one lockdown, authorities had cut off the plumbing for a week, so that contraband couldn't be flushed away, and we weren't allowed out to shower for more than a month. Since then, my attitude had always been, *I can do time on the moon if I have to.* So I wasn't about to let this lockdown, in an honor building, faze me.

Around one o'clock in the morning, the three guards of the shower squad finally got around to our building. They had full riot gear on, and a Rottweiler in tow. One by one, we were handcuffed and escorted to the shower stalls at the center of the dayroom area. As I walked past the huge dog, I turned my head to keep an eye on it, and the beast suddenly lunged against the handler's leash and barked at me with such ferocity that I actually *felt* the force of air upon my face. I walked to the shower with feigned insouciance, but my heart was pumping furiously. I knew I could forget sleeping once I got back to the cell.

Sitting on my bunk later, I thought about what was happening to this place. Information about the hostage incident had been trickling in along with reports of assaults on guards in the cell houses in the main compound, where the treatment of the inmates was said to have been more severe than here in the honor buildings. On the night of the original incident, some men in a section of one building refused to return to their cells, and in at least one section there was open rebellion, with riotous destruction and burning.

The next day a memorandum from the warden was passed out, and the warden himself appeared on the prison's TV system. He announced that there would be no visitations until sometime in October, more than two months away.

Other restrictions would be imposed, he said, including immediate implementation of new department of corrections' guidelines, stripping all prisoners of most personal property: televisions with screens larger than five and a half inches; any tape player other than a Walkman; nearly all personal clothing (jeans, nongray sweatsuits, colored underwear, etc.). And—most devastating for me—all typewriters would be confiscated. *My God*, I thought, *how am I going to write, with any hope of publication, without my typewriter?*

Confronted with this latest development, men were yelling back and forth from their cells, highly upset. Many, like myself, had done ten or fifteen years, obeying all the rules and saving the meager pay from prison jobs to buy a few personal items, possessions that we now had to surrender.

I tried going to bed early, hoping that when I got up things would not seem so dire. I awoke in the middle of the night, sweating and feverish in the humid summer air. Sitting on the edge of my bed, I looked at photographs of my family. My eyes rested upon the school portrait of Roderick, taken shortly before he died. Sorrow overwhelmed me, and I found myself giving in to grief, then to great, mournful sobs.

The tears stopped as suddenly as they'd begun. It had been years since I'd wept so, and I realized that the remnants of grief had been only a trigger, that I was really just feeling sorry for myself, and wondering if I could take much more. *This is no good,* I thought, knowing self-pity to be anathema to the prisoner, and self-doubt the deadliest of sins for the writer. *You've come too far to succumb to this now,* I told myself.

I had precious little time to complete the article on innocent men I'd been working on, and worked feverishly to finish it before guards could get around to my building with the confiscation process. In four days I had it done, and mailed it off to *The New Yorker.* It was just in time, for shortly after 8:00 A.M. the next day, three guards appeared at my cell door. One of them said, officiously, "We're here to escort you to personal property. Pack up everything in your cell, and they will sort out what you have to send out, and what you can keep, over there."

He looked through the long, narrow vertical slot in the steel door, and seeing all the books, magazines, notebooks, and piles of papers I had stacked around the cell, he shook his head in disbelief. "Looks like you're gonna need a lot of boxes," he said, "*and* some time to pack. We'll be back after lunch."

With the eight boxes they pushed into the cell further crowding my space, I sat down and looked at all the papers I'd accumulated, what a practicing freelance writer might have in his office. The only problem was that my office was about as big as a large bathroom, complete with toilet and sink, but with a steel cot where the bathtub would normally be. Now I had to kiss goodbye my accumulation of what I self-deprecatingly thought of as "intellectual debris" from fifteen years of doing time, with no idea when—or if—I might ever be free to see any of it again.

The new rules said twelve books, twelve magazines, twelve audiotapes, period. And "a reasonable number of personal and legal papers." I wondered how much of this stuff they would say was reasonable, when sometimes even I questioned the sanity of trying to hold on to it all.

I finished packing after a full three hours, then sat and smoked, waiting for the guards to return. I contemplated the stacked boxes that filled the eight feet between my cot and the cell door, wondering, *Has all of this work been just a way of staying sane? Where are all the books, plays, and film scripts I dreamed of producing?*

As I walked with the three guards to the property building on the far side of the compound, I was able to absorb rays from a brilliant sun hanging high in a cloudless sky. The air of the Virginia countryside was invigorating. Taking in deep breaths I thought of what Frank DuBose, who still believed his innocence would one day be proved, had said to me as we walked out on the ballpark one day: "Can't you smell freedom in the air?"

Looking away from the fortress-gray buildings of the prison, out through the twin perimeter fences and the gleaming rolls of razor wire, I noticed that the leaves of a distant maple had gone to orange. The season had changed since I was last out of the building.

Two guards pushed a cart laden with my boxes, grumbling. The third, an older black man I knew, walked beside me, making small talk. "Man, things are really changing here," he said, lowering his voice so that the other two couldn't hear him. He said that he was considering a transfer to work at another institution. "But that won't help," he whispered, shaking his head, "'cause it's just as bad—or worse—all over the system now."

On Christmas Eve, after nearly five months, the lockdown officially ended. I sat in the chow hall with the rest of the men in my building, eating the first real chicken-on-the-bone we'd had since summer. But things were far from being back to normal. There was the strictest control of all movement, with attack dogs and escorting guards everywhere we were allowed to go. The gym was closed, recreation time had been dramatically curtailed, and the nightly lock-in time was forevermore 8:00 P.M., instead of 11:30.

The changes were most dramatic in the chow hall. Cellblocks were fed in shifts, and we were segregated from contact with men in other sections. There were guards everywhere, and you were told where to sit. And, most dehumanizing of all, the cafeteria-style serving line had been replaced with a concrete-block wall. Now we received a standard tray, served impersonally by a hand through a small slot at the end of the wall.

I looked at the men from another building who were now in the serving line, as I hurried to finish my food in the allotted ten to fifteen minutes. There was a drab sameness to them, all dressed in the required ill-fitting uniform of prison-made jeans, coarse blue work shirts (which had to be tucked in at all times), and prison-denim jackets.

I spotted I. Sparks, my friend of more than fifteen years, whom I hadn't seen in months. I could only wave and call out a greeting to him, for "mingling" with men from another building was now forbidden. "I'm a grandfather now," he shouted to me, beaming. "I've got some pictures to show you, when we get a chance." Then his smile faded, knowing that I might never get the chance to see them.

Then I spotted a young brother named Paul Williams, the son of an old friend from Danville. Paul was serving a life sentence he'd received when he was sixteen, for firing a wild shot that killed a white man who had chased him after he'd caught Paul burglarizing his car. Though he must have been in his early twenties now, I could still remember his face as a boy, pressed close to the windshield of my truck along with my son's, as they rode with their father and me, so many years ago.

I noticed that there were a large number of young new faces in the mess hall, most of them black, with a few obviously still in their teens. One of these youths, with his lanky frame and light brown complexion, reminded me of my son—or rather of how Rod might have looked were he still alive.

During my meal I thought about how such young men were the primary reason behind the strict new prison policies, calculated to contain the "85 percenters," as they were called—those then entering Virginia's penal system, who had to serve 85 percent of their sentences under new no-parole laws.

When sent to the State Penitentiary in 1981, I was the quintessential angry young black male. But I was able to take college courses for a number of years on a Pell Grant. Vocational training was available, and literacy (or at least enrollment in school) was mandatory for parole consideration. There were a number of therapeutic and resocialization programs, and volunteers who came in from the surrounding communities helped in my effort to become a moral and less angry man.

It bothered me that the focus of the prison system was now on punishment alone. Thousands of young men entering prison, many with the long no-hope sentences (given even to teens as young as thirteen and fourteen), would never get that "last chance to change" I was able to put to good use. It saddened me to think of all the young lives that would be callously thrown away. I knew that had I been born in another time, I might well have suffered the same fate.

The blare of the whistle signaled that our fifteen minutes to eat were up. I was tempted to wrap up my unfinished square of cake in a napkin, but that could get you a stealing charge, and a stint in solitary. I took my tray up to the dishwashing room, where I encountered the youngster I'd been watching. I wanted to say something to him, but was at a loss for words. Instead, I sent a silent good-luck vibe his way as I left, for I knew he was likely to need it.

. . .

Back in the building, though the men were glad to be out of their cells, there was little real holiday spirit. Several watched whatever banality was on the dayroom TV. Most sat at the stainless steel tables, listlessly playing cards to kill time, as others waited for a place at the tables. Some waited to use one of two telephones, while others stood around in bathrobes or towels, waiting for a shower stall to become available.

Most of the men in the section were in their forties or fifties, with some well past sixty. It struck me that, for most of them, prison had become but a waiting game: waiting in line to eat, waiting for a shower or a phone call, for mail or a visit. Or just waiting for tomorrow, for parole and freedom. And for the older ones with no hope of release, waiting for the deliverance of death. I shuddered to think that, at forty-two years of age and with a life sentence, I might well be one of their number.

Recoiling from that thought, I retreated to the solitude of my cell. As I sat making notes of the day, my thoughts turned again to young men and crime. I'd been considering their plight for some time, as it seemed like Rod was on my mind evermore, and I realized that had my son grown into adulthood, I'd surely have taken a greater interest in the problems of youth.

Seeing an increasing stream of angry, sullen young bloods coming into the prison, I wondered what I might say to them in a book, something that would speak to young black men that might help them transform their lives, something a bewildered teen might one day discover while searching the shelves of some prison library, as I did so many years ago.

My journal contained many notes for a work aimed at such young men. One stuck in my mind:

Attended Nation of Islam function tonight, listened to the speeches, and went up to one young Muslim afterward to compliment him on his speech. He said, "I've been wanting to meet you since I got here. I saw the television program you were on a few years back, when I was

at the State Farm. Knowing about you, and reading Nathan
McCall's book, made me want to become a writer. . . ."

Another:

Working in the library today, I gave a young brother a book about
Chester Himes and told him how Himes had begun writing from
prison; in the 1930s. He tells me how he wished he'd been born back
when the Black Panthers and Angela Davis were active, out in Cali-
fornia. "They're my heroes," he says. I tell him that I was out there,
and a member of the Panther Party during that time. He looks at me
and says, "Then you're one of my heroes, too." I am somewhat em-
barrassed by this. Never really thought of myself as a hero. It brings to
mind the question by one of my teachers: "What kind of ancestor
will you make?"

In an effort to understand my own turn toward criminality, I had
come to see that, in a deindustrialized society in which the unedu-
cated young male could no longer support a family (which was normally the entrance into the realm of manhood), he might often find
recourse in that which would make him feel like a man—violence.
Add to that the effects of the popularization of gangsta culture, little
wonder that in many large cities one-third of young black males
were said to be under some form of criminal justice supervision—
jail, prison, parole, or probation.

I recalled the negative influence that *The Godfather* and *Superfly*
movies had upon me in my late teens, and had only to go to my cell
door to see the more pernicious influence of today: A few of the
younger men were watching a gangsta-rap video on the TV out in
the pod. The lyrics were drenched with menace and arrogant disdain, rendered by young men with angry scowls, and a bevy of
nearly naked nymphs dancing around them wantonly, abasing
themselves without shame.

I turned on my own television in an effort to find some relief from my thoughts, only to encounter a news magazine program with a story about gangs. The mother of a sixteen-year-old told of moving from Chicago to Phoenix, desperate to get her son away from a gang. Defiantly, the youth was shown displaying his gang tattoos, and telling the reporter, "I'muh be a Gangsta Disciple till I die."

The next shot was of a recruiter for the Chicago-based gang on a trip to Alabama. In the background one could see graffiti of the Gangsta Disciple's cultlike insignia—a six-pointed star with a devil's pitchfork drawn through it. "I'm here to find the ones who'll be willin' to die for the cause," the recruiter said. "You try to catch 'em 'round thirteen or fourteen," he added, looking all of nineteen himself. His words brought to mind my own recruitment, to the Black Panther Party. But I was chilled by the thought of how fundamentally different that young man's cause was from the cause for which I was once prepared to die.

I was moved to write that night:

> There is no true cause, or movement, for the youth of today, just an undefined membership in an amorphous generation of rage. And with the ready availability of all sorts of weaponry, the situation is ten times more lethal. Caught up in an alternative economy based on drugs and vice, while following irrational dreams fostered by the culture of entertainment, they become grist for the criminal justice mill—bodies for the prison-industrial complex, if not the coroner's wagon.
>
> I can sense an inarticulate rage—gone to hatred, even—among many young men, distrust of anything classified as "white." It has become but justification for nihilism and a terrible moral relativism to them, and I hear it in their rantings: "The White man's education . . . The White man's law . . . So I sold a little dope. So I robbed a man. They rob us every day, don't use no knife or gun. . . ."
>
> I tell the young bloods, when I have occasion to talk to them, "You start out hating white folks, thinking it's all right to rob them,

kill them if necessary, next thing you know you think it's all right to kill your brother, if you feel he has wronged you."

I've encountered so many men in prison who have but their hatred and rage to hold on to. The code of the streets is their only moral guide, and white, or square, society is their sworn enemy. All rebellion is rationalized as being righteous. And I must confess to once having harbored many of the same ideas of cultural rejection.

The slain rapper Tupac Shakur personifies the enraged black man of this age, believing his attitude of rebellion to be license to do whatever he wished—the ultimate existentialist. I saw him interviewed on a television program while out of jail on a million-dollar appeal bond. After blasting a silhouette target at an underground gun range, he presaged his death with the words, "They could smoke me tomorrow. My mama carried me in prison. She was a Black Panther, indicted for conspiracy to blow up buildings and tunnels and shit. I got uncles who been in prison on death row, so this shit ain't no stretch for me."

One eulogy for Shakur in New York had a preacher saying that Tupac believed that he was a revolutionary, like Malcolm X, or Huey Newton. Perhaps—in another time. But this stretched linkage causes me to ask the question: Did the militant Panther rhetoric of the sixties and seventies help give rise to the nihilism of today's youth? And did the rhetoric of justified violence influence my own descent into criminality?

With the end of the lockdown we were able to make calls again, and I rang up the editor I'd been dealing with at *The New Yorker,* Jeffrey Frank, as I'd not heard from him regarding my "The Incarceration of Innocents" piece for a couple of months.

"The bad news," he said, "is that though we think your piece is excellent, our lawyers believe we will run into too many legal problems if we publish it." After all the time they'd taken with it, this was the last thing I wanted to hear.

"But the good news is," he continued, "that we've been intrigued by the lockdown there you talked about in your letters, and we'd like to give you an assignment to do a short piece—maybe fifteen hundred words—on what a lockdown in prison is all about."

Perhaps the rejection of my long article made me hesitant to shout hallelujah. "Fifteen hundred words?" I said. "I'm not sure I can warm up to a subject like that in so little space."

Frank was amazed that a writer would hesitate to take an assignment from his magazine. "Look, Evans," he said, "I have to tell you that people are dying to get into *The New Yorker.* This can be a big opportunity for you. And we're talking about real money here, more than a dollar per word."

This mollified me a bit, but I stuck to my guns and told him, "I might be able to do it with twenty-two hundred words or so."

He said, "Go ahead and work on it, but the catch is that we need it in two weeks' time. Can you deliver by then?"

Hanging up the phone, I dropped my hard persona, shouting "Yes!" out loud.

In less than two weeks I'd written the piece in longhand and dictated it over the phone to a stenographer at the magazine. They liked what I sent so well that they asked me to make it even longer.

Just after the piece ran in the magazine's special "Crime and Punishment" issue at the end of February, I went up for parole for the fourth time. My hearing was only perfunctory, for in Virginia one never gets to go before the board, but is seen by an interviewer, who then sends in a report. Commonwealth's attorney Bill Fuller traveled once more, with my father, to talk to the board chairman, so I could only hope that they'd come through for me.

I now had to prepare myself for the waiting game. Each day I would line up for mail call with the other men in my pod, heart beating a little faster as I neared the control booth, hoping for that letter from the parole board that would yield good news, and not the devastation of another turndown.

One day the mail line seemed extra long. A new female guard was in the control room, and I suspected that several of the men in the queue knew damned well they had no mail, but just wanted to get a good look at her.

To see through the seven-by-fourteen-inch slot in what we called the "cage," you had to climb two wooden steps. As I addressed the guard, all I could see was her pelvis—a tantalizing two feet from my face. Her dowdy uniform did little to diminish her hourglass figure. I asked her a question so that she would have to bend down a bit and I'd be able to see her face and hear her voice, but neither quite lived up to that body.

She handed me a single manila envelope. It wasn't the mail from a female admirer I had been hoping for in the aftermath of my *New Yorker* article—something I'd come to expect after pieces that ran nationally—but it contained an intriguing proposition, nonetheless.

The editor of a new online magazine called *Nerve* had read my piece in *The New Yorker,* and wanted me to write an article about sex in prison, offering $1,000 for one thousand words on the subject. As I read the letter, a young brother we called Shorty who liked to hang around me was nearby, and I told him of the offer.

"Yeah, Hop, you can interview me for that one." Lowering his voice conspiratorially, he said, "I can tell you about how I screwed that faggot Sweet Tee—you know, the one with the titties? Man, I tell you, after ten years in this joint, it was just like screwing a *real* woman."

I started to tell him that I had no inclination to write about anything so sordid—though I figured that, from the editor's description of the magazine as "literate smut," that might be the sort of thing he wanted. But I couldn't help but feel sorry for Shorty; he was locked up at such a young age, I doubted that he'd even had a woman before.

Back in my cell, I thought about the editor's proposal, and the old adage of "write what you know" came to mind. Well, sex was indeed a subject I once believed I knew something about. During the early part of my incarceration, sex was something of an obsession. But after I was transferred to Nottoway, and had to deal with Nancy's death, I worked hard to relegate sexual thoughts to occasional private moments with—what shall I call it?—visual erotica. And for the last few months, I had attempted to completely rout such thinking from my mind, throwing out my girlie magazines, and resolving to remain completely celibate. So I wasn't exactly enthusiastic about the idea of penning a survey of prison sexuality (which, contrary to popular belief, was for the most part a solitary affair in private). As far as I was concerned, Philip Roth's character in his famous novel *Portnoy's Complaint* should have kept his complaint about masturbation to his damn self.

The next day I talked to an older convict named Bruno about the article proposal, talking with him about the times we shared at the old State Pen. "Those definitely were the days," he said. "A man could at least *try* to satisfy his woman with those three visits a week we had then." At The Wall there was a visiting room for children, and one for adults, and in that one many couples engaged in nonstop necking and *heavy* petting. The more daring would actually have intercourse, often by sneaking into the visitors' bathrooms; but sometimes, in the more remote parts of the visiting room, under the folds of long skirts, couples would actually conjoin. Others would slip into gaps between vending machines and have sex. The guards on duty more often than not turned their heads, whether out of sympathy, or embarrassment—or fear of confrontation.

I told Bruno that I'd been thinking of trying to pull a woman again, if only for the pleasure of correspondence, and showed him a letter from a female "fan."

"I remember how you used to be at The Wall, homeboy," he said, "when you was like me, and *always* had a woman *kickin' down the doors* to see you, *every* visiting day. Now you say you haven't had a woman in what—eight years? If you're really getting ready to go out there in them streets, and you've done without a woman for *that* long, you damn sho' don't need one now."

Bruno told me about his wife, whom he had met when she worked as a guard at the Penitentiary. "She gave up her job, and stuck with me through thick and thin on this bit, even though I can't do anything for her sexually these days, like I could at the Penitentiary. Hell, with the video cameras in the visiting room here at Nottoway, and the new rules that say you cain't even *kiss*—much less hug and get close—except at the beginning and end of the visit, I'm lucky she's hanging with me. So I *got* to be loyal to her when I get out.

"But if you pull a woman now, no way she can deserve to have you, over all the women you'll have beckin' at you when you show."

Locked in for the night at 8:00, for a half hour or so I paced the ten feet between the cast-iron cot and steel door of my cell, trying to quiet my libido for the night's work of writing, taking care not to knock over all the books and papers stacked along the wall. After a quick series of contained tennis strokes—the only exercise the old jock still enjoyed—I sat back and smoked a cigarette, thinking about my conversation with Bruno.

Contrary to the way he remembered it, I had never been the real ladies' man. In fact, I'd always been fairly shy, never having the chance to do much dating during my teenage years with the Party, and never making much time with the older comrade sisters. Consequently, my courtship skills were limited before I was locked up.

It was in prison that I had developed something of a "smooth rap," though I was hardly on the level of players like Bruno, who served as my mentors in "the game." Men like Bruno came from the streets, and being able to "mack" and "play ho's" was part of a culture in which it was both a badge of honor *and* an economic expedient. To be able to control women through the combination of psychology and sex—better known as "ho-ology" among practitioners—could often be the key to a "player's" survival.

To a man in prison, having a regular woman visitor was part and parcel of the code of manhood. It was about exercising one's power despite incarceration, and more than that, about finding someone to provide emotional comfort, financial help, and those mirages of freedom that hours in the visiting room could give.

While at the State Pen I'd learned how to attract women by placing classified ads, and would woo those who responded with long romantic letters laced with my poetry and bits of erotica. No doubt many of the women who responded had been attracted to the outlaw/rebel mystique of a man in prison, along with the promise of forbidden sex. Frequent short visits created a heightened sexual tension that seemed to be a turn-on for them—at least for a while. But I'd learned the hard way that such relationships were rarely sustainable, and usually lasted no more than a few months.

And then there was Nancy—and with her death, along with Ben's, my days as a penitentiary player came to an end.

After receiving cards and letters from women in distant states who had read my article, I finally got a live one from Northern Virginia. She wrote that she would like to correspond with a prisoner "because I want to give"—a phrase that set my mind to racing with possibilities. But while her writing was sharp and effervescent, the tone was that of an ingénue: "Is this your first fan letter?" she asked.

Years ago I would have jumped all over her with the full power of my prose. Instead, I sent a short reply, along with a copy of one of my earlier pieces from *The Washington Post,* in hope that her next letter might reveal that there was a modicum of intellectual substance there, and that maybe she was above the age of consent—

which was at least twenty-five for me—a relevant detail should the correspondence lead to something more once I was released.

Her next message answered the first question, making the second one moot. "I can't believe I'm corresponding with a *real writer!*" her letter began. She then wrote two pages of breathless prose about how she had this girlfriend who was obsessed with Stephen Sondheim and how they were going to some confab for him in D.C. that very night. Not a word about who she was or what she thought, or anything about the weighty issues of justice I had addressed in my work. Like so much of American culture, this woman existed entirely on the emotional plane.

As lonely as I was, I decided to beg off by jotting a few words on a postcard to her, telling her politely that I was busy with a deadline for an article and would try to write more when I got the chance. Still, I was glad to have heard from her, for her letter had reminded me of the enticement of the chase, and I began to relish the prospect of enjoying such thrills, with the right woman, once I was released

Another Saturday night . . . and I definitely didn't have nobody. I felt a little burnt out from trying to decide if I wanted to take the assignment from *Nerve.* I was stressed out from waiting to hear from the parole board, and maybe more than a bit lonely, too. For a distraction, I turned on my little six-inch TV, and tuned in to the videos on BET.

A love song was playing, but while the lyrics told of tenderness, the accompanying images were all about sex. In the next video, both the lyrics and the visuals were raunchy, with male singers baring their chests and poking out their pelvises, and girls in sweater-bras and hot pants were dancing around with legs spread, then pushing their rear ends back provocatively as the men grinded behind them. Next, they were on the floor, degrading themselves completely, doing some kind of doggy-style dance.

At once aroused and disgusted, I changed the station to see a series of figure skaters swirling around backward with upturned bottoms. This became too much for my libido as well, and I continued switching channels.

There was an utterly banal "edited for TV" soft-porn movie on the USA Network. On another station, a commercial for Coke had dour secretaries ogling a sweaty deliveryman. One of them wiped condensation from the Coke can the man had just drunk from, and then brought her finger to her mouth. The next channel check had me stopping at *Soul Train,* perhaps the most popular show in the prison, a regular provider of masturbatory fantasies. Though I have to confess that I, too, watched the show ritually years ago, the undulating hips proved too much for me now. It seemed that the tube was telling me tonight, as it did in some form every night, that *I've just gotta have it.*

I turned off the television, and threw a tape of Beethoven's "Eroica" symphony into my Walkman, in an attempt to get my vibe onto a higher level.

I had to ask myself, *Have you become a prude since you've been in prison?* My answer had to be no. Rather, I had chosen celibacy as an exercise, a means of withdrawing from the immediacy of the visceral world, in order to see things with greater clarity. Standing at some remove is a prerequisite for sanity in prison; the immediate world is one of clanking bars, piercing announcements from the loudspeakers, and echoing shouts from the encaged men. The discipline of celibacy would prove to be another means of escape for me—of transcendence, of maintaining self-control.

Still, I wanted a woman so bad that sometimes I would physically *ache*—longing not just for sex, but often only for the feminine voice, the gentle touch—or just the image of someone who cares for me, a photo to tape to my cell wall. But I'd come to understand that human sexuality is a precious and powerful force that affects us both in its presence and in its absence.

After recording my thoughts, I cut the light out and called it a night.

The woman from the control booth comes into my cell, says she needs to hide in the corner so no other officers or inmates can see her. When everyone else has gone to eat, she slides head-first beneath the covers of my bunk and begins to work on me . . .

I awoke to the morning clamor and recorded the dream escapade in my notebook. Writing, even *thinking*, on this subject of sex was beginning to seem to work against my plan of abstinence. But in making my notes that morning, I decided to accept the assignment from *Nerve*—if only to debunk the idea that every man in prison was fucking another man, just to get his rocks off, like the society at large told everyone we had to do. When I called the editor that afternoon, I told him that—take it or leave it—I would write a personal piece that would center on the idea of celibacy, which I would entitle "Sex and the (Somewhat) Celibate Prisoner." He accepted the idea, and I felt glad to have work while I waited for word from the parole board.

I was in the mail line again, with the same mixture of hopefulness and apprehension I'd had to contain for more than two months, waiting for that letter from the board. Adding to the strain was the upcoming anniversary of Roderick's birthday; I was usually a bit blue around that time in late April.

Vernon Joe was at the front of the line, and I watched as he received a letter, tore open the envelope, then crumpled it in his fist. He walked up to me and said, "Hop, I just got some bad news from the courts again. Can I talk to you later?" I told him "sure," and approached the guard's cage with even greater trepidation now, after seeing Joe close to tears.

Indeed, I was handed a letter with the return address of the Virginia Parole Board. I went to my cell to open it, as I was afraid to show any sort of emotion in front of others. I sat down and just looked at the envelope for a minute, steeling myself for bad news.

I finally opened the letter and read the single sheet: "After careful review of your case, the Board has decided to release you to parole supervision."

A great weight seemed to lift from my shoulders, and I knelt in front of my bunk and gave thanks. As I arose from prayer and turned toward my door, I saw that Vernon had come by to talk, and was leaning on the railing of our second-floor tier with his back turned respectfully, to give privacy to my piety. I didn't tell him of my good news, for I did not want to make him feel any worse than he must have already felt. But I thought to myself that perhaps this was a sign that, after getting out, I should never forget those whom I would leave behind.

PART THREE · LIFE AFTER LIFE

CHAPTER ELEVEN

Liberation

*T*he moment arrives. All the years, all the months and days and hours of hoping, of wishing and work and worry, this one moment in time: I walk through the outer doors of Nottoway, I breathe the air of the outside world—the smell of home and freedom in the immediate future. But the feeling of being truly free is in the distance: I am still enchained, handcuffed, and under armed guard. I am locked into the back of a prison van that will transport me to the parole office in Danville. Ironically, I won't be fully free until I am returned to the hometown I once loathed, a place that now represents my liberation.

The date was May 8, 1997. The driver of the van was a short, stocky black guard with whom I once had a fairly serious confrontation. But on this day he was all smiles, for I was no longer just an inmate, but a man who had done sixteen years of a life sentence, won out over an oppressive system, and was now on his way to freedom. While he tried to make small talk through the bulletproof Plexiglas that separated us, I did my best to make it apparent that I wasn't in the mood for conversation. I was in another world—a whole new world, it seemed. I'd not been outside the fences of Nottoway since being taken there eight years before.

I watched the passing roadside with a sense of wonderment. The cars all seemed new, the greenery of the countryside shimmered in the brilliant sunlight of a noonday sun, the roadside flowers blooming miraculously. People, *free people,* were at roadside fruit stands, a farmer was on a tractor plowing his field, a young couple in a yard playfully sprayed each other with water while washing a car. I recorded the images on a pad I'd brought along, the writing that was once my refuge now a source of new joy out in this rarefied air.

The guard asked me how it felt to finally be free, but I had no way of explaining to him that I wanted only to perceive—didn't want to feel, to even *try* to feel. I had dwelled far too long in a place where I had to repress emotion. I'd spent years agonizing about how the emotion of rage had imprisoned me, had led to a *fear* of feeling. Out of that fear had grown a subconscious recognition that the repression of the pain of injustice, of the hurt and sorrow that at every turn seemed to dash away any love I'd dared to feel, may well have been key to the preservation of my sanity. Paradoxically, the ability *not to feel* comingled with an ability to render the irrepressible emotions of the inner heart in the pages of my writing. Now, it could be that the key to my survival in the outside world would be finding a way to unlock my emotions, and learn to love fully again. But I wasn't ready to face that question on this day.

So I told the guard, "Can't really tell yet, I'm just taking it all in." I was trying to get into a more mellow approach to life, when the hard con, still in me, really wanted to tell him, *Just leave me the fuck alone, if you don't mind.*

I recalled the day he and I had locked horns. He'd been on shakedown duty outside the honor building, and while patting me down, he felt a bulge in the waistband of my underwear, felt the package of bread and cheese I was trying to smuggle in from the chow hall. It was an unwritten rule that the guards ignored such soft things, and were looking only for hard objects that might signal a weapon. But he had taken extra time to damn near fondle the little plastic-wrapped parcel, and then had asked me, "What is this?"

When a prisoner is caught in such situations, he usually just coughs up the contraband and the guard tells him to drop it in the trashcan at the entranceway—since he knows that being written up for any minor charge (like possession of contraband) will get him kicked out of the honor building, with a black mark on any chance for parole. On this particular day, however, I was not in a good mood. I'd paid two packs for that cheese (he could have had the goddamn bread), so I spun away from him quickly, looked him in the eye, and told him, "Don't start nothin', won't be nothin'." I then turned and walked into the building. While I feared he'd follow, maybe even blow his whistle to get help from other guards, he must have feared a serious confrontation over a minuscule matter. I was the high-profile writer-inmate on television and in the newspaper, and for all he knew, I might have had more pull than he with the administration.

The guard had seemingly forgotten all of that now, but it was still hard for me to think of him as anything other than one of the enemy. After finding his attempts to strike up a conversation fruitless, he turned on the van's radio to a top-40 station, the kind of music I'd avoided for years. Amazingly, the first cut up was "Fantasy," by sex kitten Mariah Carey, yet another escapist aggrandizement of sexual promiscuity. The end of the tune was a singsong question-and-answer chant that spoke about the prevalence of incarceration in the country, repeating several times: "Whatcha gonna do when you get out of jail?" The answer, "I'm gonna have some fun," struck me as going to the heart of popular culture—the desire for mind-numbing pleasure.

I resolved then to resist the temptations of the new world I was entering, to continue my self-discipline, and to remain celibate for my first weeks, or months, of freedom.

· · ·

After two hours on the road we finally came upon a sign that read DANVILLE CITY LIMITS. My mood brightened, and I could no longer remain passive. Pulling up to the parole office in the heart of the city's downtown, the guard opened the van door and helped me step down onto Market Street. Part of me wanted to do something melodramatic like kiss the ground, but then I noticed that we were just opposite of what had been the "colored" side entrance of Woolworth's, and the impulse quickly faded.

The chief of the office came out to meet us, which was perhaps a measure of the high priority given my case, and the involvement of the commonwealth's attorney. When the guard snapped the key and the handcuffs fell from my wrists, I finally felt a real degree of freedom. However, I knew that I was still in custody, now to be driven to my parents' home, where a monitoring unit would be bound to my ankle—a sort of new-age slave shackle, to my mind. But, striving to stay the optimist now, I decided to look upon this required ninety-day encumbrance as a positive tool, as it would keep me close to home. I'd have to be in by eight o'clock each evening, but I figured that would give me a chance to bond again with my parents.

We approached my childhood home on the hilly road I knew so well, the road I'd walked so many days to catch the buses that had taken me to the segregated elementary, and then the integrated high school that had changed my perception of life so drastically. It was during this last home stretch that excitement began to overwhelm me, for soon I would see the home I'd not seen in sixteen years, and embrace the mother I hadn't kissed in more than a year.

I rang the doorbell, and while we waited for Mama, in the throes of her advancing Parkinson's, to make it to the door, I worked hard not to let the parole men see my emotions. And then Mama was there, opening the door for me. With her smile at seeing me, and the length of her lingering kiss and hug, I was filled with a joy beyond measure: the celebration in her eyes was all that I needed to finally feel free.

As the parole officers hooked up the monitoring unit to the telephone (it would sound an alarm at some distant station if I was not home between the hours of 8:00 P.M. and 7:00 A.M.), I learned from Mama that Pop was still at work. She told me that, because it was Friday, he had to be there to sign the checks for the employees. Though I was able to hide it, I was disappointed that he hadn't been there to greet me.

After my watchers were gone, I felt a sense of calm satisfaction, and peace. I sat at the bar in the kitchen while Mama prepared my favorite meal of chicken and rice. I was touched to see the tenacity of the slow, deliberate movements of a woman struggling against her disability, trying hard to remain viable.

Pop arrived just as the food was done, and when we sat down to eat, he asked a special blessing upon our meal: "Thank you, Lord, for this food, prepared for the nourishment of our bodies, for Christ's sake. And thank you, most precious Heavenly Father, for delivering our son home to us, once more. Amen."

We ate in silence, just savoring being together. After dinner, we watched television, making small talk, and I soaked in the feeling of home. When the time came for me to turn in for bed, Mama said, "You know, it's strange, Derrell. I seems like you really haven't been gone so long. It's like you've just been away on a long trip."

The next morning was a Saturday, and after breakfast I rode with Pop into town in his truck. Ever the workaholic, he had his men working half a day to finish a job. But I didn't mind, as it was good just to hang out with him.

At his office building he proudly displayed the improvements he'd made while I was gone, showing off a new storage building and garage, filled with a mixture of new and badly aging equipment. Then he took me into his private office in the back of the main building and sat down with me.

"You know, Derrell, I built all of this thinking that you would one day take over," he said. "That's what I told the parole board when Mr. Fuller and I went up to see them for you. But since then I gave it some thought." Pausing, he seemed a bit nervous, and fiddled with the phone book and some of the papers on his desk. "I think that maybe you'll want to give that writing business of yours a try first, seeing how you can make four thousand dollars from one piece of writing." I'd had him cash the check I'd gotten for my piece in *The New Yorker,* and he'd been impressed. "You can make more in a week than I can clear in a month, with all my labor and overhead expenses."

He paused to clear his throat. "While it's been my dream for you to come into the business with me, especially since I'm getting a little old now"—he smiled here, as if he weren't *really* getting old—"I want you to live *your* dream now. You can have this office back here to work on your writing, and I'll do anything I can to help you."

I was touched. I knew that this was his way of passing the baton in a selfless way, since most every father wants his son to follow in his footsteps.

"Thank you, Pop," I said. "I can write back here, but I still want to help you out on the business end of things." I said this because I wondered just how long he could keep his business going. I'd talked to his secretary and his men, and they had told me, "Your father's starting to lose it. He forgets things quickly, has gotten so he can't follow what's going on in the office, and his driving is getting real bad." I feared that these symptoms might signal the onset of Alzheimer's disease, an affliction that had plagued three of his sisters already. "I think I can handle both things at the same time," I told him.

From the office we went to the bank, where Pop had opened an account for me with the proceeds of my *New Yorker* piece. Outside the bank I happened to run into a divorcée who, back during high school, had had the hots for me. After a hug that lasted a little too long, she jotted down her home number and address on the back of her business card, saying in a voice full of invitation, "Give me a call—or just come by." I pocketed the card, but the only attraction I felt was of a baser nature, and I knew that I wouldn't be calling her anytime soon.

From the bank Pop took me to Ryan's, an all-you-can-eat buffet. I was astounded by the variety of food available: fresh fruit, a salad bar with everything, all kinds of vegetables and meats, and a bakery bar that was out of this world. I ate until I was "full as a tick," as Pop liked to say. I didn't realize that all this good food would find me ballooning some twenty-five pounds in less than two months.

We then went to Danville's only mall, an addition that during my absence had become the city's major regional attraction. I felt blessed to have been released the weekend of Mother's Day, and we shopped for a dress jacket, shirt, and tie for church, for Sunday's grand occasion. It was a thrill to have real cash money in my pocket to spend for these things.

After getting everything except shoes, we went to the men's shoe department of the main store in the mall. There was something familiar about the saleswoman who assisted me. As she stooped to help me with a nice pair of loafers, I took note of her name tag, and realized that she was the girlfriend—and now, the wife—of the codefendant whose testimony had helped net me the life sentence.

I acted as if I didn't know who she was, bought the shoes, and then turned to leave. But something stopped me, and I went back and said to her, "If you see Jerry, do me a favor. Tell him there are no hard feelings."

Driving home with Pop, I felt I had passed some sort of test. A part of me had wondered if, were I ever to encounter Jerry again, remnants of hatred would spark a desire to do him the great harm I had once visualized. I knew then that I was a different man. I needn't fear the violence that used to dwell within me.

The next day Mama, Pop, and I attended the Mother's Day service at High Street Baptist. We arrived early, and I was greeted with hugs by many folk from my childhood. It was truly heartwarming. I was unused to all the embraces, such obvious affection. Then the childhood sweetheart I'd dated just before my incarceration, a woman who had continued to appear in my dreams during my years in prison, came up and drew me into a long embrace—and then began to cry. "Oh, Derrell, it's so wonderful to see you again," she said. "I'm so glad you're back."

I was nearly overcome with emotion—to have such love displayed for me, the prodigal son. I fought back tears as the choir came in singing, "We're marching . . . to Zion . . . beautiful, beautiful Zi-on." But I still felt the unwritten rule of the penitentiary: Never let anyone see you cry.

I started to work on Monday, setting up my office space with the typewriter I'd sent home, getting the phone company out to put in a business line, and working to finish the piece for *Nerve* magazine I'd begun at Nottoway—as the editors there were on me to submit a draft by the end of the week.

I'd spent the preceding evening leafing through the Virginia driver's manual, and went to take the test that afternoon, thinking I was so smart I'd breeze through it with no problem. Big mistake. Much to my chagrin, I failed the test. I had to wait until the next day to try again, and a bit of more-serious study pulled me through.

Once I had my license, Pop lent me one of his old trucks to use after I quit work at the office around six in the evening. Each night I had the eight o'clock curfew, so I had to finish my rounds quickly. Shopping for clothing essentials and food for my semivegetarian diet was first on my list. I would run through stores like I was a contestant on the old program *Supermarket Sweep,* throwing anything I saw that I wanted into the basket.

Pop accompanied me on my first foray into a grocery store, and he could not believe it when the bill at the checkout came to over a hundred dollars. He would talk about it for days: "I've been living for seventy-six years, and I've *never* heard of *anybody* spending one hundred dollars in a grocery store at one time."

Most mornings, when I would ride to work with my father in

his truck, I'd gently insist on driving—for his safety and mine, since his driving skills had become highly suspect. One morning, we passed a road gang from the city's correctional unit, commonly referred to as the "City Farm": young men using mowers and modern weed eaters (instead of sling blades) on the grass and weeds along the right-of-way, as a fat white sheriff's deputy with a shotgun watched.

"Look at that," Pop said. "Every last one of those boys is black. Now I know they all have done wrong, but you can't tell me that just as many white boys aren't doing wrong, too." This observation, coming from the man I once rebelled against because of his conservative "colored" views, blew me away. "You know," he continued, "I believe they go into our communities just tryin' to catch blacks doin' wrong, just so they can lock them up." I realized that time had a way of presenting the truth to all of us, in one way or another.

I pushed hard, working at Pop's old desk, to get work as a freelancer, and was lucky enough to land a nice gig writing a piece on my homecoming for the highly regarded online magazine *Slate*. I was also in touch with a film producer who was interested in my work. All the while I tried to stay in tune with what was happening in the office. I couldn't help but worry about Pop, who still tried to work, as he had for thirty-five years, ten to twelve hours a day. I felt that I needed to begin taking over some things for him, but I was discovering that there just wasn't enough time in the real world to do all the things one might have dreamed of.

I was spending too much time on the phone, too much time getting help with a computer given to me by a cousin, and too much time talking to editors, to think of doing much else. A conversation I had with one magazine editor lasted more than an hour, only to have my piece on innocent men again declined.

I'd never been one to deal very well with rejection, and one day, after hearing that still another publication didn't want to present my view of truth to the world, I got out of the office as fast as I could, borrowing one of Pop's trucks, then taking a meandering route home. I drove up Stuart Street, where my family had lived until I was six. The area was even more depressed, our grand old brick house boarded up. But as soon as I entered the white community on the street above, the contrast was stark: Lawns were manicured, homes immaculately maintained. I remembered working on many of the well-kept yards when I worked for my father. But I was pleased to note that a few black families now lived in the area.

As I drove on the narrow country road out near my parents' place, I passed a young white man whose car had broken down, and stopped to offer him a lift. It struck me that in years past, he probably would have never accepted the ride. Nor, perhaps, would I have given it.

After I dropped him off, I decided to stop at an old abandoned grain mill, and walked through brush down to the narrow Sandy River that winded down behind our house, the stream in which my cousins and I had had to swim, as the Pine Lake resort and pool just up the road were (and still remain) exclusively white.

Clouds and drizzle had brought on an early dusk, and in focusing on the effect of light rain and wind on the water, I didn't at first notice the thin rope, hanging from a tree limb, above the bank of the river.

My first, irrational thought was that this was a hangman's noose, and that I should cut it down. Then, remembering that I no longer carried a knife, as I had during my wilder days, I was caught in the moment—seeing clearly that the rope could bear only a child's weight. I then recalled how, as children, my cousins and I would swing from such monkey vines into this same river. Swept with emotion, thinking of how darkened the imagery in my mind had become since that simpler time, I smiled at the childhood memory, returned to the truck, and made my way home.

My parole officer had told me, "Prison is the crazy place. Out here is what's normal, so it won't be hard for you to fit back in." But I began to realize that it wouldn't be quite so simple. Trying to settle into the life of an artist, along with the responsibilities of family, proved to be challenging. While I felt that there was a higher purpose to my writing, there seemed an almost primordial necessity to take care of family. I had to recognize that there was some serious guilt involved, with my having been away for so long.

When people asked me, "How does it feel to be free?" (the question reminding me of news reporters rudely shoving microphones into the faces of folk, totally uncaring but hoping for the sensational answer), I responded simply, "I feel very sober." It was an honest answer, since I was still repressing as much emotion as possible, while fighting against culture—and emotional—shock.

One day, while going into the office, I spotted a man driving by in a Cadillac. He looked so familiar that I ran down the sidewalk abreast of his car until it stopped at the corner—and lo and behold it was my old friend Mike Fisher. "Mike," I yelled, as the light changed. He glanced at me as he pulled off, quickly made a dangerous U-turn against traffic, and pulled into the driveway of the office.

"Derrell, I can't believe it's you," he exclaimed as he got out of the car, hugging me and actually kissing me on the cheek. "Man, you don't know how much I've thought of you, how glad I am to see that you're back."

As it happened, Mike had worked in television news until he became bureau chief for a CBS affiliate in Fort Worth, Texas, but had recently come back to Danville to help run the funeral home his dad had cofounded. "You don't know what it means to me to have you back, to have someone in this country town to talk to about writing." Indeed, it would turn out that Mike would become the one true friend I'd have in Danville, the only source of serious conversation I'd find in the blue-collar mill town.

Other friends from my previous lives would stop by the office during those first weeks, after hearing that Hop was back in town. One man gave me the deal on many of the old gang I used to hang with, a group I'd scrupulously avoided since my return.

"Man, half are in prison, and a lot of them are dead," he said. Then he started ticking off the names of those who were "out there on that crack," and I got a picture of just how devastating the cocaine scourge had been, even in a community as small as this. "Man, that cook-'em-up came through Danville like Grant went through Richmond," he said, "and it ain't let up yet." Then he asked if I had a few dollars I could lend him, and gave me his phone number—which I "misplaced" as soon as he was out the door.

Another old reefer-smokin' partner stopped by, with the question I was often asked: "You get any yet?"

He laughed when I told him, "I'm just taking it slow, brother, checking out my options."

"Man, that ain't no way to be after all the years *you* been gone. You want me to set you up, just let me know. Won't be no problem hookin' you up with a ho. The price of pussy is at an all-time low, down to the cost of a rock of cocaine now," said the notorious ladies man.

When I told him I was holding off on sex for a while, he just shook his head in disbelief, and tried to get me to change my mind by recounting an escapade from high school, when we'd double-dated twin sisters. He was equally shocked when I declined his offer of going out for a drink, having no comprehension when I told him that I'd sworn off *all* forms of getting high.

After he left the office, I reflected on my determination to abstain from drinking—which didn't seem to be all that hard—but I knew that remaining celibate would really be a test. Was I afraid to surrender my mind to the intoxication available in a sex-crazed world? Or was it simply emotion I feared? Somehow I felt a need to make sure that my first sex after prison would be wedded, at least, to the hope of love.

Not that I wasn't tempted in those first days, just to get my wick wet, as the saying goes. I was set up on a luncheon date with a young woman by one of the men who worked for my father. While drinking iced tea she'd told me, "I just want to be up-front with you, so I've got to tell you that I'm pregnant." I played it off, saying that I thought bringing a child into the world was wonderful. But the next day the workman who'd introduced us told me that the girl had asked him to come replace the locks on her apartment so that the baby's daddy couldn't get in anymore. I knew then that this was a situation with too much drama for me.

My father had made his attractive secretary available to me for typing, filing, and other duties. She had been a fantasy voice on the phone for years, but I knew better than to try to mix business with pleasure. ("You never want to screw around with your secretary," Pop had told me some years ago. "It's bad business to let a woman who *knows* what's in your pocket to be *in* your pocket, too.") Then, there was this stone fox who lived in one of the apartments below the office that Pop rented out. She emerged periodically, sirenlike, in Daisy Duke short-shorts and a halter top, large nipples showing through as if they were throbbing with fever. Though I thought of scenarios with these women, I was too shy—or too cautious—to approach any of them.

My friend the womanizer stopped by the office again one morning, wearing last night's liquor as his morning cologne, singing a song of woe about how two of his women had bumped heads at his house the preceding evening. "I'm thinking about trying out that celibacy thing you seem to be into," he said. "These young broads are nothin' but trouble. After you get your thing off, there's nothing left."

His comments reinforced my thinking about sex. The desire for sex is often a guise for the broader need for human joy, but it seldom satisfies that hunger. I had learned to satisfy my deepest passions through writing. I didn't need the periodic comfort of another's flesh to feel at one with the world. While I continued to long for a soul mate, I needed just to think of myself as at one with the universe of freedom that was unfolding before me.

• • •

Midnight, alone on the porch of my parents' home in the country, I began celebrating my 43rd birthday, my first in freedom in more than sixteen years. I felt content in the enchantment of flowering shrubs and trees bathed in the moon glow of the June night. The trees had grown to giants in my absence, and brought to memory the six-year-old Derrell who had "helped" his father plant these trees as saplings. A warm breeze began to blow, and the magical imagery, along with the song of crickets punctuated by the bark of a dog in the distance, brought on a great peace. I was prompted to pen the first poem I'd conceived in many a year.

This birthday gift from the Muse gave me a renewed sense of hope, taking me back a decade or more, to when I'd been a serious poet. Back then the verse had seemed to dry up, during my last years inside—though I suppose it continued to inform my prose. I remembered what my friend Greg Donovan had told me at the time. "Don't worry. Poetry is based upon beauty, and you've precious little of that in prison. But believe, it *will* return someday."

Reading over the poem, I wasn't quite pleased with my effort. But I felt good about it, for the verse had been inspired by the hope of new love. On my first visit to Richmond I had connected with Michelle, a college instructor with whom I'd corresponded, on a Platonic level, while I was at Nottoway—whom I'd now taken to calling "my beautiful professor." She was coming in the morning to visit me for my birthday, then to take me back to her home.

Michelle arrived early, for we planned to spend part of the day in Danville before driving up to her place in Richmond. In an act of chivalry, I went to the large magnolia tree in the yard and picked a blossom for her, taking delight in her smile and the gentle reward of a kiss when I presented it to her.

She allowed me to drive, and I felt a thrill at being behind the wheel of a sporty car with a stick shift, relishing the sense of power and control as I maneuvered through the curves of the country roads on the way into the city. While Danville has relatively few scenic locations, Michelle seemed to take joy in the simplest of pleasures: stopping to see the decayed remnants of the great house in the neighborhood where I grew up; taking photos with a little girl on the footbridge in a small picnic area by the city's river; being held as we watched ducks gliding in V formation on the wide expanse of water.

Impulsively, she removed her sandals and waded a little way out into the river, which was shimmering in the early summer sun. "I just want the feeling of being in the river of your fathers," she said. Taking a photo of her as she held up the hem of her powder-blue sundress to keep it from getting wet, I felt a moment of tenderness: a little something melting within, which at once warmed—and frightened—me.

On the road to Richmond she nestled beneath my arm and dozed, while I contemplated this new intimacy, after years of celibacy. While the heartbreak I'd endured inside prison was still with me, it was hard to keep my guard up with such a dear woman. It was almost like being in high school again, with the unreal feeling of a dream come true, of moments in time that couldn't *really* be real.

On this first long drive I enjoyed the liberating spirit of being on the highway, as if I were soaring toward a new life. I recalled how, at Nottoway, I would sometimes try to get this feeling of rolling freely by hopping onto the utility cart, when I had to move my possessions from one building to another. I would propel it like a scooter, and think of the thrill children must feel on tricycles, skates, and bikes.

Thoughts of Nottoway were inescapable, as route 360 from Danville to Richmond goes past the prison. As I drove that hundred miles, I could not help but think of how my parents had so dutifully made that trip to visit me every month, until my mother became so infirm that she could not travel.

Arriving at the turnoff to the prison, on impulse I decided to circle the facility, in order to recall the feeling of walking out through the gates, to relive the sense of accomplishment. On the outside of the fences laced with razor wire, I thought of the eleven hundred men still trapped there. Especially in my thoughts were the innocent men whose cases I'd written about, as I still felt the pain of not having gotten their stories published.

Michelle awoke, but remained silent until I got back on the highway. Then she said, "Don't you think you're torturing yourself a bit? I mean, I know you left friends there, but—"

"No," I told her, cutting her off, feeling a little chill come over my demeanor, as I explained to her how I never really developed real friendships inside. "You learn early that it's best not to have very many friends in prison," I said, "because it's like being a slave on a plantation—you never know when someone you've become attached to might get shipped off.

"It's more about needing to stay in touch with where I've been, because I've got to continue writing on the subject," I said with resolve. "There's no need in having freedom, if you're afraid to use it."

How to describe first sex after sixteen years? Rushed and fevered, an expression of power and manhood. Then slow and loving, the feeling of melding with another, the miracle of touching, naked torsos entwined, giving and yielding; and then the release of pent-up passion melting away in an aftermath of gentle languor—the feeling of being fully human, once more.

CHAPTER TWELVE

Even Freedom Means Struggle

In August I became fired up when I learned that famed Pulitzer Prize–winning playwright August Wilson was going to be in Winston-Salem, where he was having a production of his very first play presented at the National Black Theatre Festival. After contacting *Emerge,* the national news magazine owned by the cable conglomerate BET, an editor there arranged for me to interview Wilson for a profile. This gave me the added incentive I needed to face a responsibility I had put off—to return to the city to visit Ruth, and to go by Rod's gravesite.

I drove the familiar eighty miles to Winston-Salem in a sturdy, fifteen-year-old Toyota Cressida my uncle Carroll had given me. Arriving in the city's downtown area, I discovered noticeable growth, most especially the new, grand skyscraper hotel, the Adams Mark. The headquarters of the festival was there, and entering the lobby I found it filled with hundreds of black folk, many of them in flamboyant African regalia, most dressed in the tony garb of a new black middle class I had never seen before. There were people from all over the country, theater and arts supporters who migrated every two years to this ten-day event featuring plays by production com-

panies from all over the country. I was impressed, to say the least, to
see so many involved—and *believing in*—black theater, sending the
latent playwright in me to dreaming once more.

I had revered Wilson ever since I'd read about him in *The New
York Times* theater section, which I had read religiously in the
prison library. One day I had mustered the nerve to write to
Charles Dutton—a former prisoner who'd received acclaim on
Broadway in Wilson's plays before going on to become a TV star in
the series *Roc*—telling him of my interest in writing for the stage.
He had sent me all of Wilson's published works, which I had used
to further the work on my historical play about Maggie Walker. But
reading Wilson's plays had not prepared me for the impact of viewing my first serious theater production: his *Jitney*—which, as fate
would have it, was presented in the auditorium of my alma mater,
R. J. Reynolds High School.

Memories of my time at the school during my early Panther
days melded with the relevance of Wilson's story to my own personal life: the militant son of the owner of a jitney (or gypsy cab)
business comes home after a stint in prison; and after confronting
personal demons and encountering friction with his father, he has
to take over the business in the wake of his father's death.

While interviewing Wilson in the restaurant of the hotel after
the play, I told him about my Panther past in Winston-Salem; about
how I'd encountered his work through Charles Dutton, while in
prison; and of my current situation, with my aging father and the
likelihood that I'd soon face the decision of taking over the business
he'd established during an era when black businesses had to overcome great odds.

Wilson warmed to me after hearing my personal story, and said,
"Well, I guess this has been a double—or triple—homecoming for
you." Over the next hour he opened up to me about many things,
including how *Jitney* was his first play, the one in which he'd discovered his voice. He had transcended the formalist language of the
poet he'd been, by listening to the cadences of the down-to-earth

language of the black community he'd grown up in. He expounded upon how the visions of his work presented themselves almost miraculously, as if of their own volition; how such visions came to him as he wrote on notepads in bars filled with people, later transcribing it all while standing before his typewriter in the basement of his home.

I left the interview with the feeling that I had not only the material for a wonderfully revealing piece about the man many critics proclaimed to be "America's greatest living playwright," but I had also gained inspiration to continue my efforts to realize my own visions, someday, on stage.

The play and the interview had taken longer than I'd thought, so it was early evening by the time I reached Ruth's home. The route I drove took me by the site of the old Panther headquarters, which I discovered had been torn down and replaced by a home for the elderly. I stopped anyway, in homage to my time there. Getting out of the car, I discovered that part of the inscription I'd carved into the sidewalk still remained: "If ever I should break my stride/or falter at my comrade's side/This oath will surely kill me!"

Ruth had a very nice two-story home not far from the old office. She greeted me at the door with a warm hug. We'd not seen each other since the time, a few months after Rod's death, when she'd come to visit me at the State Penitentiary in Richmond.

When I told her that I still wanted to go to the cemetery to visit Rod's grave, she said, "Don't try to put too much on yourself, Derrell. I've had to learn," the emotion in her voice threatening to trigger tears from me, "that at some point you have to realize that Rod has left us. He's gone. And that's the only way you can go on dealing with those of us who are still living, and move on with your own life."

I realized then that she'd given me the greatest gift that I could receive, as beset with latent grief as I was: an offering of absolution, of forgiveness, along with the understanding that I *would* have to go on living, though I still felt an overwhelming sense of guilt at not having been there for Rod, and for her—more guilt than I felt the strength to endure.

Talking with Ruth was one of the hardest things I'd ever had to do. It became apparent that she still had hope for our marriage. When I told her that I'd begun a relationship with a woman in Richmond, someone I'd befriended while still incarcerated, the pain she felt was palpable.

"I don't know why you couldn't wait to see if things could work out with us," she said. "Didn't you want to even come see me first, and realize what we might build upon here in Winston?" Indeed, I could not help but see how well Ruth had done, especially considering all she'd gone through. She was the principal of a charter school that had been founded by her sister Hazel, my former Panther comrade. But while I felt proud of what she'd done, and knew that Winston would be a fine place to begin again, I just couldn't handle the emotion it would take to try to make it with her once more.

She saw it in my eyes, and said, "I think I know what the deal is, Derrell. I know Rod's death was hard on you, being locked up like that. So I'll just have to try and understand. But I have no doubt that if Rod were alive today, things would be different for you and me."

During the drive back to Danville that night, I felt swamped by feeling—and emotion was something I still wasn't equipped to deal with very well. In prison, emotion had been an enemy, and love was something I'd grown to fear. But out here in the free world, I felt as if I were melting down, for the emotions of love and fear were releasing that of pain, as well.

Back in Danville, the old nemesis of rejection reared its head once more. Though I had a dynamite interview with Wilson in hand, the editor at *Emerge* told me that her editor-in-chief demanded that I write the profile on spec (that is, without formal assignment, so that the publication could reject the piece and leave the writer without compensation for any work done).

"Bullshit," I told her, and immediately had to apologize for letting the convict/street language come out. I tried to explain to her: "Look, I've written for *The New Yorker*, and I've got people wanting to publish me all over the place. You've got a chance to publish something on a level you don't see every day, and I don't have the time to write something for you that you just *might* not see fit to accept." But she kindly let me know that that was just how it was with the politics of magazine publishing, and apologized that she could not sell her boss on the idea of assigning the piece to me.

Then I received word from an editor I'd made contact with at *George,* the magazine founded by John F. Kennedy, Jr. "I'm sorry," he told me, "we can't use the piece you sent us about the innocent men. But we like the proposal you sent about writing a piece on Geronimo Pratt, and would like to give you an assignment to go out to California to do it." I was elated. Geronimo, the former Black Panther Party leader who was perhaps the nation's most famous political prisoner since Angela Davis, and a hero in Panther lore, had just been released from prison in California. He'd been exonerated after twenty-seven years of incarceration in a racially charged case of murder.

And so it was, just after my return from confronting memories of my Panther past in Winston-Salem, I was now going back to Oakland. With a renewed sense of mission, I would be able to relive the thrill that I'd had as the young revolutionary correspondent, twenty-five years before. I would also, however, have to face the demons of my past in California.

The airliner lifted from the runway, soaring above the North Carolina countryside, settling just above a sea of clouds. A metaphor for my new freedom, I thought, before remembering that clouds have no substance to cushion a fall, and that I was strapped inside a crowded, hollow machine no larger than some of the cellblocks I had seen.

Sit back and enjoy your first plane ride in twenty-five years, I had to tell myself. Then early turbulence brought me close to trembling.

The flight was a re-creation of the route I'd taken to the West Coast as a young Panther. But now I had an assignment for a top magazine to get a story set large both in my past and my present: the story of a Panther leader who was a living symbol of the injustices visited upon radicals during the turbulent years of the Black Power Movement. Geronimo had become well known because of the support of groups like Amnesty International, as well as his having had the most famous of attorneys, Johnnie Cochran, who called the release of "my good friend and brother Geronimo" his greatest victory. My Panther connections had gotten me access to Geronimo, allowing me to get to the head of the line despite his having a legal team fielding scores of proposals from folk wanting to do books and films about the case.

My job was to find out how Geronimo was adjusting to freedom and sudden celebrity after nearly three decades of imprisonment. It had finally been proved that the LAPD and the FBI had conspired to "neutralize" him. With a sentence of twenty-five years to life, he'd spent eight years in solitary confinement, then years and years fending off attacks from both authorities and inmates while doing hard time inside California's worst prisons: San Quentin, Folsom, Pelican Bay.

FBI files had revealed the extent of the conspiracy against Geronimo, all a part of the FBI's COINTELPRO program. The campaign against the Panther Party was foremost in my mind, for just before I'd embarked on this assignment, I was introduced to the Internet, and had discovered COINTELPRO files that documented how the FBI had tracked *me,* beginning with the period I worked with the Party in Winston, and continuing with surveillance of my movements when I went out to Oakland.

While we'd always been told that we were being watched, actually learning of how they had tracked a rank-and-file member like me helped in my understanding of the FBI's focus on leaders like Geronimo, and how it had culminated in his being framed for the murder of a Santa Monica schoolteacher during a robbery. Most damning of all was the fact that he'd been at a Panther meeting in Oakland when the crime he was accused of had taken place.

The FBI held back wiretaps of that meeting which would have acquitted him. And, because of the internecine rivalry between Geronimo and Huey Newton fostered by COINTELPRO's dirty tricks (they'd sent forged letters that led each of them to believe that the other was planning to assassinate him), Party members who might have cleared Geronimo of the charges were ordered not to testify at his trial.

I'd followed Geronimo's story, even while I was in prison with wounds still festering from my own Panther experience in Oakland. I thought then, *How could a man handle such an onslaught, from former comrades and the government, without being consumed by hatred and rage?* And now, as I flew back into my own past life as a Panther, I had to wonder: *What shadows might such treachery leave upon the soul?*

It was a cool day for late August, and the welcome-home rally for Geronimo, held in a small park in West Oakland, was a grand gathering that took me back to my past life in the Party. There were hundreds of people, with information booths, free food, poetry and music, and impassioned speeches and young rappers chanting out their rage against the system. This limited expanse of grass, in the heart of the inner city, had been called "Bobby Hutton Park" by Panthers in the old days, named after the organization's first martyr. (I wondered, in the midst of the assembly, if the ghost of Huey Newton was walking about the park. He'd been shot dead in a street altercation over drugs in 1989, only a few blocks away.)

But, different from those days when I covered such events for the Party paper, now I couldn't really count myself as one of the revolutionaries, since I was working as a paid journalist for a more-or-less Establishment publication (however iconoclastic *George* might have seemed), and I felt somewhat like a spy. Looking around me, I wondered if there were any *real* informants there, like the infamous Julius Butler, whose false testimony against Geronimo had been a basis of his conviction.

I had been brought to the rally from my hotel in San Francisco by Emory Douglas, an artist of tremendous talent who had been the Party Minister of Culture, and who had been instrumental in keeping grass-roots ferment alive in the Bay Area for Geronimo's release. Emory's warm welcome when he'd picked me up had set me at ease for encounters with other former Party members at the gathering, including some who had been members of the dreaded Security Squad. But, twenty-five years later, this was a reunion for us all, and when Emory told old comrades that I'd served sixteen years of a life sentence back in Virginia, I was embraced like a long-lost son.

Geronimo arrived in a black SUV with tinted windows, and emerged with his family: wife, son, daughter, and toddler granddaughter. With them was a small woman I recognized as ex-Panther Afeni Shakur, mother of the slain rapper Tupac, to whom Geronimo had been godfather, as well as Angela Davis, the Movement icon. A throng enveloped them, with Geronimo embracing old friends, while teens surrounded Afeni to get an autograph from the mother of their rap idol.

Wearing a stylish safari jacket and a T-shirt emblazoned with the head of a magnificent lion, along with reflector sunglasses and a straw Panama, Geronimo looked more like a celebrity than a revolutionary firebrand. But when he took the stage he launched into an hour-long speech that used terms I hadn't heard in two decades: *liberation, self-determination, self-defense.*

"First of all, my name is not Pratt. Pratt was some racist-dog plantation owner. My name is ji Jaga, meaning I am of the Jaga people of West Africa," he told the crowd. Then, with a folksy manner and the Louisiana accent he still retained, he assailed the crowd for continuing to give their children "slave names," and for being "bought off by poverty-program money."

"Y'all know me from the sixties, I don't bite my tongue. And if you don't like it, then step to my face!" he yelled. Yet, he didn't come across as an embittered man. There was no personal condemnation of the FBI or LAPD—or, most surprisingly to me, of Huey Newton.

I followed Geronimo and his entourage to an even larger rally in San Francisco for Mumia Abu-Jamal, the former Panther and prison journalist/author on death row in Pennsylvania, whose proclaimed innocence in the shooting death of a Philadelphia policeman had elicited worldwide attention, prompting thousands to take to the streets in Europe and America in his behalf. I'd followed Mumia's case closely while I was in prison, for we were the same age; had joined the Party while very young; and with all that I'd gone through to write from the general population of prison, I had nothing but respect for how he'd been able to publish a book, and do commentary for National Public Radio, from the solitary confinement of death row.

More than fifteen hundred people filled the high school auditorium to hear the speeches by Geronimo and other luminaries of the left like author Alice Walker. Geronimo's speech was as strident as ever. "I talked to Mumia over the phone when I got out," he said, "and I told him that he just had to be strong in there. I told him to remember that we didn't join the Revolution to live, we joined the Revolution to *die.*"

The next day I interviewed Geronimo at the modest apartment he was sharing with his wife, Ashaki, a woman of exotic beauty inherited from her Hawaiian mother and black father, whom he had married while in prison. Their teenaged son and grown daughter were both conceived during conjugal visits between the couple during his incarceration. We sat out on the apartment's small terrace in our stocking feet, and G. (as he is called by his friends) was totally casual, as if I'd just dropped by to watch a football game.

Emory introduced me as a comrade from the Winston-Salem chapter, and Geronimo told me that as field marshal for the Party, he had organized the chapter there. I let him know how the comrades there were doing—that Ruth was the principal of a charter school organized by Hazel, who was now a lawyer; that Larry Little was a law professor at Winston-Salem State University; and that Nelson Malloy, though in a wheelchair, was serving as a member of the city council. He said it made him feel good to know that his old comrades were still carrying on the struggle, in some way, and that I also was carrying on as a journalist, after enduring such a long imprisonment—a comment I really appreciated.

We traded humorous stories about our transitions back to society after so long. "Man, I'd never seen a waterbed before, never seen a pro football or basketball game; and trying to drive these new cars—what a trip!" he said. "I got behind the wheel, after getting my license, and didn't know heads or tails about how to use the thing on the side, what was the high beams for the lights, or what controlled the windshield wipers."

"Yeah," I said, "I know what you mean. I almost got decapitated by the automatic seatbelt in my car." Then we laughed about what Dennis Miller said, on national TV, about his release: "Yeah, that's just what we need, another brother bewildered by the ATM machine, and holding up the line."

Then I had to turn to the hard questions. As I still felt animosity for Huey Newton and how he had fucked up the Party, I asked Geronimo about his absence of rancor for Newton.

"It was so clear to me that they had sent Huey to San Quentin, out of all the other prisons in the California system, because they knew I was there," he said. "They knew of the bad blood they'd fostered between us, and of the influence I had there, and they fully expected that he would be killed. But what they didn't know was that

I had learned the lessons of COINTELPRO, so instead of falling into their trap, I put out the word that Huey should be helped. We got him on vitamins, got his strength up, so that when it was time for him to be released, he wanted to demand that I go free also."

It was hard for me to understand how Geronimo could be so forgiving of the man who had more or less cooperated in his long imprisonment. But it hit me that if Geronimo was able to forgive Newton, then I certainly should be able to exorcise the bitterness I felt toward a man who now was no more than a memory, a memory that should possibly be revered for the organization and movement he founded, rather than scorned for his human failings.

When I asked Geronimo how he had been able to keep his anger in check, his response made him sound like a cross between a mystic guru and a Marxist general. "Emotionalism is not conducive to rationality," he said. "You cannot analyze anything if you are operating from extreme stress. You have to maintain your balance mentally in everything you do."

So then the big question came, and in asking it, it hit me that I might ask the same question of myself: "How were you able to survive so many years in prison, and come out without an overwhelming sense of rage?"

"I was sustained by a base in the Eastern ways of discipline," he said. "I stayed rooted in those realities that kept me balanced, kept me standing straight up, kept me from falling into things like drugs, or ego-tripping. And the same thing that sustained me through those twenty-seven years is still keeping me going now."

Riding back from Geronimo's home in Marin County with Emory, I reflected on the calm fire that G. had exhibited in the interview, and at the rallies. I was inspired by the continued strength in the brother's voice against the System, for it had been a long time since *I* had felt such fervor and dedication. I realized that it may well have been a similar dedication, cemented in my Panther past, that had been my sustaining force during my incarceration, and had kept me writing, speaking truth to power.

As we crossed the Golden Gate Bridge, viewing its magnificence and the vista of San Francisco Bay, I thought of how wonderful the creativity of man was, to erect such a structure, to exert such a command over nature. Then I looked left, and saw the island of the former Alcatraz prison, now one of the area's main tourist sites. Amid all this glory of industriousness and freedom, I could not help but recognize that there, before me, was yet another monument of man's inhumanity to man.

On the morning before I was to leave San Francisco, I was stricken with pain—*serious* pain. After checking out of the hotel, I left my bags at the front desk and caught a cab to the emergency room of the nearest hospital. After an interminable wait, I was seen and diagnosed as having a large blood clot in my lower gastrointestinal tract. I was quite alarmed, thinking that I might need hospitalization, for I had no health insurance. But the doctor assured me that I could still fly back to North Carolina that evening.

I arrived home in severe distress. After being checked out by doctors in Danville, I would spend weeks bedridden, and months more recuperating.

I was in bad shape, having to endure pain I had never imagined. But I had a deadline for my article, and perhaps it was the necessity to write that kept me from succumbing to the self-pity of illness. I found a way to write while in bed, on a legal pad, and even conducted phone interviews, while prone, with Stuart Hanlon, Geronimo's lead attorney; Jim McCloskey of Centurion Ministries, the investigator who broke open the case; and of course Johnnie Cochran. (When I told Cochran that I was dealing with illness, he was ever the warm personality, telling me, "Well, we're just going to have to get you well, won't we.")

Somehow I got the piece for *George* finished, only to learn from my editor that there had been a changing of the guard at the magazine, and he was waiting for his new boss to okay the piece. In the meantime, I wasn't able to get reimbursement for my traveling expenses, which left me broke. Then, still laid up, my lady in Richmond sent me a Dear John letter, saying that she could no longer handle a long-distance relationship, not even having bothered to come visit me while I was sick. This brought about emotional and psychological pain that increased my anguish. I'd finally been able to open up to love again, but once more, as in prison, I was left stranded and alone.

On top of it all I was hit with an infection that extended my convalescence. Next, the new editor at *George* rejected my piece, and my devastation was complete. I fell into a chasm of depression nearly as bad as I'd experienced after Rod's death, feeling as if I were again imprisoned. My bedroom was my new cell, with me now trapped not only by emotional distress, but by physical pain as well.

I blamed myself for having allowed my warrior's heart to weaken. How could I have given in to romantic love, the emotion that had always seemed to cripple me in the past? How could I ever come to trust women—or my emotions—again?

I also wondered, during the nights and days of physical suffering, *What is my body doing to me?* I felt betrayed by the athletic physical form I'd taken such pride in maintaining. Had I endured two decades of hell, only to succumb to such illness? Nightmares of my imprisonment returned, torturing my sleep. I'd lost the illusion of eternal youth, and I began to think that my death was not as far away as it had seemed, that my freedom might easily be cut short by mortal sickness—and then the nothingness of oblivion.

During my convalescence, I drew special courage from phone conversations with relatives and friends. My uncle Carroll gave constant counsel, as did my cousin Monifa, and her husband, the well-known sculptor and professor at Florida State, Ed Love. "Look, Derrell," Monifa told me, "you have great work to do. You could have died when you were in prison, or on any number of occasions when your life was in danger. Just know now that you *will* heal, and you will soon be able to continue your work."

Ed talked to me about the relationship of the body to stress, and how it took years for former prisoners he knew to deal with post-traumatic stress after getting out. My friend Stacy contacted me and sounded a similar note: "You have to give yourself time, brother man. It's just like when our ancestors got out of slavery, and after a few years white folk were saying, 'You been free long enough, why is it taking you so long to catch up?' You can't expect to recover from sixteen years in prison in sixteen weeks."

As I struggled to recover, I witnessed my mother's own struggle with her advancing Parkinson's disease, and how she endured, without complaint, to accomplish simple tasks like making it from the bedroom to the bathroom to the kitchen. It was at once depressing, and inspiring. Perhaps it was seeing her courage that got me going again. I knew it was time to complete my recovery, to begin taking charge of my parents' lives as their health declined. My sister, who was in Baltimore, hardly ever visited. I knew it was up to me to come through for them, just as they had been there for me during all the years of my incarceration.

I brought in a contractor to erect railings in the hallway, so that Mama could move about more easily. Overriding her stubborn refusal, I brought in a wheelchair, and got Pop to hire an aide, a woman named Anita Tomasso, to come in during the day to assist her. Realizing that my father was going downhill as well, I drove him to see a specialist at Duke University's hospital, in Durham, North Carolina, to undergo tests for his increasing forgetfulness.

After a battery of testing, the neurologist came into the waiting room to tell me of the news. "My diagnosis of your father is that he is in the early stages of Alzheimer's disease." The words hit me like a sledgehammer. Though I suppose I knew it was coming, I had not wanted to believe that my family might be beset by such calamity, that I would have to deal with two seriously ill parents. "You need to prepare for his advancing dementia," the doctor said. "Someone will have to take over all of his business affairs, and you will *definitely* have to stop him from driving, as soon as possible. It won't be easy, but I have to tell you frankly, you have no choice but to deal with it."

The doctor's words reverberated in my head during the ensuing months, as I found myself constantly battling with my bullheaded father, whose domineering attitude would not allow him to believe that there was anything remotely wrong with him. I was fortunate to have the counsel of my uncle Carroll in Washington, whom I talked to regularly, and who had become something of a surrogate father. Carroll was busy caring for his wife, who had been suffering with Alzheimer's for several years and was now in the advanced stages. "You'd better get ready to deal with much worse," he told me. "But you need to remember, you've got to take care of yourself, because if you don't survive, they don't survive."

Carroll offered to let me live in a house he owned on Stuart Street, the neighborhood where I grew up, where the family still owned most of the houses. It was one of the old houses my grandfather had built, where I'd lived with my now-deceased uncle Harry during my junior year of high school. Though I would be living in a fairly impoverished community, the house would provide my first real taste of independence, my first chance to be alone, to write.

Soon after my move to Stuart Street, Pop dropped by to see my new digs. I tried to talk to him about the need for my coming into the business with him, though it was the last thing I wanted to do. My father, proving that he still had more of his cognitive faculties than I'd believed, said, "Derrell, you don't want to give up your writing business. You don't have to pay anyone but yourself, and you get paid thousands of dollars to work out of your home. You'd be crazy to get into landscaping, where I have to pay four or five employees, while worrying about overhead, and when—or if—people pay me on time. I think you better stick with what you know best."

So, while it still seemed like Pop could run things, I set about furthering my career as a writer. But during 1998 I found little work in my craft. The main problem was just being in Danville, where nothing existed for a freelance writer, and there was precious little in the way of intellectual ambience to keep the creative juices flowing. I still sent out dozens of proposals and articles, with little success. I was lucky enough to get a job writing a documentary film for a producer on an unsuccessful and largely unknown slave rebellion led by Gabriel Prosser in Richmond, during the year 1800. But after months of research and effort, and a partial payment for a preliminary script, the producer's effort ran out of steam, and I was once again without work.

Somehow I was able to keep believing in myself, and worked on my long-term fiction project about the turn-of-century heroine Maggie Walker. I also kept a journal chronicling my life, believing in the dictum I'd learned in prison, that the poet's first duty is to keep a journal. I often turned the entries into literary vignettes, which blended my past with my present, in an effort to keep my writing instincts alive. One such effort was titled *The Glove:*

When she said to me, "I knew something was wrong, when that glove didn't fit O.J.," I was tired of hearing that view, so popular with so many black people who simply wanted to believe that the white justice system was wronging a black man again. I resisted replying with impatience, understanding the collective sense of injustice felt by so many black people, how many might be reluctant to condemn O. J. Simpson, even this many years hence. Even when my editor at The Washington Post *asked me to write a view of the verdict, I had hesitated to say, unequivocally, "The bastard did it," and only suggested that the police may have tried to frame a guilty man. But now I decided to confide a bit of personal history to my lady friend, to drive home the point.*

"Look," I said, "I once committed a crime with gloves which were two sizes too small, a pair of woman's gloves that took me much too

long to put on, and which made handling a shotgun difficult—but not impossible." I didn't share with her the details of the bank robbery, my first felony; nor did I reveal the greater shame I felt when I remembered that the gloves had belonged to my mother.

A few weeks later I was visiting my parents, and went into the basement to smoke a cigarette. In the little room filled with junk from my childhood, memories flooded back with each item: the old Victrola from Grandmother's house, the tennis racket that once belonged to Arthur Ashe, an old volume of poetry from high school years, and the small cot-like bunk I'd slept on, now piled high with old clothes. And among the clothes, I spied an old glove, its blue leather now molded grayish white, crumpled and stiff. Was it one of that pair I'd worn twenty-six years ago, discovered by police in my briefcase, and brought home by shamed and bewildered parents after my arrest?

Picking it up, I thought of trying it on again. Had time and moisture caused it to shrink? Would it possibly still fit?

I tossed it aside, thinking, "It never did fit me," and went back upstairs to attend to my aged parents.

I sat in the restaurant, crowded on the little couch in the corner at Applebee's, waiting on a table, and waiting for Gerald Stovall to arrive.

Gerald Stovall. My oldest friend from the beginning of my life sentence, my brother whom I'd not seen in more than ten years. I'd surfed the Department of Corrections website on the Internet, had found out that he had been paroled, and had gotten his number from Doc Johnson, the elderly man who had coordinated the drug program twenty years ago, when Gerald and I were at the State Penitentiary together. I could sense the excitement Gerald felt when I'd called him—"Hop, is that really you, man?"—and sat now remembering his words: "I tell everyone about you. I keep that article they wrote on you with me, I know you're going to be famous one day. . . . It's so good to hear your voice again. I love you, man."

I love you, man. *The words echoed in my brain as I waited, flashing back to 1981, a time when, as hardened convicts, we never used the word love—though Gerald had talked to me about the bonds formed between men in prison. And here I was, at a crossroads of freedom, wondering why I was having such difficulty feeling love, in any sense—for my family, my friends, and moreover, for my readers and maybe myself—having so much trouble with the concept of this thing called love that I had come to view the quest to regain it (for, most certainly, I was* once *able to feel the emotion) that feeling it again had become the theme of my life, and the holy grail of my writing. . . .*

And so Gerald arrived. We embraced in that manly way initiated with a handshake that pulls into what one might call a hug, if one were not so ingrained in the culture of machismo. "Hey, Hop—you still look the same, man," he said.

"Yeah, and you ain't grown no taller, I see," I replied.

We smiled and laughed, when he said, "I see you still comin' on with the short jokes." And it all seemed to flash back in an instant, the degree of humor and camaraderie—the sense of humor I seemed to have lost in my most serious struggle. Sitting at the table, sipping on tea and Pepsi, we reviewed old times, his spirit and humor causing me to rethink the sense of dire drama with which I tended to see my life. He had lived through such a serious case of tuberculosis that it was rumored he had died. We were both atheists long ago, yet he smiled as he told of his near-death experience, of seeing angels around him, and his calling upon God to reveal Himself. Then he joked about how, after emerging from his coma, he was barely able to emit—in a hoarse whisper he now mimicked his words to a fellow-traveler he encountered from the State Pen days, "Send me a Qu'ran." He converted to Islam after that, and changed his name to Khalid.

I could see that this was a man who felt lucky to be alive, and doubly lucky to be free. If he was able to come through so much, should not I be able to smile about the past, remember that there were good times, even then, and see how—in comparison—I was in an exalted position to do some good in the world, with my writing? Compared to Gerald, I was livin' in "high cotton," as they say. He was a recovering drug addict, yet he recounted—still with a smile—how he violated parole by having dirty urine, and was re-incarcerated for another nine years. All told, he had spent twenty-eight of his fifty-four years in prison. But when folk asked him, "Aren't you mad about it?" he said that his reply was, "Yeah, I'm mad—but I'm mad at myself."

Seeing him gave me a new perspective on things. I recalled how he had helped to comfort me upon the death of my girlfriend in the visitation van accident, how we now shared the loss of a son—his having been shot to death. But most of all, his smile reminded me of the fact that I, too, was still able to smile, when I was with those who love me, and whom I cared for. . . .

A few days later, I happened to see The Shawshank Redemption, *a picture I'd not been able to watch for a number of years—eschewing any type of prison picture that might take me back. . . . But watching it then, I thought of Gerald, and the bonds that can form between men under such circumstances. And I thought of his perspective: "I firmly believe that we pay our debt to society after we get out. We owe it to those left behind to show that we are not monsters, that the worse-case-scenario shit they see on TV is not the case, to show that those still behind bars deserve a chance at freedom."*

Such writing kept me going during 1998 and into 1999, but my existence was beset with loneliness. (Ruth and I had never gotten back together, and soon our long separation would be finalized by divorce.) I had never really learned the rituals of dating, having gone straight into the Party in adolescence, and then into prison just after that. So I had little experience to draw upon in approaching the opposite sex. Just *trying* to date in Danville was rough. It was a mill town with no place for a man of some education to meet eligible singles, and few educated women from which to choose a mate. It made me feel as if I were in a larger social prison, made all the worse for the fact that I was now free of the strictures of incarceration. I was also still a very shy man, and didn't seem to have the boldness to approach women with a fast line.

I felt like a loser, without a woman after almost two years of freedom. Then, on a trip to Richmond, I met Shelia, a woman a bit younger than I, but with eyes full of fire, and stars of hope. After long conversations by phone, we had our first date, an assignation at an Applebee's near her home. I presented a dozen roses to a woman clothed in a clinging brown dress that highlighted her complexion, and was immediately beguiled by her almond-shaped eyes, as well as her curvaceous figure. We hit it off right away, and after getting together regularly in the months that followed, we began a serious relationship.

She lived in a town house on Brandermill Lake, which was like a dream home away from home to me, when I was able to break away from Danville to see her. The lovemaking was wondrous, but the long-distance aspect of the relationship kept me on the defensive. I seemed unable to relinquish the baggage of my past, our intermittent periods together reminding me of monthly visits while I was in prison. And after having so many attempts at love broken up, I was fearful of my own emotions, and fearful of the wild emotional swings that the women in my past had exhibited.

I was driving back from Washington, D.C., in April 1999, after having lunch in a ritzy hotel restaurant with Jodie Allen, my former editor at *The Washington Post*. I'd finally met her after years of phone conversations and her invaluable help in shaping the career I'd been able to further while inside. I decided to take the scenic route out of town, and drove down Pennsylvania Avenue, past the White House and the Washington Monument and all the symbols of freedom—symbols of a freedom I now had, but which I still could not feel.

Every trip out of Danville was a revelation for me. During this trip I had made my first public speech since my release, at a memorial held at Howard University—a sad eulogy for my kinsman, Ed Love, who had suddenly passed away the week before from a heart attack, devastating my cousin Monifa.

The highway seemed to me a metaphor of my long journey, all of these miles of road, scenery, folk traveling alongside me, a highway leading back to the place I wanted to call home, but was still not a place I could embrace—and which certainly had not embraced me.

Passing through Richmond, I took a detour past the place where the State Penitentiary had stood, my "home" for eight years, now but a plot of land owned by Ethyl Corporation. The highway back to Danville reminded me of all the years my parents had driven this road, faithfully every month, and the highway where Nancy and Ben had lost their lives, while traveling to visit me.

Passing the turnoff to Nottoway, I decided to drive past the prison for the second time since my release. Slowly passing the entrance, I recalled my emergence through those doors, still handcuffed, but able to taste the freedom to come. Just south of the prison, I looked at the woods just beyond the recreation yard, woods I once dreamed of running through, during my fantasies of escape.

After I turned my car around, a vehicle drew up close behind me, and suddenly I was beset with fear: Was it a state trooper or county cop who would pull me over, run my tags, and discover that I was on parole and had veered off the assigned route home? Would he arrest me and return me to the hell of this place?

Then the car behind went in another direction, and I realized that I'd been tripping—another taste of the post-traumatic stress syndrome that had plagued me since my release. *No one is after you, you are no longer under the police-state scrutiny of prison,* I had to tell myself, taking a few deep breaths before lighting a cigarette.

A few miles later I found myself braking hard, seeing blue lights flashing at the side of the road, though I was not speeding. I was surprised to see that the state trooper, who had stopped another motorist, was a black man, as I had never seen a black trooper in the state of Virginia. My mind, still racing from my recent scare, assimilated this new information and suddenly, looming before me, was the beginning of a new novel.

> *It is just before dusk, and the trooper has driven through the other side of a rain. He sees a plastic bag blow across the highway, paying little attention to it—until, on his return trip, he spies a dog nosing into a trash bag, on the side of the road. Turning around to investigate, the dog scampering before his spotlight in the darkening mist of dusk, he discovers the body of an African-American male, whom he recognizes as having been an officer at the nearby state prison where he once worked. . . .*

And there it was, that feeling of creative discovery I'd not had for some time: a murder mystery in the making, with the protagonist on the other side of the law from where I'd previously been—a state trooper.

With the idea of having to identify, through imagination, with characters from another world, it hit me: *This is what I've been missing:* a sense of empathy with others—a sense of identification, not only with characters but with a whole new audience and with people in general—something I hadn't had since being immersed in my personal story and tragedies. It was just what I needed, to begin thinking of myself as an artist once more.

It was March 2000 when I received a call from my father's secretary, Sylvia. "Your father is very upset," she said. "A client just came by and has threatened to sue him about a big job that has gone bad. Mr. Hopkins is just sitting in his office, trembling. You need to get over here, now."

I had known the time would come when I would have to take

over for Pop, but I wasn't really prepared, emotionally or mentally, for the suddenness of the task. My father had made a mistake in a job costing several thousand dollars, and I had to step in to try to clean it up. Luckily, I was able to do so, but he was badly shaken by the experience. All of my writing had to be put on hold, for it was apparent that I now had to take charge.

But Pop, true to form for a man in the early stages of Alzheimer's, refused to relinquish command of things, and I became embroiled in a battle to reestablish some order to his affairs. Foremost on the list of things was a big job landscaping the new building being erected by the city's black bank, an institution established nearly a century before, whose board of directors was headed by my uncle Julian.

While I had little or no training for the task, I made a quick study of the architect's plans, and commanded the execution of the thirty-thousand-dollar project. All the while I pretended, for Pop's sake, that he was actually the one in charge.

Somehow I succeeded, completing the project so well that my head "blew up," and I believed that I could actually make enough money with the landscaping business to eventually support my writing. It was not lost upon me that I, a former bank robber, was now able to do a *different* sort of bank job, contracting with a bank for tens of thousands of dollars.

After we finished, I stood with my father upon a high embankment of the property we had just finished beautifying, which overlooked a busy thoroughfare. "I don't know how you did it," Pop said to me. "With no experience you took a blueprint and laid out all of this, and it *really* looks good. I'm real proud of you, son. I always dreamed that you would take over the business from me one day, and now I feel like my dream has come true."

I was moved by his words, especially knowing that he was able to say this before all such memories, for him, would be gone. I was just happy to know that he had this moment of peace with his son. I put my arm around him on that hilltop, and told him the words

I'd not been able to muster in all the years of my adolescence and adulthood. "I love you, Pop," I said. "And I'm just glad to be able to be here to help you now."

I was approaching the auditorium of the University of the District of Columbia, there to attend the Thirty-fifth Anniversary Reunion and Conference of the Black Panther Party, and I felt both excitement and a degree of anxiety—for once again I would encounter aspects of a painful past.

When I reached the door of the building, a man was coming out whom I vaguely remembered. "I can't recall your name, brother, but I think we were out in Oakland together. I'm brother Derrell Hopkins," I told him, as I offered my hand.

"Comrade Derrell," he said with a degree of pleasure in recognizing me, pulling my handshake into a hug. "I'm Flores," he told me, and with the name came recognition: he had been of the dread security cadre. But as the memories came back, I recalled that he and I had gotten along well, when he was driver for Elaine Brown during the campaign of '73.

That greeting broke the ice on my reservations about those I might encounter at the reunion, for we were all old comrades now. I entered the large foyer of the auditorium, which was replete with posters and photos from the old days. More than two hundred folk were milling about, young and old, students and former members talking in groups, some manning tables with leaflets and displays of vintage Party newspapers, leaflets, and buttons.

My comrade from Oakland, Billy X. Jennings, greeted me at the registration desk, all smiles. He was the reunion's chief organizer and the primary force behind the BPP alumni, publishing and distributing a newsletter around the country, and running the alumni website, itsabouttimebpp.com. Next I was warmly embraced by a group from my Oakland days, each of them quickly catching me up on what they were now doing: my friend Omar Barbour, who was now a prominent developer in the black community of Jersey City; Sultan "Big Herman" Ahmed, who became a force in Philadelphia as a poverty program director; and James "Bubba" Young, who had become a successful businessman. They'd all done very well after leaving the Party, and had continued to carry on the organization's legacy of activism and service, in one way or another.

They were pained to learn that I'd spent twenty of the intervening years in prison. My conversation with Sultan was especially poignant, for it turned out we both had had to endure the pain of losing a son, his having fallen prey to gun violence. While we were talking, up walked Aaron Dixon, who gave me such a hug he damn near lifted me off the ground.

Bobby Seale came into the auditorium, still full of energy, though well into his sixties. Then Bobby Rush, the former leader of the Chicago chapter, now a U.S. congressman from Illinois, joined the throng.

While videotaping a wonderful photographic display of the earliest days of the Party, I met Roz Payne, a middle-aged white professor at a college in Vermont, who had taken many of the photos. I wanted to hear more about her time in New York during the anti-war protests of the late sixties, as she had established an archive of photos and films of the period; so I invited her to join me for a cup of tea at a nearby restaurant.

"The Black Panther Party inspired us all," she said, after telling me how she had become a supporter while working alongside the SDS (Students for a Democratic Society) and other radical organizations. "The Movement took its cues from the Panthers, taking on the cry of 'Power to the People,' even borrowing its name—as in the case of the White Panthers, and the Gray Panthers who fought for the rights of senior citizens."

But she noticed the lack of enthusiasm in my voice when I told her a bit about my days in California, and she asked me, "Why do I sense that you seem to be *mad* at the Party, for some reason?"

Before then I'd never thought of it in those terms, but I realized that, in a way, she was right. "I guess you could say that I was disillusioned, and maybe somewhat bitter about seeing an organization of beautiful, bright young men and women betrayed by a corrupt leadership," I told her. "And yes, it still leaves me a little sad, especially looking at the state of the world, and the country under George Bush. I can't help but get the feeling that we failed."

"But you didn't fail, Evans," she said. "Think of all the pride you instilled in people who had no hope, how you got them to start taking action in their own behalf. Think of all the programs you started—how you were the first to do widespread feeding of children before school—like so many school systems offer now—and how you had free health clinics doing sickle cell anemia testing, before most people even *knew* about the disease. Don't let your bad experience in Oakland make you forget the great things the Party accomplished, how this one organization inspired *millions.*"

Driving through the Washington streets to my uncle Carroll's home, where I was staying, I thought about what Roz Payne had said. I realized that perhaps I had still felt the need to blame something other than myself for my having veered off into crime. I'd learned in prison that anger stems from a perceived slight or injustice, how often rage comes from wounds so deep in one's past that you end up expressing it toward someone or something other than that which initially inflicted the initial hurt.

It hit me then that disillusionment is one of the deepest hurts, for it causes you to feel like a fool—mad at yourself for being a dupe. Such inner rage then tends to be expressed outwardly, and often irrationally, since the unconscious knows that self-loathing will eventually destroy you.

Well, instead of destroying others, I'd nearly destroyed myself. But somehow I'd been able to emerge from anger and despair by learning to accept and forgive. It was high time for me to quit blaming others and, in facing up to my mistakes, learn to *fully* forgive myself—and love *myself* as much as I'd selflessly loved the Party and the people we had sought to serve.

I felt in a lighter spirit the following evening, when I attended the event's closing gala in a room filled with more than one hundred fifty former Panthers and their family members. I was joyously reunited with members of the editorial cadre, who had worked with me on the Party newspaper: JoNina Abron, Gloria Abernethy, and Sherry Brown. We all expressed disappointment that our beloved editor, David DuBois, was not there with us. But I was able to report to them that he and I were in contact once more, and that his duties with the W.E.B. DuBois Foundation, and his teaching at the University of Massachusetts at Amherst, had kept him from attending.

I also met former comrades from other chapters, including Paul Coates from Baltimore. There he had achieved great success as founder and publisher of Black Classics Press, which had recently published an edition of Walter Mosley's first novel. He had also put out the most comprehensive book on the BPP, *The Black Panther Party Reconsidered,* edited by University of Georgia professor Charles Jones.

After Party leaders Bobby Seale and Elbert "Big Man" Howard spoke, Kathleen Cleaver, wife of the deceased Eldridge Cleaver and now a law professor at Emory University, gave the keynote address. Her presence, along with members of the New York chapter, was evidence of how time had helped heal the Cleaver/Newton rift that had once divided the Party.

At the end of her speech she seemed to speak directly to the feeling of failure I'd expressed the night before: "We should never feel like we failed in our struggle to achieve justice. Remember, some may have thought that John Brown failed after his raid on Harper's Ferry. But it was that action which brought about the Civil War."

Driving back to Danville, I stopped to spend some time with Shelia in Richmond. Looking out at sunset on the lake behind her home,

I reflected on my reunion with my Panther past as well as my long incarceration. *You've come a long way,* I thought to myself, as I watched a flock of geese descend from a western sky colored with pink and magenta streaks, then alight on the silvery-blue surface of the water. I felt such peace in the beauty of the moment that I longed to begin a poem—only to have the thought arise, *With all that you face back in Danville, when would you ever find the time to finish it?*

Indeed, the situation at home with family and business was more challenging than ever. The business was not doing well, and my parents' health was deteriorating rapidly. The last time I'd been able to visit Shelia was Valentine's Day, two months before, and I had received a call from my parents' caregiver, Anita, to rush back home: they both were being sped by ambulance to the emergency room, suffering from severe flu. Looking out at the fading rays of day, I thought of how I'd attended to them both in the hospital room they had shared. I recalled helping a nurse wrestle with Pop when he had tried to yank out his IV, in such a delirium he kept repeating that he didn't want to "stay at the funeral home" any longer; and remembered the gentleness I felt in washing my mother's fevered face.

I realized that I was becoming a man of greater tenderness, from my having to care for them. But I was also having to bear witness that they were slowly dying: the Parkinson's was robbing Mama of the use of her body, and had begun to affect her mind as well. With his Alzheimer's, I watched the agonizingly slow death of my father's brain, with the attendant loss of the memory that had given him identity. It was like having to mourn the passing of one's parents while they are still alive, and it was breaking my heart. And while I believed that caring for them was a welcome aspect of my penance—and I was glad to be there for them—I still knew, deep inside, that the fullness of redemption lay somewhere within the realm of my writing.

Shelia came to my side, then, and perhaps sensing my mood, she wrapped her arms around me. Our relationship had grown into the deepest love, despite the long periods of separation. As we gazed out upon the sky and lake in silence, I was content in the moment once more, this bit of joy willing me to move here someday, and make this place my home.

One afternoon in the fall of 2002, I sat at the table in my little kitchen, looking out the window at the vacant lot next door, watching the human traffic going in and out of the house just beyond, where it was obvious that drugs were being sold. My fingers were poised above the keyboard of the used laptop I'd bought at Monifa's suggestion. "It will get you back on track with your writing," she had said, "because you'll find you can use it every day to begin your journal again, whether in the bedroom or living room or kitchen. Just remember that you are born to write, Derrell, so just sit down and let the words come."

But the words were not coming. I even tried reworking another article on Vernon Joe. But the fact that he was still having to fight for freedom made me even more frustrated. It was hard to write about because it reminded me of my own imprisonment. Feeling a little stir-crazy, I decided that I had to get out of the house. I grabbed the $4.95-at-Wal-Mart basketball I'd personified with the name of Spaulding, and beat/dribbled him into the pavement on the small street outside my home, pausing to look at the glorious sky filled with billowy clouds this spring day. I then made my way from this spot in the neighborhood of my birth, out onto West Main Street, where the white folks with money lived.

At the top of the street I encountered Jimmy B., a man who had been a dealer I'd bought reefer from in the old days, an ace chess player whom I remembered as a better student than I in high school chemistry. He'd been in jail with me, twenty years ago, but now had the emaciated form of a cocaine addict. Like many old drug users, he had descended into alcoholism, for he was obviously intoxicated. Still, he greeted me with great relish.

"Every time I see you, Hop, I just got to shake your hand," he said. "You one helluva man, I got to tell you, to get out of prison with a life sentence like you did. I saw you on TV while you was still inside, and I told my girlfriend, 'Look at this here dude. He in the *penitentiary* and on TV. I told her how you wanted me to try and escape with you, how you told me right after you got that life sentence that you won't ever going to get out, unless you broke out.' You remember that?"

I told him that so much had happened to me in my life, I didn't remember everything—though the images of the rope of sheets, and all the fantasies of escape, came back in a flash. While I didn't want to prolong my conversation with him, I had to feel for Jimmy. When he'd gotten out of prison, he had not been blessed, as I had been, with a strong family support system. He got only the twenty-five dollars and a suit of clothes the prison system gave to each inmate they discharged. While there were now a few halfway houses and one or two small organizations that tried to help a man just out of prison to find work, by and large a released prisoner was still on his own—and faced with all manner of temptations, on all different levels. (I'd had to put one "old friend" out of my house, after he'd stopped by with an offer of sharing his "big rock" of crack. Another man, whom I thought to be a legitimate businessman, once asked me if I wanted to "double a few grand real quick." I'd been able to resist such offers; many like Jimmy weren't so strong.)

Now he jokingly said, "I know you still got some of that bank robbery money you buried somewhere before you fell, Hop," all smiles now. I laughed with him, knowing what was coming next: "Maybe you can let me hold five dollars. I'll pay you back next week."

I could not help but have some compassion for the brother, thinking, *There but for the grace of God go I*. I reached past the ID I carry when I'm out walking or running (for, as a black man, one never knows when you might get pulled up on by the police), and handed the brother a ten-dollar bill I carry for emergencies. I thought he was through with the praise I'd figured had only been a lead-up to asking for his "loan." But he held on to my hand as he took the money, looked into my eyes with sincerity, and said, "I also remember when you was with the Black Panthers, while you was still in school. You said the things a whole lot of us felt, but was just afraid to say. You spoke out for us, brother."

I walked on, dribbling fast now, past the brownstones and brick-storied homes, past the spot where there was once the big house my grandfather moved, brick by brick, back into the neighborhood where he was allowed to live. Then, settling down a pace, I cradled Spaulding and walked along the front of the antebellum mansion that now housed the Danville Museum of Fine Arts, the revered former home of the "Last Capitol of the Confederacy," as the historical marker declared. It was still the city's claim to fame. The flag of the Confederacy flew from a monument on the lawn, and Civil War reenactors in heavy woolen gray uniforms were cavorting with muskets on the lawn beneath it.

Remembering how the building now heralded in tourist brochures as a museum had been the public library thirty years ago, from which I was banned during the Jim Crow years of my youth, I gave in to the urge to spit on the manicured lawn. Turning north, I walked for three or four blocks, stopping before a condemned apartment building that once had housed the two rooms of the "colored library," the place where I used to spend Saturdays leafing through volumes discarded from the main library.

I began pounding the ball into the pavement once more, and started a long run back southward, finally arriving in a sweat at the office of Hopkins's Landscape Gardening, Inc., the company I had inherited from a father still alive, but so diminished by dementia that I was having to mourn the slow death of his mind, even as I rejoiced just to have him still in the land of the living, at age eighty.

This office, sitting upon a parcel of land liberated by my enterprising grandfather from the soil of oppression more than seventy years ago, was a gift from my predecessors, yet it still seemed an albatross around my neck. I'd resisted closing down the business for months, though I knew it was losing money, and a review of the books of the last ten years revealed that Pop had been in the red for six of them. So now, as I entered the structure I'd helped him build twenty years ago, I just wanted to check the mail, and get back home as quickly as possible.

But on that day, with the mood engendered by my walk, I decided to finally open some of the boxes I'd sent home from prison, boxes full of notes, papers, partial manuscripts, books, whatever. I had not had the courage to open those boxes up until then, afraid to wrestle with the memories of all the years of incarceration, fearful of examining the paper trail of my past.

I retrieved a dust mask (the sort my employees used when working on the tractor, or spreading straw after seeding a lawn), and a knife, and slit open a box labeled with my prison number in bold Magic Marker ink: **106824.** From that first box I pulled out notes from my last year in prison, old articles and news clippings, and then a sheaf of poetry, priceless verse from a time when I believed that *feeling* was the key to my artistic life.

I pulled out a copy of the *Richmond Times-Dispatch,* my color photo on the Sunday cover, seeing again the headline blaring, CAN LIFER WRITE HIS WAY OUT OF PRISON? Next was the discovery of the videotape of my parole interview, and a tape of the television documentary (still airing, I'd recently learned) in which I was featured. There were photos: a much younger Evans with my parents in the visiting rooms of the State Penitentiary and Nottoway— and then one of me with my son, taken the week before he died. I had to ask myself, *Is this why I've not dared to delve into these boxes before now?*

Another box revealed a folder of more than a dozen articles I'd written while I was under the gun—literally. I took that folder of clippings, along with the photo of my son, into the office my father had first given over to me upon my release, so that I would be able to concentrate on my writing. On the desk now was my business computer, stacks of invoices, and a photo of Shelia, surrounded by cards she had sent to help bridge the distance between Danville and Richmond.

Pushed to one corner of the desk were dust-covered files of writing projects I'd been working on before taking over the business, and on another corner four books, anthologies that contained reprints of some of my articles. Three of them were readers for college-level writing students. I thought of the encouraging words Shelia had said to me when I expressed doubts about my writing: "How can you doubt yourself, knowing that students in colleges and universities are already studying your work?"

I sat and pondered my feeling of malaise. I was saddled with a failing business, with the task of ensuring the care of a father lost in the fog of his dementia, and a mother who was now bedridden much of the time, in a town still filled with racism, with no cultural milieu to sustain my spirit. I felt trapped, as if in a new prison, paradoxically boxed in like the papers of my past life that still languished in the cardboard boxes in the next room. I'd never dreamed, during all those years in prison, that I would feel so unfree after five years in the outside world.

I leafed through the folder of my old articles, dating back from that first attack upon capital punishment published in *The Washington Post* in 1982, all the way to the crowning achievement, *The New Yorker* piece. Memories flooded back with each photocopy as I relived the toil and triumph of each meager accomplishment—as well as the trepidation I'd felt, for I had always had to wonder if a piece might call down the wrath of my keepers. Pondering this evidence from my past, I asked myself: *If you summoned the courage to write under such conditions, why aren't you still creatively productive now?*

Had my past writing been fueled only by my rage against injustice? Or had there been a supreme kernel of love for humanity—and for art—that had kept me going for sixteen years? I was glad that the rage was gone, but what had happened to the love?

And then I had to realize: It was, indeed, the love that had overpowered the rage, a dream and love for a world of readers I had continued to believe in, readers who might take in my words and return to me the love I'd always longed for during my past lives of racial oppression and condemnation to life in prison. I saw then that during life after life, from childhood through incarceration, it was *love* that had somehow carried me through. Now, I just *had* to believe that such love was still there, in my heart.

Opening the boxes had confronted me with the painful truth: I'd been avoiding thinking back on the hardest times, such as when they took away my typewriter, or the occasions when I actually wrote poetry and notes on napkins and toilet paper. But now I had everything I needed at my fingertips, all the tools of my trade—including computers connected to the Internet, and to the world. *You have to get out of this business, shut it down for good, and get back to the real business of writing, of storytelling, beginning with your story first. The legacy bequeathed to you is larger than the land and soil and offices that once belonged to your forefathers. You must start to sing again. . . .*

I booted up my computer, dumped some old business files, and opened up one labeled NEW BOOK. It was time to begin a new life. Writing was the only path to full freedom for me. Now I could see that my past lives, embodied in those boxes, held the keys to how I might transcend into this new life. From my past I would glean lessons of that which had sustained me, had taken me through and given me the spirit and love to grow in a wilderness of concrete and steel, of fury and despair. I would have to relive the recklessness, pain, and rage of that past, and somehow transform it all into a story of redemption.

ACKNOWLEDGMENTS

As this work comprises virtually the whole of my life, all those who have provided aid, friendship, and inspiration are to be thanked here, for in some way all of you have assisted in the making of this book.

Giving thanks first of all to the Creator, I'd like to extend specific thanks to my publishers at Free Press, Martha Levin and Dominick Anfuso, and my editor, Liz Stein, and to my agent, Gail Ross, who always believed in me. Also, my gratitude is extended to Chuck Adams, Emyl Jenkins, John Michael Fisher, Robert Sexton, and the members of the Nectar Writing Workshop; to George Gibson, Jenna Land, and Philip Rappaport, whose encouragement and guidance have been invaluable; and to Shelia for when I needed a gentle push to keep going.

I am forever indebted to the support of my family, especially my late mother, Marguerite, who passed on before the book's publication; my father, Daniel Hopkins; my uncles Carroll, Frederick, and Julian Swanson; my aunts Anne Drew, Catherine Barlow, and Cletis Swanson; and my cousins Monifa Love Asante, Nana Kweku Asante, Fred Swanson, Jr., Fred and Connie Drew, Lottie Adams

Hayes, and the late Ed Love; and to Anita Cruz Tomasso, for her loving care of my parents.

For Ruth Mack Hopkins, who gave me the gift of a son, and has always remained in my corner, my enduring honor and gratitude.

For encouragement during the darkest of times, I am thankful to the late Carole Kass, and to Stacy Burrs, Ben Cleary, Gregory Donovan, Nathan McCall, Marita Golden, and Patrice Gaines; as well as to Janine Bell, Beatrice Bush, Lois Brooks, Patrick McCurnin, Jill Talbot Derby, the late Mary Tyler McClenahan, Marie Deans, Mary Kaylor Patterson, Michael Billington, Martha Randolph Carr, Chris Dickon, Helen Butler, Itabari Njeri, Jeanne (Mrs. Arthur) Ashe, Paule Marshall, the late Marianna Wertz, and the late Reverend and Mrs. Robert Jones.

And thanks to all others who extended the kindness of conversation, correspondence, and visits to me during those twenty years, including those good brothers I knew on the inside: Khalid (Gerald) Stovall, I. Sparks, Charles Satchell, Marvin Brown, Ashim (Rasta-Man) Ricks, and especially Vernon Joe, whose continuing struggle for justice remains inspirational.

For help in achieving my freedom, I have William Fuller and Dr. Miller Ryans to thank, as well as all those who wrote letters in my behalf.

To all the editors who worked with me over the years, most especially Jodie Allen, Jeffrey Frank, Hendrick Hertzberg, Rufus Griscom, Judith Shulevitz, Katherine Boo, Lorna Wyckoff, Salim Muwakkil, and the late Wendy Bishop, I say *Thank you.*

For my comrades who have remained brothers, Omar Barbour, David DuBois, Nelson Malloy, Larry Little, and Bernard Patterson, thank you as well. And for the words of encouragement from new comrades in the world of writing, especially Kalamu y Salaam and Sonia Sanchez, I also note my thanks.

To my extended family, the Crews, and all others who lent love and support upon the passing of my mother, you have my deepest gratitude.

And for the world of readers: The thought of you has kept the flame of my writing spirit alive, and I am pleased to be able to say here that I owe you the greatest debt of all.

About the Author

Evans D. Hopkins grew up in Danville, Virginia, and now resides in Richmond, where he works as a freelance writer. His pieces have appeared in *The New Yorker, The Washington Post, Slate,* Nerve.com, *The Atlanta Journal-Constitution, In These Times,* and *Southern Exposure,* among others. His writing has been anthologized in several volumes, including the *Prentice Hall Reader,* Graywolf Press's *The Private I,* and *The Best of Nerve.com. Life After Life* is his first full-length book. He can be reached at www.evanshopkins.com.

Printed in the United States
By Bookmasters